CONSCIENCE AND
CATHOLIC EDUCATION

CONSCIENCE AND CATHOLIC EDUCATION

Theology, Administration, and Teaching

KEVIN C. BAXTER AND

DAVID E. DECOSSE, EDITORS

ORBIS BOOKS

Maryknoll, New York 10545

Founded in 1970, Orbis Books endeavors to publish works that enlighten the mind, nourish the spirit, and challenge the conscience. The publishing arm of the Maryknoll Fathers and Brothers, Orbis seeks to explore the global dimensions of the Christian faith and mission, to invite dialogue with diverse cultures and religious traditions, and to serve the cause of reconciliation and peace. The books published reflect the views of their authors and do not represent the official position of the Maryknoll Society. To learn more about Orbis Books, please visit our website at www.orbisbooks.com.

Library of Congress Cataloging-in-Publication Data

Names: Baxter, Kevin C., editor. | DeCosse, David E., editor.
Title: Conscience and Catholic education : theology, administration, and
    teaching / Kevin C. Baxter and David E. DeCosse, editors.
Description: Maryknoll, NY : Orbis Books, 2022. | Includes bibliographical
    references and index. | Summary: "Collected essays from a symposium on
    the prominent issue of conscience and how it is related to Catholic education"
    — Provided by publisher.
Identifiers: LCCN 2021038636 (print) | LCCN 2021038637 (ebook) |
    ISBN 9781626984523 (trade paperback) | ISBN 9781608339150 (epub)
Subjects: LCSH: Conscience—Religious aspects—Catholic Church—Congresses.
    | Christian ethics—Catholic authors—Congresses. | Catholic Church—Doctrines
    —Congresses. | Catholic Church—Education--Congresses. | Catholic schools
    —Congresses.
Classification: LCC BJ1278.C66 C6549 2022 (print) | LCC BJ1278.C66
    (ebook) | DDC 241/.1--dc23
LC record available at https://lccn.loc.gov/2021038636
LC ebook record available at https://lccn.loc.gov/2021038637

We dedicate this volume to Kim,

who has helped form Kevin's conscience for almost thirty years,

and to Paul G. Crowley, SJ (1951–2020), the late Jesuit Community Professor of

Religious Studies at Santa Clara University; editor in chief of Theological Studies;

and a much beloved practitioner of Catholic education.

Contents

Acknowledgments

Many people have been instrumental in the origin and completion of this project but none more so than Michael and Phyllis Shea. Their generous gift years ago launched the Project on Conscience and Roman Catholic Thought at the Markkula Center for Applied Ethics at Santa Clara University. Since that time, they have continued their wonderful support. Mike and Phyllis exemplify the dignified, kind, and wise commitment to conscience and Catholicism that is the animating idea behind this book and behind the earlier books in this series. We are deeply grateful.

We also thank Jill Brennan O'Brien, our editor at Orbis, for her patience and constant good counsel throughout this project and especially in the face of the difficult, pandemic-related circumstances of the last year. And we thank, too, all those at Orbis who have assisted with seeing this book into print and making it a success. We do not underestimate the hard work and insight of all those in the production, copyediting, marketing, and sales departments.

At Santa Clara University, numerous people have helped with every aspect of this project including Don Heider, the executive director of the Markkula Center; Monica DeLong, the operations director of the Markkula Center; Julie Garcia of the university's general counsel's office; and all those in the counsel's office and university finance who made this project happen. We are deeply grateful to all of them.

And we also cannot thank enough each of the contributors to this volume. Pulling together a book like this one during a global pandemic was a challenge in innumerable ways. And it is not lost at all on us how each of our contributors had to navigate lockdowns, quarantine, child care, quick learning curves for teaching on Zoom, and more while they also kept their essays moving forward to completion. We deeply honor their efforts.

On an individual note, we each wish to thank the following.

Kevin Baxter: "I am grateful to my wife Kim and our children, Ella, Scott, Sean, Meg, Nick, and Phoebe, for their love and patience in all things. Thanks to my colleagues at the National Catholic Educational Association for their effort and work supporting Catholic schools, especially during the pandemic.

And for the clergy, educators, staff, parents, and students in the Archdiocese of Los Angeles—my passion was nurtured and grown through my work there, and I will be forever grateful."

David E. DeCosse: "I am grateful to my dear mother, Sheila Flynn DeCosse, my whole family, my dear friends, my Markkula Center colleagues, the Los Angeles Catholic Worker community, and the many wonderful teachers and mentors I have had in many years of Catholic education. In the end, the conscience of a Catholic lives in an ambient world of grace. I am so grateful to all named here for the gifts of love and wisdom that have revealed that world."

INTRODUCTION

Kevin C. Baxter and David E. DeCosse

How might recent developments in the theology of conscience in the Catholic tradition be better incorporated into the administration and teaching of K-12 Catholic schools and in Catholic colleges and universities? This question is the driving force behind *Conscience and Catholic Education: Theology, Administration, and Teaching*, the third book in a series from the Project on Conscience and Roman Catholic Thought at the Markkula Center for Applied Ethics at Santa Clara University, the Jesuit university in Silicon Valley.

The first two books in the series were called, respectively, *Conscience and Catholicism: Rights, Responsibilities, and Institutional Responses* (Orbis 2015) and *Conscience and Catholic Health Care: From Clinical Contexts to Government Mandates* (Orbis 2017). Both books followed the same model as *Conscience and Catholic Education*: a collection of essays by top theologians who draw on and deepen the Catholic moral tradition on conscience by paying special attention to social, cultural, and structural contexts. Thus, the first book in the series, *Conscience and Catholicism,* featured contributors from global Catholicism and essays that explored race and gender in the American context. *Conscience and Catholic Health Care* took on such topics as the "reciprocity of consciences" in a Catholic hospital and the interplay between conscience and the roles of employees in Catholic institutions whose leaders opposed the accommodation offered by the Obama Administration to facilitate the availability of contraception for women. With *Conscience and Catholic Education*, we continue the exploration of the social, cultural, and structural dimensions of the theology of conscience in the context of Catholic education. We also offer practical classroom tips for K-12 and college and university teachers. More than in the first two books in the series, *Conscience and Catholic Education* includes contributions from practitioners who are not professors of theology.

Several crucial contexts shape the contributions in this volume. One is the recent, aforementioned development in the Catholic theological tradition of conscience. By "development," we mean the coherent deepening of implicit and explicit aspects of a concept; such a deepening often happens in response to new questions. With the theology of conscience, we have seen this development move in different directions. One movement has been back in time to recover more robustly what is called the "primacy" or "freedom of conscience," an idea powerfully articulated in the thirteenth century by St. Thomas Aquinas and part of the Christian tradition from its first decades.[1] According to this idea, one has a duty to form one's conscience and then, before God, to follow it. The Catholic Church has never formally rejected this moral doctrine, even if during the papacies of John Paul II and Benedict XVI the idea of such freedom was seen often as evidence of a problematic subjectivism.[2] By contrast, Pope Francis had in mind the positive significance of the freedom of conscience and the negative experience of Catholic authoritarianism when he said in *Amoris Laetitia* that it was the task of the church to "form consciences, not to replace them."[3] Another key aspect of the recent development of the theology of conscience is captured by a paradox: conscience is both the utterly singular place where each person is "alone with God, whose voice echoes in his depths," in the words of *Gaudium et Spes*,[4] and conscience is also inalienably social and historical. Thus, to think with theological accuracy about conscience requires engagement with such aspects of human existence as embodiment, relationships, context, culture, history, and structure. Finally, the third major factor in the development of the tradition has been the teaching on conscience of Pope Francis himself. Beyond renewing the tradition of the primacy of conscience, he has created more space and responsibility for the exercise of conscience on the part of all Catholics as a manifestation of the *sensus fidelium* of the universal church.[5]

---

[1] See, for instance, Thomas Aquinas, *Summa Theologica*, Question 19, Article 5, "Whether the Will Is Evil When It Is at Variance with Erring Reason?" and Paul's *Letter to the Romans* 1:16–2:29 and 14.

[2] See, for instance, Joseph Ratzinger, "Conscience and Truth," in *Crisis of Conscience,* ed. John M. Haas (New York: Crossroad, 1996), 1–19.

[3] Pope Francis, *Amoris Laetitia*—"On Love in the Family" (2016), no. 37, www.vatican.va.

[4] Pope John XXIII, *Gaudium et Spes*—"Pastoral Constitution on the Church in the Modern World" (1965), no. 16, www.vatican.va.

[5] See *Sensus Fidei in the Life of the Church*, International Theological Commission, 2014; https://www.vatican.va/.

The remarkably challenging social and political events in the United States and around the world in the last years marks another crucial context for this volume. As of this writing, nearly 600,000 Americans have died in the COVID-19 pandemic. The total deaths worldwide stand at almost four million. The pandemic revealed vast structural inequalities that left millions of poor and vulnerable human beings exposed to the virus. The pandemic also revealed the deception at the heart of radically individualistic notions of conscience, common in the United States, invoked in order to refuse the use of proven measures of public health like wearing masks and getting vaccinated. In one way of putting it, COVID-19 was an empirical and ethical reality check. Like it or not, as an empirical matter, the virus showed that we are all connected to everyone else: getting infected in one part of your city could plausibly mean, via a chain of transmission, that you infect someone on the other side of the city whom you will never know. A notion of conscience was incoherent apart from taking such a context into account. Then, in the late spring of 2020, George Floyd was murdered by a Minneapolis police officer who, in order to restrain Mr. Floyd, kneeled for nine-and-a-half minutes on his neck to the point of asphyxiation while Mr. Floyd was already lying on the ground with his hands handcuffed behind his back. Looking at the murderous police restraint of Mr. Floyd in the videos that went around the world stirred the conscience of millions: how could such a casual, homicidal act of indifference happen at all, much less be perpetrated by a public authority charged with the duty of public safety? But looking at the scene of Mr. Floyd's death also raised in unprecedented fashion searing questions about White supremacy and racism and the malformation of conscience, not only of (now former) Minneapolis Police Officer Derek Chauvin but also of American society and societies around the world with long histories of racial oppression. What long-held cultural assumptions about the value of Whiteness and the value of Blackness have shaped and distorted our judgments of conscience about criminality, guilt, and innocence? What legal structures of restrictions and opportunities in every phase of life—from schools to housing to criminal justice to politics—have over centuries shaped the way we make judgments of conscience about who is equal, who is free, and who is responsible? The Catholic conscience in the United States has been painfully slow to engage White supremacy and racism. One last aspect of context for the book warrants mention: the democratic political crisis in the United States driven by the rise of an ethnic Christian and populist nationalism. Here concerns about conscience took a paradoxical twist. On the one hand, many

Catholics rallied to the "Catholic conscience" to support a president who backed laws against abortion but who disdained telling the truth to American citizens, repeatedly denigrated persons of color and supported the separation of immigrant families, and whose shocking degree of moral indifference and policy ineptitude contributed to tens of thousands of COVID-19 deaths in the United States. Moreover, throughout the country in the weeks after the November 6, 2020, presidential election, many Democratic and Republican election officials took heroic stands of conscience in the face of pressure from President Trump to lie and cheat in service to keeping him in power.

Finally, for this book, we wish to note the context of Catholic education, especially in the United States. The pandemic blazed an economic fire through many Catholic educational institutions, resulting in closures or at least serious financial struggles at the primary, secondary, and university levels.[6] But Catholic schools were already facing a myriad of challenges that have been decades in the making. In 1965, there were 5.5 million students in Catholic schools across the United States, and today that number is down to 1.6 million.[7] Over the past two decades, over one million students have left Catholic education. The reasons for this decline are many, and they are often debated among those who work in the Catholic school sector. The decline of vocations to religious orders over the past thirty to forty years has resulted in the loss of the low-cost labor force that allowed Catholic schools to offer a high-quality product at a very low cost. The priest abuse scandal has damaged the reputation of Catholic schools in the minds of young parents. New models of public education, like charter schools, have directly competed with many of the aspects of Catholic schools that are appealing to parents, like strong discipline and uniforms. Finally, parents are having fewer children today than they did even a generation ago, so the potential population for all schools is down.

It should be noted that the decline in Catholic school enrollment is mirrored in the decline in participation in the church overall. It is not that there is a Catholic school "problem" in a thriving church, but rather that Catholic school decline is a microcosm of engagement with the broader faith.

---

[6] See Alex Welsh, "Catholics Schools Are Losing Students at Record Rates, and Hundreds Are Closing," *Wall Street Journal*, May 10, 2021; https://www.wsj.com; and Jesse Remedios, "Catholic Colleges Strapped for Cash during Pandemic, Struggle with Re-opening Plans," *National Catholic Reporter*, May 4, 2020; https://www.ncronline.org.

[7] For background and data on Catholic schools, see "Catholic School Data," *National Catholic Education Association*; https://www.ncea.org.

Much has been written about the rise of the "nones," and the fact is that the disengagement and disaffiliation experienced by (mostly young) Catholics also has a consequent impact on Catholic school enrollment. The disaffiliation of young people also should be viewed through the lens of conscience, which can be seen in how certain decisions are made by church hierarchy that in turn impact how Catholic schools are viewed in the wider society.

Finally, it is important to note background tensions between hierarchical directives and the judgments of the community that constitutes a Catholic school or university. Or, in other words, the collective conscience of a Catholic school community is often not considered when major decisions are made. The principle of subsidiarity dictates that those who are most immediate to a problem are best situated to solve it. This principle allows for both individual and collective conscience to be considered when decisions are made that potentially impact the community in a significant way. Those who are closest to a particular situation are more likely to make judgments that include a variety of views within the community. If those decisions are made by those who are detached from that community, the message that is often communicated is detached from the interests of those closest to the situation.

Having set the context for *Conscience and Catholic Education*, it is now time to introduce its rich array of contributors and their essays. In the first essay, moral theologians Michael Lawler and Todd Salzman lay out a theological roadmap for this book. Lawler and Salzman have written widely on the theology of conscience, and here they show how Popes John Paul II and Benedict XVI affirmed in principle the freedom of conscience but also were constantly concerned to limit the legitimate grounds for an appeal to such a concept, especially with regard to moral laws and norms affirmed by the hierarchical teaching office of the church. In doing so, Lawler and Salzman argue, John Paul II and Benedict XVI risked turning back to a mode of thinking common in the decades before the Second Vatican Council in which the conscience of a Catholic was free to do little more than obey such hierarchical edicts. By contrast, Lawler and Salzman note, Pope Francis has recovered the ancient and more spacious theological tradition of conscience oriented to moral truth found both in and beyond the explicit moral teachings of Catholicism. Here misunderstandings abound. Critics of this ancient view of conscience dismiss it as the fruit of liberalism, or as warmed-over subjectivism, or as the leading edge of ethical relativism. But to affirm the doctrine of the freedom of conscience within Catholicism is to affirm, among other things, an inalienable moral responsibility belonging to each person who in any case is to be formed by the teachings, stories, symbols, and sacraments of the Catholic tradition. Is Catholic education meant, in the words of Pope Francis, to "form" or to "replace" the conscience of its students? By making clear the theological tradition of conscience, Lawler and Salzman also make clear the theological grounds for the task of formation—not replacement!—faced by every Catholic educator.

Jesuit moral theologian James Keenan has done crucial recent work on the recovery and renewal of the Catholic theological tradition of conscience—a process he calls "redeeming conscience."[8] In his essay in this book, he builds on this work by turning to the challenge facing every Catholic educator dedicated to the formation of conscience of their students: what is the best way to do this so that behavior actually changes? Keenan, himself a Catholic educator of many decades, argues that it's not enough simply to approach this as an intellectual problem. Instead, he draws on such thinkers as Thomas Aquinas and Judith Butler to argue that we need to think of the formation of conscience in three key steps: first, to start from the awareness of a shared vulnerability with others; second, to move from such a shared awareness to a recognition of a shared humanity; and, third, to turn to conscience for the moral and prudential resources to respond. For Keenan, the story of the Good Samaritan provides a model for conscience formation. The Samaritan allowed himself to be touched by the plight of the robbed man by the side of the road and to see in such a plundered victim a person precisely like himself. "Only after being vulnerably disposed to the other, and then subsequently recognizing the other, do we in conscience act," Keenan notes.

One aspect of Keenan's call for redeeming conscience is his insistence that we think of conscience as both personal and social: indeed, the social dimension emerges from the relationality at the heart of personhood. In her essay for this book, moral theologian Darlene Fozard Weaver builds on these personal and social dimensions of conscience to argue for imagining the contemporary Catholic university as a "community of accountability." Weaver, now associate provost at Duquesne University, takes on the specific theme of conscience and academic freedom at Catholic universities. She reviews the recent history on this matter that pulls in different directions: the autonomy for Catholic universities favored by the Land of Lakes statement from 1967; the clearer Catholic identity called for by John Paul II in

---

[8] James F. Keenan, "Redeeming Conscience," *Theological Studies*, 76, no. 1 (2015): 129–47.

his 1990 document *Ex Corde Ecclesiae*;[9] the social media-driven censorious-
ness of the present day; and American university faculty's expansive claims
to academic freedom, which are not always consistent with key texts in the
tradition of American thought on academic freedom. In response to these
approaches, the notion of conscience understood in terms of a community
of accountability provides a way for a Catholic university to affirm its Cath-
olicity and its freedom in light of a vivid sense of communal obligations.

The work of conscience formation in Catholic schools always proceeds,
for good or ill, on the basis of some scientific understanding about how
persons feel and think and choose. The field of neuroscience has provided a
great deal of new data about such mental processes. In her essay, moral theologian Elizabeth Sweeny Block reviews recent advances in neuroscience in
light of Catholic moral theology and applies her reflections to the task of
conscience formation in Catholic schools. In particular, Block explores what
is called "embodied cognition" as a way to understand better how conscience
formation should proceed, especially in the face of the social and cultural
dimensions of the chronic injustices of racism and poverty. Conscience
formation understood as imparting the intellectual content of moral teaching
may cast a light on such realities but finally doesn't touch their sinful center.
Conscience formation that incorporates a wide range of embodied practices,
rituals, and physical solidarity with the dispossessed holds significantly more
promise of transformation.

The essays opening the book by Lawler and Salzman, Keenan, Weaver,
and Block lay down some theological markers: the Catholic moral tradition
of conscience is in a period of renewal, and their essays articulate that renewal
in light of the challenges of conscience formation in Catholic education. The
next essay in the book moves the conversation in a more decisively applied
direction. Sister Mary Angela Shaughnessy has for years been widely consulted
on matters of state, federal, and constitutional law by Catholic schools around
the country. A lawyer and accomplished educator, in her essay Shaughnessy
offers a magisterial overview of the key concerns regarding conscience and
law that any Catholic school administrator ought to know. What about the
constitutional rights of the Catholic school as an institution compared to the
constitutional rights of employees at a Catholic school? Or the contractual
security of employment of gay, lesbian, or trans persons working in a Catholic school? Or the expanded inclusion of all employees—from teachers

---

[9] Pope John Paul II, *Ex Corde Ecclesiae*—"Apostolic Constitution on Catholic
Universities" (1990).

to janitors—under the designation of the "ministerial exception" affirmed in the last decade by the U.S. Supreme Court? Shaughnessy's essay provides a crucial blueprint to Catholic school administrators for understanding the legal dimensions of such ongoing, vexing matters of conscience.

In 2019, one such vexing issue of conscience was splashed across the national news: Archbishop Charles Thompson of Indianapolis ordered two Catholic high schools in the diocese not to renew the contract of a gay male employee at each school because these men were married to each other contrary to Catholic teaching against gay marriage. Faced with canonical penalties including the possible loss of their designation as a Catholic institution, Cathedral High School complied with the archbishop's directive. But Brebeuf Jesuit Preparatory School did not. In her essay for this book, legal scholar and moral theologian Cathleen Kaveny engages the Brebeuf case as an occasion to reimagine the way we think about such conflicts of conscience. Often, she says, such conflicts are reduced to the case of a heroic holdout refusing to comply with oppressive force. To be sure, there *are* such cases. But there is also a way in which the assumption of such a bipolar conflict is imposed on situations that in fact have a greater degree of moral and relational complexity. So, in the Brebeuf case, Kaveny reconsiders it as a case of conscience involving the ethical obligations and prudential judgments pertinent to the roles and spheres occupied by the key players in the conflict. Kaveny's reimagination of this noted case offers a way for Catholic educators to reimagine their own approaches to similar conflicts.

As the Superintendent of Schools for the Catholic Archdiocese of Los Angeles, Dr. Kevin Baxter engaged issues of conscience that ranged from high-level policy to the hopes and dreams of the students in the largest Catholic school system in the United States. In his essay, Baxter, a Catholic layman, offers a window into challenges faced by administrators in Catholic school systems across the country: the struggles of lay leadership with clericalism; battles within the church over the Common Core standards; and the realities of LGBTQ persons working in the school system, even as rumors in the chancery about their sexual orientation risk costing them their jobs. For Baxter, the insistence by many in the church on making conscience simply a function of Catholic hierarchical teaching has led to significant missed opportunities. He grapples with how to get the best out of employees in the school system if each person is inculturated not to trust their conscience unless it is in strict conformity with hierarchical directives. He also reflects on how to reach the vast number of students with consciences sincerely searching for truth, even if these "nones" may decline for now a more complete embrace of the Catholic tradition.

Dr. Brandi Odom Lucas is the Principal of Verbum Dei High School in the Watts neighborhood of Los Angeles. A Black American woman born and raised in LA, Lucas in her essay speaks from her experience and from her theoretical expertise to offer a model of conscience formation on racism for Catholic schools. For Lucas, her experience growing up in the Macedonia Baptist Church in LA deeply informs her current antiracist work. At that Black church, each member was made to feel respected, free, and beloved by God. Racism was called out—and opposed. Solidarity, honesty, and courage were practiced and made real. And all this took place within the larger reality of the Christian story of hope. In her essay, Lucas draws on the practices and spirit of her treasured church to advance a process of conscience formation to foster equity around race in Catholic schools. Overarching the whole process is the story of the Road to Emmaus: Lucas creatively interprets that famous passage in the Gospel of Luke in which disciples on the road from Jerusalem to Emmaus come slowly to recognize the Risen Christ. She recasts conscience formation around race in terms of three key movements in the story: courageous companionship, the vulnerability of truth telling, and a commitment to restoration.

If racism presents one significant challenge to conscience formation in Catholic schools, diversity presents another. In his essay for the book, former Catholic high school teacher Paul Kuczynski reflects on a powerful empirical fact: students at Catholic schools are more diverse than ever. How at a Catholic school does a singular tradition—Catholicism—engage in conscience formation with students from many different traditions? Drawing on his own experience in the classroom and on the work of educational theorists like Robert Kegan and Luigi Giussani, Kuczynski argues for reimagining Catholic schools not so much as vessels for imparting a single vision of the good but as places that foster a Pope Francis–inspired "culture of encounter" that facilitates fruitful engagement across traditions. There's no simple solution to conscience formation amid such diversity, he says. The work is challenging and can go wrong: The apparent dissonance of diversity can drive adolescents more deeply into silos. But there's also no way to hide from this challenge. And there is great promise in this work, too. The critical engagement of a student with her own tradition that occurs in a culture of encounter can be a decisive step in the development of a responsible freedom about one's own tradition and about the common good. "The question," Kuczynski says, "is whether or not we provide any intentional support as students engage these challenges and develop the capacities capable of handling this complexity."

As a matter of conscience, how should administrators at a Catholic school respond to a trans student? Moral theologian Lisa Fullam uses her essay to assist trans students, their families, and administrators who may face such a situation. She proceeds in three steps: an analysis of "Male and Female He Created Them,"[10] the 2019 document from the Vatican on "gender theory," a review of relevant scientific literature on the biological bases of trans persons, and a reflection on tools from the Catholic moral tradition that can assist everyone involved in these matters. On the one hand, these vexing cases are shaped by the Vatican's strong claims for gender essentialism (that is, one's assigned sex at birth determines one's gender identity) and gender complementarity. On the other hand, Fullam notes, the normative approval of a broader continuum of sex and gender is increasingly common among many; moreover, the testimony of trans persons who don't "choose" their gender so much as "consent" to who and what they already are tells a very different story from the demands of gender essentialism. One tool from the Catholic moral tradition that could be of use in such cases is called "probabilism." This piece of moral theology holds that a "probable," if not "certain," judgment of conscience may be held; probabilism is well suited for complex situations when, for instance, the findings of science may be pointing to new realities contrary to long-held Catholic assumptions about what is "natural."

Patrick O'Kernick's essay for the book takes on the challenge of conscience formation of students at a Catholic college or university. As with other writers in this book, O'Kernick, a doctoral student in Catholic theology, rejects an approach that relies exclusively on the recitation of Catholic moral doctrine. The problem isn't the moral doctrine; it's the exclusive approach that sidesteps the complex worlds of emerging adulthood and the pluralism of students at many Catholic universities. Instead, O'Kernick argues on behalf of what he calls conscience formation understood as the "cultivation of conscience." By this, he means a process of formation that begins with an acknowledgment of the complexity of emerging adulthood, that considers conscience a reality relevant to all aspects of life and not only isolated decisions, that the bedrock of conscience formation first involves engagement with basic values of truth and goodness common to general human experience, and that the experi-

---

[10] Congregation for Catholic Education, "'Male and Female He Created Them': Towards a Path of Dialogue on the Question of Gender Theory in Education" (Vatican City, 2019).

ence of conscience has an inescapably sacred dimension even when it may not be explicitly religious. In turn, O'Kernick provides here an entire teaching module keyed to a sixteen-week semester and ready for use by college, university, and even high school teachers.

For centuries, Catholicism has affirmed the doctrine of the freedom of conscience. But how might the liberating possibilities of such a doctrine be received by persons who have long endured oppression? In her essay for the book, Catholic theologian Pearl Maria Barros takes on this question as it pertains to Latinx and marginalized college and university students. Drawing on the work of thinkers like *mujerista* theologian Ada María Isasi-Díaz and philosopher Eduardo Mendieta, Barros argues that "appeals to inner authority [like conscience] that do not take account of systemic injustice ring false to most people who belong to marginalized communities." In place of such an ahistorical appeal, Barros advances a concept she calls conscience understood as "critical consciousness." By this, she means that the affirmation of the freedom of conscience of the marginalized should occur alongside the critical project of unmasking oppression and the liberationist effort of exploring reimagined communities of justice. Barros, who teaches university-level Latinx and other students, also shares crucial pedagogical tips for teachers who undertake this essential task: be aware of one's own privilege and positionality with regard to oppression; be willing to make mistakes and reject perfectionism; and be unafraid to cultivate hope.

Daniel Castillo is a Catholic moral theologian who specializes in environmental matters. In his essay for the book, Castillo argues that, in response to the challenge of climate change, Catholic schools and universities should engage in a comprehensive process of conscience formation in order to become communities of "integral ecology" (the concept of integral ecology, taken from Pope Francis's 2015 encyclical *Laudato Si'*,[11] requires a community to be organized in response to the cries of the earth and of the poor). Importantly, Castillo connects this process of conscience formation with the Christian imagination. How can Catholic schools and universities not only teach moral thought about the environment but also foster the affectivity of Christian care for the things of creation? Castillo notes that we first have to understand how our pervasive habit of instrumentalizing the natural world does not properly find its justification in Catholic thought, even if some

---

[11] Pope Francis, *Laudato Si'*—"On Care for Our Common Home" (2015), www.vatican.va.

people claim it does.[12] By contrast, Catholic educators need to engage the ancient Catholic theological tradition that articulates the sacramentality of the world (a tradition renewed in *Laudato Si'*). And Catholic schools and universities must also place imaginative engagement with Christian symbols and stories at the center of this process of conscience formation. For centuries, Catholics assumed that the command in Genesis 1:28 to have "dominion" over the world meant they could dominate creation. But what if we drew instead on Genesis to teach that each student is to be a "gardener" responsible to "till and keep" a world now teetering on the edge of disaster?

Julie Hanlon Rubio is a Catholic feminist and professor of social ethics; she has taught at Catholic universities for the last twenty-five years. In her essay for this book, she turns to the theology of conscience as a resource for Catholic feminists in education (and beyond) as they reflect on being in a church with a patriarchal structure resistant to change. To be sure, other Catholic feminists like Anne Patrick and Linda Hogan have written on the theology of conscience. But, Rubio argues, there has to date not been a sustained Catholic feminist reflection on conscience *per se* as a means by which to engage the challenge of being Catholic and feminist. Thus, Rubio puts key categories in the theology of conscience—conscience as an "inner sanctuary," conscience as "formed and malformed," conscience as "creative fidelity," and more—into conversation with feminist thought. For instance, conscience understood in sacred terms as an inner sanctuary where the divine call can be heard indistinctly is likened to Virginia Woolf's noted "room of one's own" where a woman can find the space and solace to engage her creative power. The appeal to conscience doesn't make all dissonance of being Catholic and feminist and working in Catholic education go away. "Purity is not possible in this space," Rubio says. But it clarifies what is at stake, both the challenge and the beauty.

These are the essays of Conscience and Catholic Education. This is a book to be read, studied, and applied. We offer this book in service, with immense gratitude, and with great respect to all those in Catholic education—students, parents, administrators, teachers, professors, and staff.

---

12 For a prominent early example, see the infamous essay by Lynn White Jr., "The Historical Roots of Our Ecologic Crisis," *Science* 155 (1967): 1203–1207.

The Theology of Conscience in the Papacies of John Paul II, Benedict XVI, and Francis

Michael G. Lawler and Todd A. Salzman

The Catholic Church today is in the midst of a profound renewal of its theological tradition of conscience, a renewal that is both provoked and supported by the writings of Pope Francis. At the heart of this renewal are the ideas of the freedom, the authority, the inviolability, and what we will call the subjective-orientation of conscience. In keeping with a general theme of this book, the essay is directed especially to Catholic educators at every level and in every discipline; they should be aware of and respect this development. We hope this essay will help them in doing so. We conclude the essay by exploring communion for the divorced and remarried without annulment to illustrate the practical implications for the freedom and authority of conscience.

Popes John Paul II, Benedict XVI, and Francis all reject ethical relativism. Pope Francis's perspective on the freedom, authority, and inviolability of personal conscience, however, is more closely attuned than that of Popes John Paul and Benedict to the teaching on conscience long embedded in the Catholic tradition and resonantly reaffirmed by the Second Vatican Council. The Council achieved a recovery of the Catholic moral tradition of conscience, a tradition that had become stunted in the centuries before the Council, by an emphasis on the impossibility of conscience arriving at a moral truth different from the moral truth formulated by the magisterium of the Catholic Church. The perspectives of all three popes include both a subject-orientation and an object-orientation of conscience (which we will explain later) but Francis's perspective prioritizes the former over the latter and has a broader understanding of the object-orientation that includes not only some moral norms but also all the relevant circumstances in which the norm is to be applied.

1

Conscience

In the thirteenth century, Thomas Aquinas argued most powerfully for the ancient tradition on the authority and inviolability of conscience.[1] "Anyone upon whom the ecclesiastical authorities, in ignorance of the true facts, imposes a demand that offends against his clear conscience, should perish in excommunication rather than violate his conscience."[2] For any Catholic in search of the good and the true, no clearer statement on the authority and inviolability of personal conscience could be found. Seven hundred years later, the last hundred of which saw the rights of personal conscience much ignored and even suppressed in the Catholic Church, the Second Vatican Council (1962–65) renewed this theological tradition of the primacy of conscience. The conciliar document *Gaudium et Spes* issued a clarion cry in its defense. "Conscience is the most secret core and sanctuary of a man. There he is alone with God whose voice echoes in his depths. In a wonderful manner conscience reveals that law which is fulfilled by love of God and neighbor."[3] The conciliar *Declaration on Religious Freedom* went further to assert the inviolability of conscience. "In all his activity a man is bound to follow his conscience faithfully, in order that he may come to God for whom he was created. It follows that he is not to be forced to act contrary to his conscience. Nor, on the other hand, is he to be restrained from acting in accordance with his conscience, especially in matters religious."[4] In the 1960s, these were words seldom heard in Catholic magisterial circles, but Catholic educators at every level should understand that the freedom, authority, and inviolability of conscience are not ideas that have filtered into the Catholic moral tradition from some modern liberal theory but are ideas deeply rooted in that tradition and, indeed, constitutive of it.

For Aquinas, conscience is related to reason, and its understanding is situated in his assumptions about the nature of the human person. Closely following Aristotle, Aquinas considers the human person to be a unitary being endowed with a body and a rational soul that vivifies it. Reason distinguishes

---

[1] The ancient teaching on conscience in the Christian tradition finds its roots in the Hebrew Scriptures (Jer 17:10; Sir 42:18) and New Testament in St. Paul's writings, who clearly believed in the inviolability and primacy of conscience (1 Cor 10:25–27; 2 Cor 1:12; 4:2).

[2] Thomas Aquinas, *In IV Sent.*, dist. 38, q. 2, a. 4.

[3] Pope John XXIII, *Gaudium et Spes*—Pastoral Constitution on the Church in the Modern World (1965), no. 16. Hereinafter *GS*.

[4] Pope Paul VI, *Dignitatis Humanae*—Declaration on Religious Freedom (1965), no. 3. Hereinafter *DH*.

humans from all other animals, and the rational soul has two powers, intellect and will, intimately related and involved in the process of knowledge. All knowledge begins with experience[5] and proceeds through understanding to judgment and decision, which is then actualized in action. Conscience is the act of practical judgment that something is right or wrong, moral or immoral, to be done or not done. Conscience is, as Robert Smith comments, "the act of practical judgment on a particular moral issue . . . that commands us to do this or not to do that."[6]

Conscience, then, is a process of experience, understanding, judgment, and decision. This process includes a natural grasp of moral principles that Aquinas calls *synderesis*, though the Greek is more correctly *synteresis*. "Though the habits which inform conscience are many," he argues, "nevertheless they all take effect through one chief habit, the grasp of principles called *synderesis*."[7] Aquinas never makes these principles clear anywhere because, in a sense, he doesn't think it's necessary to do so. Or, as Jean Porter argues, his "general theory of goodness requires him to hold that the first principle of practical reasoning is self-evident to all."[8] Cardinal Joseph Ratzinger, in a 1991 speech, interpreted the medieval tradition as offering two levels to the concept of conscience, *synteresis* and conscience. *Synteresis* is "an inner repugnance to evil and an attraction to the good. The act of conscience applies this basic moral inclination and knowledge to particular situations."[9] To make a practical judgment of conscience, then, involves both a grasp of the first principles of practical judgment (*synderesis*) and a gathering of as much evidence as possible, consciously weighing and understanding the evidence and its implications, and finally making as honest a judgment as possible that this action is to be done or not. It is commonplace theologically to insist that, in order to be right and moral, conscience must be informed; formation is precisely the process from gathering the necessary informational evidence to the final step of judgment we have just outlined.

---

[5] See *Summa Theologiae*, I, q. 79, a. 2. For an excellent summary, see Kenneth L. Schmitz, "St. Thomas and the Appeal to Experience," *Proceedings of the Catholic Theological Society of America* 47 (1992): 1–20.

[6] Robert J. Smith, *Conscience and Catholicism: The Nature and Function of Conscience in Contemporary Roman Catholic Theology* (Lanham, MD: University Press of America, 1998), 12.

[7] *Summa Theologiae* I, q. 79, a. 13.

[8] Jean Porter, *The Recovery of Virtue: The Relevance of Aquinas for Christian Ethics* (Louisville, KY: Westminster/John Knox, 1990), 85–86.

[9] Cardinal Joseph Ratzinger, "Conscience and Truth" (1991), https://www.ewtn.com/catholicism/library/conscience-and-truth-2468.

We have described here the basic theology of conscience of the Catholic moral tradition. We would next like to address one of the sources of contemporary dispute over the theology of conscience made evident in the writing of Popes John Paul II, Benedict XVI, and Francis, namely, the threat of ethical relativism. In a reductionist but common way of putting it, is the appeal to the authority of conscience among Catholics simply an appeal to ethical relativism?

Relativism and Perspectivism

Throughout their pontificates, all three popes have raised concerns over relativism, a metaethical theory that claims that there are no universal ethical truths. Relativism fundamentally threatens conscience's search for truth in general and moral truth in particular. In his homily at the opening of the 2005 papal conclave, Cardinal Joseph Ratzinger spoke of the "dictatorship of relativism," which "does not recognize anything as definitive and whose ultimate standard consists solely of one's own ego and desires."[10] Concern about relativism is undoubtedly warranted in the twenty-first century. In 2002, Barna Research Group conducted two national surveys, one among adults and one among teenagers, which asked participants if they believed that there are unchanging moral absolutes or that moral truth is relative to contextual circumstances. In the adult group, 64 percent responded that truth is always relative to the person and his/her situation; in the teenage group, 83 percent responded that truth is always relative to the person and situation, and a mere 6 percent responded that moral truth is absolute.[11] A 2016 Barna study reported that about two out of every three Americans (65 percent) see morality as a matter of cultural consensus, though some 59 percent believed that the Bible provides us with absolute moral truth permitting no exception.[12] These statistics verify our perception that most students entering the university today believe that truth is relative.

---

[10] Joseph Ratzinger, "Cappella Papale Mass 'Pro Eligendo Romano Pontifice' Homily of His Eminence Card. Joseph Ratzinger of the College of Cardinals" (April 18, 2005), http://www.vatican.va/gpII/documents/homily-pro-eligendo-pontifice_20050418_en.html.

[11] Barna Research, "Americans Are Most Likely to Base Truth on Feelings" (February 12, 2002), http://barna.org/FlexPage.aspx?Page=BarnaUpdate&BarnaUpdateID=106.

[12] Barna Research, "The End of Absolutes: America's New Moral Order," https://www.barna.com/research/the-end-of-absolutes-americas-new-mpral-order/

Every semester at the beginning of our Christian ethics courses, which enroll students of diverse national, cultural, religious, and ethnic backgrounds, we show three slides: one shows children in a Nazi concentration camp who have been used for human experimentation; another shows noted physician Paul Farmer treating patients in a hospital facility in Haiti; and the last one shows Terri Schiavo, a permanent vegetative state (PVS) patient, whose case drew national attention in the United States in the early 2000s, hooked up to artificial nutrition and hydration (ANH) in a hospital bed. After describing the ethical issues surrounding each slide, we ask the students, all things being equal, whether the act indicated in the slide is right or wrong. Are the Nazi experimentations on children right or wrong? Is Paul Farmer's medical treatment serving the poor in Haiti right or wrong? Is removing Terri Schiavo from ANH, which will lead to her death, right or wrong? With the first two slides, there is always unanimous agreement: it is wrong what the Nazis did; it is right what Paul Farmer is doing. The third question always has a mixture of responses, with some saying it is right to remove Terri from ANH, and others saying it is wrong.[13]

What is the point of this exercise and what can we learn from it? First, the exercise demonstrates that, though there are diverse social, cultural, religious, and ethnic backgrounds among our students, there is universal consensus on what is right or wrong on *some* ethical issues. This consensus among people of diverse backgrounds challenges claims that relativism is a dominant ethical stance. It also points toward the Catholic tradition's understanding of conscience, which "can recognize with sincerity and honesty what for now is the most generous response which can be given to God, and come to see with a certain moral security that it is what God himself is asking amid the concrete complexity of one's limits."[14] What God is always asking is the fulfillment of the gospel law decreeing love of God and of neighbor (Lk 10:27).

A second and related goal is to discover how different people can agree that there are universal truths, like what is good or right facilitates human dignity and what is bad or wrong frustrates human dignity, and yet disagree on the definition of human dignity and on the formulation and justification of norms that facilitate and do not frustrate it. All our students agree that some acts can never be justified, such as Nazi's experimentation on human subjects. They disagree, however, on the rightness or wrongness of other acts, such as removing ANH from a person in a PVS. What accounts for these

---

[13] Terry Schiavo died in 2005 when she was, in fact, removed from ANH.

[14] Pope Francis, *Amoris Laetitia*, "The Joy of Love" (2016), no. 303. Hereinafter *AL*.

disagreements are often-unarticulated, social and personal commitments about the nature of reality and relationships, and cultural, contextual, political, religious, and ethical beliefs that yield different ethical perspectives. These commitments and beliefs contribute to both shaping definitions of human dignity and formulating and justifying norms for what facilitates and does not frustrate attaining human dignity. It is at the level of foundational commitments and beliefs and conscience's discernment of their anthropological and normative implications that interesting and important ethical discussions in the classroom can occur.

As our survey indicates, even though the vast majority of teenagers may claim that truth is relative to the person and situation, students do agree that some actions are always right and some are always wrong. The tension between the Barna surveys and ours may indicate a simple difference in how relativism is defined. When Popes John Paul, Benedict, and Francis have expressed their concern over the controlling prevalence of relativism in the contemporary world, they have often failed to note the difference between *relativism*, which rejects all universal, objective, and absolute ethical truth, and *perspectivism*, which acknowledges universal, objective, and absolute ethical truth but insists that humans can attain that truth only partially if reliably. In the view of perspectivism, whatever truth persons or communities attain is both a ground on which to stand and a ground in need of further clarification, development, and understanding.

We explain perspectivism via the visual analogy of a man in a multistory building. He looks out a first-story window and sees what that window allows him to see; he then looks out a tenth-story window and a twentieth-story window and sees what those windows allow him to see. What he sees outside the three windows, though different and clearly partial to the extent that our viewer can see only what each window allows him to see, puts into adequate, reliable, but partial focus what truly lies outside each window. When you look out a first-story window, you see what truly lies outside the window; when you look out a twentieth-story window, you see what truly lies outside the window. In terms of the theology of conscience, the view of perspectivism is especially apt. We live in a complex, changing world, and we all inhabit different stories in the building of that world during different periods of cognitive and moral development. We may see the same things, a building outside the window, but depending on the fifth- or twelfth-story perspective, that building may be taller or shorter. Similarly, we can see human dignity, norms, and duties as foundational concepts in ethics, but depending on our perspective, the definition of human dignity and the norms and duties that flow from that definition may differ. We would next like to engage another way of understanding the theology of conscience and its current, contested status. We call this way the object-subject approach to the theology of conscience.

Object-Orientation and Subject-Orientation of Conscience

It is common in contemporary theological ethics to distinguish between what is called the object-orientation and the subject-orientation of conscience. Indeed, keeping in mind this distinction is a helpful way to understand the different approaches to the theology of conscience in the writings of Popes John Paul, Benedict, and Francis. In brief, the object-orientation of conscience refers to the relationship of an individual conscience to objective laws and norms, including church laws and norms, and may include a consideration of circumstances: The subject-orientation of conscience refers to the relationship of an individual conscience to the individual's prudential discernment of a situation. Subject-orientation is about the person or subject *who* is acting and about her/his moral goodness and judgments in a moral situation. Object-orientation is about *what* objective norms a subject must consider in order to be morally correct or right in the situation.

On the basis of different perspectives, the three popes highlight different orientations when explaining the interrelationship between church teaching and conscience formation and moral judgment. Those who prioritize conscience's object-orientation argue that moral norms *must* always be followed and, therefore, that such norms in effect control the subject-orientation of conscience. For instance, in this way of thinking, the emphasis is put on the duty of conscience to comply with a norm no matter what the circumstances are of a particular situation. The norm tells the conscience what to do. By contrast, those who prioritize the subject-orientation of conscience argue that the conscience is free and that, when it makes a moral decision, the subject is guided more by the subject's prudential discernment of a situation than by obedience to a norm. Both models of conscience are evident in the Catholic theological tradition. A problem arises, however, when the object-orientation overwhelms the subject-orientation—when, for instance, the demand for every Catholic conscience to comply with church teaching against the use of artificial contraception confronts the prudent, conscientious disagreement of a Catholic married couple. Catholic educators must learn and teach about these two models of conscience and how they are to be discerned in every concrete situation. Which of these two models of conscience, the primacy of the object-orientation or the primacy of the subject-orientation, is in the forefront in the perspectives of Popes John Paul, Benedict, and Francis?

Pope John Paul II

In his encyclical *Veritatis Splendor*, Pope John Paul II provides a detailed answer to this question that is in tension with the vision of conscience in *Gaudium et Spes* and *Dignitatis Humanae*.[15] He cites St. Paul's assertion that "the law of God is written on the heart."[16] Conscience is an intrinsic dimension of the person's human dignity and the moral law, *"the universal and objective norm of morality,"*[17] and is an essential component of that dignity; "to obey it is the very dignity of [humans]."[18] Conscience knows the foundational principle of this law, to do good and avoid evil, and the magisterium teaches the ethical truths of this law, which the Christian conscience "ought already possess."[19] In this way, the magisterium is at "the service of conscience" and, especially with difficult ethical questions, helps it "to attain the truth with certainty and to abide by it"[20] by applying "the *objective* law to a particular case."[21] John Paul juxtaposes the objective and subjective in relation to a "correct conscience," which is "the *objective truth* received by man"; whereas an erroneous conscience is "what man, mistakenly, *subjectively* considers to be true."[22] He continues, "it is never acceptable to confuse 'subjective' error about moral good with the 'objective' truth rationally proposed to man in virtue of his end."[23] The formation of conscience and its judgment to choose this specific act, for John Paul, follows syllogistically. Conscience is formed by the objective norms taught by the magisterium that have a principle of obedience imprinted upon them, which establish and condition "the corre-

---

[15] See Mary Elsbernd, "The Reinterpretation of *Gaudium et Spes* in *Veritatis Splendor*," *Horizons* 29, no. 2 (2002): 233–34.

[16] Pope John Paul II, *Veritatis Splendor*—"The Splendor of the Truth" (1993), no. 59; Rom 2:16. Hereinafter *VS*.

[17] *VS* no. 60 (emphasis in original).

[18] *VS* no. 54; *GS* no. 16.

[19] *VS* no. 64.

[20] *VS* no. 64.

[21] *VS* no. 59 (emphasis added).

[22] *VS* no. 63 (emphasis in original).

[23] *VS* no. 63.

spondence of [conscience's] decisions with the commands and prohibitions which are at the basis of human behavior."[24] He rejects positions that propose a "creative character of conscience" whereby the "concrete existential considerations" or the circumstances of a situation could justify "certain exceptions to the general rule and thus permit one to do in practice and in good conscience what is qualified as intrinsically evil by the moral law. Such positions attempt to legitimize "pastoral" responses to ethical situations that are "contrary to the teaching of the magisterium";[25] they prioritize the subjective intention over the objective truth of the law.

Pope Benedict XVI

To explain Pope Benedict's perspective on the formation and judgment of conscience and its relationship to church teaching, we must distinguish between his early writings as theologian Joseph Ratzinger and his later writings as Cardinal Ratzinger and Pope Benedict. Although there is scholarly debate about whether there is a radical evolution in Ratzinger's theology throughout his various careers, his evolving writings demonstrate a "continuous and ever more severe assessment of the content and reception of *Gaudium et Spes* [and other Vatican II documents] in the post-conciliar church."[26] This severe assessment is clearly evident when comparing his initial and subsequent analyses of conscience.

In his early commentary on *Gaudium et Spes* theologian Ratzinger states unequivocally,

> Over the Pope as the expression of the binding claim of ecclesiastical authority there still stands one's own conscience, which must be obeyed before all else, if necessary even against the requirement of ecclesiastical authority. Conscience confronts [the individual] with a supreme and ultimate tribunal, and one which in the last resort is beyond the claim of external social groups, even of the official church.[27]

---

[24] *VS* no. 60.

[25] *VS* no. 56.

[26] Lieven Boeve, "Introduction: Joseph Ratzinger: His Life, Thought, and Work," in *The Ratzinger Reader: Mapping a Theological Journey: Joseph Ratzinger*, ed. Boeve and Gerard Mannion (London: T&T Clark, 2010), 12.

[27] Joseph Ratzinger, "The Dignity of the Human Person," in *Commentary on the Documents of Vatican II*, Vol. 5, ed. Herbert Vorgrimler (New York: Herder, 1969), 134.

He argues that conscience should be informed and guided and that church teaching is a helpful guide in this formation, but he recognizes the limitations of church teaching and tradition. "Not everything that exists in the church must for that reason be also a legitimate tradition. . . . There is a distorting as well as legitimate tradition." The long-standing church teachings prohibiting taking of interest on loans and religious freedom and permitting slavery are well-known examples of distorting traditions that the church now rejects. Ratzinger concludes to what is obvious: "Consequently tradition must not be considered only affirmatively but also critically."[28] The object-orientation of conscience affirms the objectively true and good and it is the duty of the subject-orientation of conscience to critically analyze and consider if and how the objective norm applies.

As head of the Congregation for the Doctrine of the Faith (CDF) and as Pope Benedict, Ratzinger's hermeneutic of Vatican documents, shaped in large part by perceived threats of a "dictatorship of relativism," became more critical of what he considered lax trends in the theology of conscience. His writing at this time of his life signaled a shift from the primacy of a subject-orientation of conscience to discern the true and the good in a situation to an object-orientation of conscience in which the church's objective norm reveals the true and the good to the discerning subject. "Conscience signifies the perceptible and demanding presence of the voice of truth in the subject himself."[29] This truth "is first of all *given* to us. In every cognitive process, truth is not something that we produce, it is always found, or better, received. Truth, like love, 'is neither planned nor willed, but somehow imposes itself upon human beings.'"[30]

This evolution from the primacy of subject-orientation to the primacy of object-orientation of conscience is also evident in Ratzinger's assessment of Cardinal John Henry Newman and the authority of conscience. In his commentary on *Gaudium et Spes* and the relationship between conscience and authority, theologian Ratzinger would seem quite comfortable with, and supportive of, the primacy of conscience over the pope and ecclesiastical law. In the words of Newman and his famous comment in a letter to the Duke of Norfolk, "If I am obliged to bring religion into after-dinner toasts . . . , I shall drink to the Pope if you please, still to conscience first and to the Pope

---

[28]   Joseph Ratzinger, "The Transmission of Divine Revelation," in *Commentary on the Documents of Vatican II,*" Vol. 3, ed. Herbert Vorgrimler (New York: Herder, 1969), 185.

[29]   Ratzinger, "Conscience and Truth."

[30]   Pope Benedict XVI, *Caritas in Veritate*—"Charity in Truth" (2009), no. 34.

afterwards."[31] Newman was of the opinion that in the modern age the papacy wrongly came to be seen as an objective authority controlling the subject. This view of Newman was incorrect, Ratzinger later judged, because conscience points toward an openness to the objective truth the papacy presents. It's a sort of seamless back and forth. If conscience truly searches for the truth, it will actually find the truth already articulated in the magisterial teaching of the church. Object-orientation is primary; subject-orientation conforms to and obeys the object-orientation.

Pope Francis

In *Amoris Laetitia,* Pope Francis brings squarely to the moral forefront the Catholic teaching on the freedom, authority, and inviolability of personal conscience. With Francis, the subject-orientation of conscience is, in our judgment, restored to its rightful place in that teaching. He writes that "Individual conscience needs to be better incorporated into the Church's praxis in certain situations which do not *objectively* embody our understanding of marriage,"[32] or, we add, many other ethical issues. Francis also notes that the church is called to form, not replace, consciences.[33] His introduction of "new pastoral methods" qualifies John Paul and Benedict's prioritization of a narrow object-orientation and their focus on conscience's conformity to absolute proscriptive norms. Francis's emphasis on the connection between conscience and discernment shifts the priority to a subject-orientation. We consider now how Francis's introduction of new pastoral methods and his emphasis on discernment influence the Catholic theology of conscience.

New Pastoral Methods

Whereas John Paul II is suspicious of "pastoral" solutions that may contradict magisterial teaching,[34] Francis introduces "new pastoral methods" in *Amoris Laetitia* that "respect both the church's teaching and local [and individual] problems and needs."[35] These methods embrace the existential, lived reality of persons in all their complexity. He quotes Thomas Aquinas

---

[31] Cardinal John Henry Newman, "Conscience," http://www.newmanreader.org/works/anglicans/volume2/gladstone/section5.html.

[32] *AL* no. 303.

[33] *AL* no. 37.

[34] *VS* no. 56.

[35] *AL* no. 199.

frequently throughout the document and, for the first time in an official papal document, he refers to Aquinas's axiom that the more we descend into the details of any situation, the more general principles will be found to fail.[36] As the popular saying goes, the devil is in the details. There is an "immense variety of concrete situations" and situations can be so vastly different that church teaching, the pope confesses, cannot "provide a new set of rules, canonical in nature and applicable to all cases."[37] The only moral solution to any and every situation is a path of careful discernment and a final judgment of educated personal conscience that commands us to do this or not to do that.[38] Only such an informed conscience can make a moral judgment about the details of any and every particular situation. Francis's new pastoral method transforms John Paul's and Benedict's narrow understanding of object-orientation and a deductive, absolutist application of norms to concrete situations, which ignore morally relevant circumstances, to a broad, inductive understanding that includes all morally relevant circumstances. In addition, his emphasis on discernment shifts the priority of conscience from object to subject-orientation.

Discernment

Although it is hardly surprising to find discernment used frequently by a Jesuit son of St. Ignatius of Loyola, it is surprising to find it used so centrally in official church teaching as a basis for forming conscience and guiding responsible decisions in the realm of ethics. In the Jesuit tradition, discernment is the art of prayerful decision-making that relies upon spiritual practices,[39] and this approach is clearly reflected in *Amoris Laetitia*. In his commentary on *Amoris Laetitia*, Archbishop Andre Vingt-Trois of Paris writes that it invites all pastoral workers in the church and, we add, all Christians, to return to "meditating on the message of Christ and the Christian tradition of the family and to seek to understand how this message could help to accompany families in the challenges that face them today."[40] Discernment, Francis writes,

---

[36] *AL* no. 304; Aquinas, *Summa Theologiae*, I-II, q. 94, art. 4.

[37] *AL* no. 300.

[38] *AL* nos. 300–305.

[39] James Martin, "Understanding Discernment is Key to Understanding *Amoris Laetitia*," *America* (April 8, 2016), http://www.americamagazine.org/issue/discernment-key-amoris-laetitia.

[40] See Anne-Bénédicte Hoffner, "*Amoris Laetitia* Requires an Effort of Formation of Discernment," *LaCroix International* (October 19, 2016), https://

requires "humility, discretion, and love for the church and her teaching, in a sincere search for God's will and a desire to make a more perfect response to it."[41] Discernment, however, is much more than simply following absolute norms. It moves us from a legalistic-type ethic to a virtue-type ethic, grounded in the theological virtues of faith, hope, charity, compassion, mercy, justice, and prudence. These virtues do not seek simply to conform to a moral law but instead help us to see and judge from a uniquely Christian perspective and to act in a uniquely Christian way. In turn, a discerning process of conscience formation involves seeing and judging in a way that may lead to acts that follow norms presented by the church or they may lead to the act of challenging those norms. Authentic discernment in the subject-orientation of conscience allows for, and sometimes may even demand, conscience's dissent from magisterial teaching.

Clashing Theologies of Conscience: Communion for the Divorced and Remarried without Annulment

Both models of conscience are evident in the Catholic Church and in the theologies of its professional ethicists. Those who prioritize an object-orientation argue that conscience *must* follow established ecclesiastical moral norms that control the subject-orientation. Those who prioritize a subject-orientation argue that conscience is free and authoritative and that, when it is in the process of discerning a moral decision, it *must* take into consideration not only relevant ecclesiastical norms but also relevant concrete circumstances that can override those norms, cause one to choose a different norm, or lessen moral culpability. The two models are clearly evident in efforts to interpret and apply church teaching on communion for Catholics who are divorced and have remarried without their earlier marriage having been annulled.

In *Familiaris Consortio* Pope John Paul II explicitly teaches the norm that the divorced and remarried without an annulment cannot be admitted to communion.[42] As head of the Congregation for the Doctrine of the Faith and as Pope Benedict, Joseph Ratzinger affirms this same norm. "The conscience of the individual," he declares, "is bound to this norm without

---

international.la-croix.com/news/amoris-laetitia-requires-an-effort-of-formation-for-discernment/4085.

[41] *AL* no. 300.

[42] Pope John Paul II, *Familiaris Consortio*—"The Fellowship of the Family" (1981), no. 84.

exception."[43] John Paul and Benedict assert a moral truth in itself, a narrow object-orientation of conscience obligating Catholic subjects simply to obey the objective moral norm. In their eyes, the conscience of a Catholic who is divorced and remarried without an annulment simply may not entertain as morally acceptable under any circumstances the possibility of receiving communion.

But the subject-orientation of conscience requires both the discernment of moral truth and the discernment of such truth precisely amid any and every relevant circumstance. Pope Francis clearly teaches this in several different ways in *Amoris Laetitia.* Speaking of those in the "irregular situation" of being divorced and remarried without annulment, he acknowledges that they "can find themselves in a variety of situations, which should not be pigeon-holed or fit into overly rigid classifications leaving no room for personal and pastoral discernment."[44] In a footnote that became instantly famous, he cites the Second Vatican Council's judgment that if they take the option of living as brother and sister the church offers them, "it often happens that faithfulness is endangered and the good of the children suffers."[45] For these reasons, the pope continues,

> a pastor cannot feel that it is enough simply to apply moral laws to those living in "irregular" situations, as if they were stones to throw at people's lives. This would bespeak the closed heart of one used to hiding behind the church's teachings, "sitting on the chair of Moses and judging at times with superiority and superficiality difficult cases and wounded families."[46]

Francis rejects prioritization of a narrow object-orientation of conscience and prefers a new pastoral method that prioritizes a subject-orientation focused on discernment.

This new method leads to a broader object-orientation that includes the existential, circumstantial reality of people's lives and leads the people

---

[43] CDF, "Concerning Some Objections to the Church's Teaching on the Reception of Holy Communion by Divorced and Remarried Members of the Faithful" (January 1, 1998), http://www.vatican.va/roman_curia/congregations/cfaith/documents/rc_con_cfaith_doc_19980101_ratzinger-comm-divorced_en.html.

[44] *AL* no. 298.

[45] *AL* no. 298; *GS* no. 51.

[46] *AL* no. 305.

themselves to a more personal love of God, neighbor, and self. His response to this and other ethical issues emphasizes a return to Catholic tradition and teaching on the freedom, authority, and inviolability of personal conscience, which "needs to be better incorporated into the church's praxis in certain situations which do not *objectively* embody our understanding of marriage."[47] His argument, of course, applies not only to marriage and divorce and remarriage without annulment but also to every other concrete personal moral situation.

Conclusion

As we pointed out in our introduction, John Paul II, Benedict XVI, and Francis all reject ethical relativism. Pope Francis's perspective on the freedom, authority, and inviolability of personal conscience, however, is more faithful to Catholic tradition than are the perspective of Popes John Paul and Benedict. Both perspectives include a subject-orientation and an object-orientation of conscience, but Francis's perspective prioritizes the former over the latter and has a broader understanding of the object-orientation that includes not only the church's narrow definition but also all the relevant circumstances in which the norm is to be applied. It is crucial for all those working at every level of Catholic education to note that Pope Francis highlights, as we have shown, not some modern liberal intrusion into the Catholic moral tradition but a genuine recovery of the true theology of conscience in that tradition. For too long, the leadership of the church and Catholic educators at every level obedient to it have ignored this tradition on conscience and have taught a version of conscience-theology that has left no room for the informed consciences of Catholics across a wide range of church teachings. Educating according to this narrow understanding of conscience has the immediate consequence of turning out unthinking and obedient Catholics. Unfortunately, it has the long-term drawback of turning out obedient and unthinking Catholic children and adolescents, ill-equipped to deal with the multiple moral questions that face them in the modern adult world. It is time, we suggest, for the Catholic Church and Catholic educators to go back to the Catholic tradition on the freedom, authority, and inviolability of conscience recovered by the Second Vatican Council and reaffirmed by Pope Francis. This tradition teaches that following one's conscience on moral and religious

---

[47] *AL* no. 303 (emphasis added).

matters facilitates one's human dignity and development, and violating one's conscience on moral and religious matters frustrates one's human dignity and development.[48] It provides a firm guide that demands that Catholic believers must, first, responsibly inform their consciences and, then, equally responsibly follow their inviolable conscience-judgment on every moral issue.

---

[48]   *GS* no. 16; *DH* no. 3.

Building Blocks for Moral Education

Vulnerability, Recognition, and Conscience

James F. Keenan, SJ

I want to share with you an ongoing discovery.

Years ago I became worried about teaching conscience formation. It seemed to me that we were designing conscience formation as if the students just needed a number of instructions. I began to see that we were thinking of conscience as a faculty, as something the students had, that we wanted to form.

Now I am beginning to think that conscience is an act and that it follows from some other disposition.

I say this because I see some students who are responsive to the need for moral assistance, others not. If all have consciences, why do some respond and others do not? Moreover, if they all take courses on conscience formation, why is it that afterward some respond to the need for moral assistance and others do not?

Failing to respond *in the first place* seems to be the predominant failure in human history. At least it appears that way in the Bible. People do not fail having responded; rather, they fail beforehand: they fail to bother to respond *in the first place.* The priest and the Levite pass by the man on the road in Luke 10:30–37; the goats don't see the hungry and the naked in Matthew 25:31–46; and the rich man steps over Lazarus in Luke 16:19–31. None of them respond.

Is there something that starts the ball rolling? Is there something about conscience formation that precedes the act of conscience that considers what am I to do? Is there something we are not forming that eventually gets one to act?

I think the problem is that we think of the beginning of moral action as the conscience, but I now believe that only after being vulnerably disposed to the other, and then subsequently recognizing the other, do we in conscience

17

act. In other words, I think there are two steps before acting in conscience: being vulnerably disposed and then actually recognizing. These are the preconditions to the conscience act.

Let's return to the Good Samaritan parable. I do not know if the priest and the Levite could have acted in conscience, but I do know two things. Neither in their humanity were vulnerably disposed to the injured man, and neither gave him the recognition that he was injured and in need.

On the other hand, the Good Samaritan's first recognition of the injured man gives evidence of his vulnerability to the wounded man. Then, after he recognized the man as being in need, he conscientiously went about the details of what he needed to do: clean the wounds, get him to a safe place, make inquiries about the appropriate place in which to leave him, negotiate and secure from the innkeeper his oversight of the injured man, dispense with his funds, redesign his return so that he could return to this particular inn so as to take the man with him, etc.

The Good Samaritan's conscience got a workout, but the work of conscience was the particular reflection of not whether to respond but what to do. Whether to respond happened when his vulnerable disposition *recognized* the man; the recognition led then to the conscience question: now what do I do?

One reason why we do not see what precedes the conscience is because, disregarding Thomas Aquinas, we think of conscience as essentially both a faculty and an act. We think of conscience as something one has *and* as something one does. I know I did. But I do not anymore. I think something precedes conscience: a vulnerable disposition and then the act of vulnerability that is recognizing another.

I think now that conscience is not a power or a faculty but simply an act, just as Thomas argued.[1] I think we act in conscience when we try to descend into the particulars about what our moral response should be.

All ethics courses are effectively about conscience, of what constitutes the right conduct toward the other, the common good, or even the self. Ethics effectively helps form conscience for its right action. That moral response is what I now am calling the conscience act, which is much different from the previous matter that I am now calling the recognition.

In the article prior to the one on conscience, Thomas asked about a closely related aspect of the moral life called *synderesis*. There he argued that *synderesis* is a habit that inclines us to the good and that while it incites us to

---

[1] Thomas Aquinas, *Summa Theologiae* I. 79. 13.

the good and murmurs at evil, this initial habit is for Thomas what eventually launches the act of conscience deliberating.[2] Like Thomas, I want to argue that something precedes conscience that inclines us toward the good. Thomas called this inclination synderesis. I want to explore what that something is in different, more contemporary terminology, so that we can better educate our students in conscience formation.

What the goats, the rich man, the priest, and the Levite have in common is that they were not vulnerable to and did not recognize the other, that is, the homeless and the naked, poor Lazarus, and the wounded stranger. If they had recognized these humans as such, then they would have needed in conscience to figure out what ethics wanted from them. I believe that these instances of "overlooking" others happen precisely because these agents were not prompted to see or imagine the others as like them. In that same moment, they gave themselves permission not to be bothered by the others or by their situation. Lacking the vulnerable disposition and the habit of recognizing these people, they passed them by.

They knew ethics, but only for those whose dignity they recognized: the priest and Levite for their colleagues, the rich man for his business partners. But they are not interested in ethics for those whom they do not recognize. If they recognize them as worthy, then they need ethics.

What we have to address is their particular indifference, their lack of vulnerability and recognition. We need to tap their vulnerability and then train them to recognize others beyond family, friends, and caste.

In what follows, I want to do three things. I want to first examine vulnerable dispositions and then recognition. Then I want to return to the question that is the focus of this book.

For those of you well read in theological ethics and conscience, let me situate my argument between one made forty-five years ago and another, much more recently. Timothy O'Connell distinguished conscience 1, 2, and 3, which represented the nascent call (1) of conscience, the process of (2) deliberation in conscience and the commitment (3) to conscience. What I refer to as vulnerability is somewhat analogous to his conscience 1 (or Thomas's *synderesis*), and what I call conscience is his conscience 2. But recognition is a commitment that happens prior to conscience, not at the end as O'Connell suggests.[3]

---

[2] *Summa Theologiae* I. 79. 12.

[3] Timothy O'Connell, *Principles for a Catholic Morality* (Minneapolis: Seabury Press, 1976), 83–97.

I think that my argument eventually advances the insight of Daniel Fleming who also argues that conscience 1 is akin to vulnerability, that a student's encounter with conscience 1 is a threshold experience, and that the work of conscience education is to help students to cross that threshold of conscience 1. My differences with Fleming are threefold. First, in his work on vulnerability, he relies on Emmanuel Levinas, and I on Judith Butler; I believe her understanding of vulnerability is much more capacious. Second, Fleming's crossing the threshold is what I, and others, call recognition. I will suggest that those working in moral education ought to attend more to the multiple works on recognition so as to help students develop the habit of recognition and thus enable multiple crossings of the threshold. Third, unlike Fleming, I suggest that we move beyond O'Connell's "conscience 1, 2, 3" and speak instead of the vulnerable disposition, the habit of recognition, and the work of conscience.[4]

Vulnerability

Like many others, when I first thought of vulnerability, I considered it singularly as being wounded, as primarily a condition that raises alarm and concern. From the writings of Judith Butler, among others, I began to see vulnerability as more responsive.

When I recognized that the word "vulnerable" does not mean having been wounded, but rather being able to be wounded, then I began to see how it means being exposed to the other; in this sense vulnerability is the human condition that allows me to hear, encounter, receive, or respond to the other even to the point of being injured. Being human is being vulnerable.[5]

Being vulnerable should not be reduced to being precarious, that is, being in an unstable or risky situation where the possibility or the continuation of harm occurs. Butler realizes that too many people think of vulnerability as primarily being in an unstable context. She rather wants us to understand that all of us as human beings are vulnerable to one another and precisely when one's vulnerability is at risk, we vulnerably respond. So wisely she distinguishes precarity as a moment of risk for the vulnerable human. She notes, "Precarity exposes our sociality, the fragile and necessary dimensions of our interdependency."[6]

---

[4] Daniel Fleming, "The Threshold of Conscience: A Radical Challenge for Education in Theological Ethics . . . and Beyond," *Journal of Adult Theological Education* 13 (2016): 103–16.

[5] See the helpful insights in Erinn C. Gilson, *The Ethics of Vulnerability: A Feminist Analysis of Social Life and Practice* (New York: Routledge, 2014), 31–38.

[6] Judith Butler, "Precarious Life, Vulnerability, and the Ethics of Cohabitation,"

Certainly, in being vulnerable, we have the capacity to encounter and respond to another whose vulnerability is precarious, as in the Prodigal Son parable (Lk 15:11–32) where the son's own precarity is evident. But, while the beginning of that parable focuses on the younger brother's precarity, the center of the parable emerges as we recognize the vulnerability of the Father who recognizes his son in the distance; embraces him; reincorporates him; and works to restore all that was unstable, threatened, exposed, and jeopardized. Like the vulnerable Good Samaritan, the vulnerable father recognizes his son as the precarious one, a humanity not recognized by those who left him to eat with the pigs.

Butler recognizes how fundamentally foundational vulnerability is: "Ethical obligation not only depends upon our vulnerability to the claims of others but establishes us as creatures who are fundamentally defined by that ethical relation."[7] Vulnerability is what defines and establishes us as capable of being moral among one another.

Again, emphasizing the priority of vulnerability, she contends,

> This ethical relation is not a virtue that I have or exercise; it is prior to any individual sense of self. It is not as discrete individuals that we honor this ethical relation. I am already bound to you, and this is what it means to be the self I am, receptive to you in ways that I cannot fully predict or control.[8]

Vulnerability essentially is what most qualifies my self as one among others.

She returns to the priority of vulnerability, as prior even to the moan from another in need:

> You call upon me, and I answer. But if I answer, it was only because I was already answerable; that is, this susceptibility and vulnerability constitutes me at the most fundamental level and is there, we might say, prior to any deliberate decision to answer the call. In other words, one has to be already capable of receiving the call before actually answering it. In this sense, ethical responsibility presupposes ethical responsiveness.[9]

The Journal of Speculative Philosophy 26, no. 2 (2012): 134–51, at 148; See also her *Precarious Life: The Power of Mourning and Violence* (Brooklyn: Verso, 2004).

[7] Butler, "Precarious Life," 141; See also her *Giving an Account of Oneself* (New York: Fordham University Press, 2005).

[8] Butler, "Precarious Life," 141–42.

[9] Ibid., 142. See also Judith Butler, Zeynep Gambetti, and Leticia Sabsay, eds.,

Our vulnerability is our answerability, what allows and prompts us to recognize, to respond, to communicate—in short, to love.[10]

Theologically, Butler's natural, created answerableness resonates with a variety of creation narratives that capture the vulnerability of the human. Though not from a theologian, T. H. White's wonderful *The Once and Future King*[11] provides an account of creation that captures it beautifully. God gathers all the embryos of each and every species of animal life and on the sixth day offers each embryo the opportunity to ask for an addition that will distinguish their species. The giraffe embryo gets a long neck for tree food, the porcupine asks for quills for protection, and so it goes for the entire animal kingdom. The last embryo is the human who when asked by God what he wants, responds, "I think that You made me in the shape which I now have for reasons best known to Yourselves, and that it would be rude to change. . . . I will stay a defenceless embryo all my life." God is delighted and lets the human embryo have no particular protection, to be the most vulnerable of all newborns, and says, "As for you, Adam . . You will look like an embryo till they bury you."[12]

Behind White's imaginative portrayal of creation is his remarkable vision of the human embryo as the bearer of human vulnerability. By positing the human as willing to remain vulnerable, White is able to disclose further God's delight in that the human now is in God's image, precisely because of the deci-

---

Vulnerability in Resistance (Durham, NC: Duke University Press, 2016); Catriona Mackenzie, Wendy Rogers, and Susan Dodds, eds., *Vulnerability: New Essays on Ethics and Feminist Philosophy* (New York: Oxford University Press, 2013).

[10] See other theological ethicists who have turned to vulnerability as providing a foundations for theological ethics: Linda Hogan, "Vulnerability: An Ethic for a Divided World," in *Building Bridges in Sarajevo: The Plenary Papers of Sarajevo 2018*, ed. James Keenan, Kristin Heyer, and Andrea Vicini (Maryknoll, NY: Orbis Books, 2019), 217–22; Enda McDonagh, *Vulnerable to the Holy: In Faith, Morality and Art* (Dublin, Ireland: Columba Press, 2005); Vincent Leclerq, *Blessed Are the Vulnerable: Reaching out to Those with AIDS* (New London, CT: Twenty-Third Publications, 2010); Roger Burggraeve, "Violence and the Vulnerable Face of the Other: The Vision of Emmanuel Levinas on Moral Evil and Our Responsibility," *Journal of Social Philosophy* 30, no. 1 (1999): 29–45; Hille Haker, "The Fragility of the Moral Self," *The Harvard Theological Review* 97, no. 4 (2004): 359–81; Daniel J. Fleming, *Attentiveness to Vulnerability: A Dialogue between Emmanuel Levinas, Jean Porter, and the Virtue of Solidarity* (Eugene, OR: Pickwick Publications, 2019); Charles Mathewes, "Vulnerability and Political Theology," in *Exploring Vulnerability*, ed. Heikke Springhart and Günther Thomas, (Bristol, CT: Vandenhoeck & Ruprecht, 2017), 165–84.

[11] T. H. White, *The Once and Future King* (New York: Ace Books, 1987).

[12] Ibid., chap. XXI.

sion to "stay as a defenceless embryo all my life." White concludes his account with God revealing to the human, "Adam . . . eternally undeveloped, you will always remain potential in Our image, able to see some of Our sorrows and to feel some of Our joys. We are partly sorry for you, Man, but partly hopeful."[13] Human dignity, rooted in the image of God, participates in the vulnerability of God.

This insight of our vulnerability being connected to God's resonates with Enda McDonagh's work, *Vulnerable to the Holy: In Faith, Morality and Art.*[14] There he begins his treatment on vulnerability with God. God reveals to us God's self as vulnerable by the birth of Jesus in Bethlehem, his life in Nazareth, and his death on Golgotha. Thus, sounding like White, McDonagh writes that to be made in God's image is to be made vulnerable. Our dignity is rooted in God's vulnerability.

Recognition

Besides theology and philosophy, the literature on vulnerability expands elsewhere.[15] For this essay, I want to turn to the work on gender and domination by the psychoanalyst and feminist theorist Jessica Benjamin, who reflected on infancy and mutual recognition among infants. Mutual recognition is the central experience of infants among infants; after being the object of the attention of people much bigger than themselves, mutual recognition is where an infant finally encounters another that seems much like itself and yet, not.

Benjamin writes, "Mutual recognition is the most vulnerable point in the process of differentiation." She adds, "In mutual recognition, the subject accepts the premise that others are separate but nonetheless share like feelings and intentions."[16] In this work Benjamin sought to explore ways of restoring mutual recognition as a defining key for understanding right relationship between the genders. In a more recent work in 2017, she turns again to mutual recognition and among other matters finds the language of vulnerability key for recuperating and restoring the experience of mutual recognition.[17]

---

[13] Ibid.

[14] McDonagh, *Vulnerable to the Holy.*

[15] Brené Brown, *Daring Greatly: How the Courage to Be Vulnerable Transforms the Way We Live, Love, Parent, and Lead* (New York: Avery Publishing, 2015).

[16] Jessica Benjamin, *The Bonds of Love: Psychoanalysis, Feminism, and the Problem of Domination* (New York: Pantheon, 1988), 53.

[17] Jessica Benjamin, *Beyond Doer and Done to: Recognition Theory, Intersubjectivity, and the Third* (New York: Routledge, 2017).

As we mature, the experience of mutual recognition can and should happen time and again as part of our growth as moral agents. The mutual recognition in infancy becomes the foundation for subsequent expressions of due recognition whenever we encounter humanity in its greatest precarity or neglect. From that first recognition where we acknowledge the other's and our own humanity, we learn to develop a sense that the other in need is another human being. Of course, as we saw earlier in the biblical stories, overlooking the humanity of another is what gives us "permission" to withhold due recognition. Thus, the work of education is to help one another to be vulnerable and vigilant enough so that due recognition and appropriate response to the other is actualized as the worthy alternative to the customary, but harmful stance of overlooking or neglect.

The philosopher Paddy McQueen explains recognition as an insight and a practice that develops, going from first being an awakening; second, to making a form of identification; and, finally, to appreciating a responsible relationship that broadens our self-understanding:

> The term "recognition" has several distinct meanings: (1) an act of
> intellectual apprehension, such as when we "recognize" we have made
> a mistake or we "recognize" the influence of religion on American
> politics; (2) a form of identification, such as when we "recognize" a
> friend in the street; and (3) the act of acknowledging or respecting
> another being, such as when we "recognize" someone's status,
> achievements or rights. . . . The philosophical and political notion
> of recognition predominantly refers to (3), and is often taken to
> mean that not only is recognition an important means of valuing or
> respecting another person, it is also fundamental to understanding
> ourselves.[18]

McQueen's move from recognizing someone familiar to giving recognition to one to whom it is due is, I think, the threshold into the moral life. What we learn in infancy is literally a first lesson: in our vulnerability we can recognize that we are related one to the other. Then, we move from an awakening to a form of identification. Later, as children, we realize that that form of identification calls us to a form of responsiveness, especially when the other is neglected, in need, or oppressed. The awakening to and the identifi-

---

[18]   Paddy McQueen, "Social and Political Recognition," *The Internet Encyclopedia of Philosophy*, https://www.iep.utm.edu/recog_sp/#SH3a.

cation with another's humanity are therefore the first steps across the moral threshold.

We can return to the prodigal son parable to uncover recognition's rich relationship with both the vulnerable and the familiar. In the parable, as the vulnerable father attends to the prodigal, he remains vulnerable to his older son who does not suffer from precarity but from dominance, which expresses itself in his resentment. Still, we should not think that the father is surprised by the older son's resentment. When he sees his younger son in the distance, he knows that his movement toward that son will surely trigger the older son's own insecurities that are covered by his dominance. Here then we recognize the father's own vulnerability that anchors both sons. The stability in the story is the vulnerable father, as the precarious son returns and the resentful one tries to leave; the enduringly vigilant, attentive, and responsive Father is so because he is vulnerable.[19] So when the older son refers to his brother as "that son of yours," the father wants him to *recognize* his brother, "this brother of yours was dead and has come to life." But the brother needs to be vulnerable before he can recognize; without it, due recognition just does not happen.

One of my doctoral students reintroduced me to the notion of due recognition. In a paper he delivered in Rwanda in the summer of 2019, "Twenty-Five Years after the Genocide: Can Rwanda Embrace an Ethics of Recognition?," the Nigerian Hilary Nwainya developed this fundamental insight because he wanted to recognize not only the victims of the genocide but also the reformed, penitent perpetrators. He noted that in Rwanda there was recognition for those harmed but not for those who, through restorative justice, were seeking reinsertion back into their community, wanting to be recognized as such; till now they remain ignored, overlooked, and neglected.[20]

Nwainya notes that our human dignity is established socially by an appreciation of our interrelatedness. Borrowing from Charles Taylor, he argues that in the context of shared human dignity, due recognition is not then just a courtesy we owe people, which we can confer or reserve at will, but rather a vital human need.[21] When we fail to give due recognition, we

---

[19] James F. Keenan, "Vulnerability and the Father of the Prodigal Son," Alfonsiana Blog, September 27, 2019 https://www.alfonsiana.org/blog/2019/09/27/vulnerability-and-the-father-of-the-prodigal-son/.

[20] Hilary Nwainya, "Twenty-Five Years after the Genocide: Can Rwanda Embrace an Ethics of Recognition?" presented at an International Conference held on June 20–22, 2019, at the Center Christus in Kigali, Rwanda, on the 25th Anniversary of the Genocide in Rwanda Kigali conference.

[21] Charles Taylor, "The Politics of Recognition" in *Multiculturalism: Examining*

often add to the oppression of the other, whose own situation might well be related to our own, though we fail to acknowledge it. Recognition becomes then a moment not only of the engaged awareness of another's situation but also of the self-reflective awareness of my relationship to that other and her or his situation.

Reverting the Gaze

In 1932, Reinhold Niebuhr warned ethicists that they lacked "an understanding of the brutal character of the behavior of all human collectives, and the power of self-interest and collective egoism in all inter-group relations."[22] There, in *Moral Man and Immoral Society: A Study in Ethics and Politics*, he insisted that we do not see "the limitations of the human imagination, the easy subservience of reason to prejudice and passion, and the consequent persistence of irrational egoism, particularly in group behavior."[23] In many ways we go on teaching today nearly ninety years later failing to heed the forces that empower "the inequalities of privilege (that) are greater than could possibly be defended rationally."[24] It is in the interests of such forces that we continue to fail to recognize those whose inequities pay the price of our privilege. No wonder that we rarely recognize.

And yet, reason is often invoked precisely to defend such inequalities of privilege and thus to keep us from giving due recognition to others. In her stunning critique of Adam Smith's *Theory of Moral Sentiments,* Kate Ward describes Smith's contempt for "'those whining and melancholy moralists' who call attention to the suffering of distant others," noting how he considers the moralists' sympathy for those with misfortunes "absurd and unreasonable" and irresistibly unnatural.[25] The father of capitalism understood well the importance of keeping our gaze from those who are victims of our privilege.

Isabel Wilkerson, in her magnificent *Caste: The Origins of Our Discontent,* takes us further than Niebuhr and provides us with the image of the "wordless

---

the *Politics of Recognition,* ed. Amy Gutmann (Princeton, NJ: Princeton University Press, 1994), 26. See also David Pellauer and Paul Ricoeur, *The Course of Recognition* (Cambridge, MA: Harvard University Press, 2007).

  [22] Reinhold Niebuhr, *Moral Man and Immoral Society: A Study in Ethics and Politics* (Louisville, KY: Westminster John Knox Press, 2001), xxxiv.

  [23] Ibid.

  [24] Ibid., 117.

  [25] Kate Ward, "'Mere Poverty Excites Little Compassion': Adam Smith, Moral Judgment and the Poor," *Heythrop Journal* (March 2015), DOI: 10.1111/heyj.12260.

usher," whose flashlight keeps our gaze focused, not letting our eyes avert to any lower caste whom we dare not recognize.

> As we go about our daily lives, caste is the wordless usher in a dark-
> ened theater, flashlight cast down in the aisles, guiding us to our
> assigned seats for a performance. The hierarchy of castes is not about
> feeling or morality. It's about power—which groups have it and
> which do not. It is about resources, which caste is seen as worthy
> of them and which are not, who gets to acquire and control them
> and who does not. It is about respect, authority and assumptions of
> competence—who is accorded these and who is not. [26]

The power of these arguments is that they remind us how prevalent the forces are that keep us from reverting our gaze and discovering a mutual recognition in the other whose condition we are socially trained to ignore. Recognition is therefore the act that liberates the vulnerability of the agent and the other in the face of the distorting power of the castes that structure our lives.

Yet, before we teach recognition, we need to educate our students about just how pervasively the wordless usher deflects the gaze of due recognition.

Let me give a few examples of my own discovery of the prevalence of the politics of overlooking, from the church's sexual abuse scandal, from the cover-ups and shields at universities, from racial injustice, and finally from the most ignored people in the world, the homeless.

In 2002, as a priest in Boston, I learned, for instance, how the many letters of Margaret Gallant reporting to the chancery the abuse of her nephews and others went unanswered and unrecognized for decades. [27] We later learned that the practice of overlooking these arresting reports was universal, hitting its zenith in early 2018 when the pope himself refused to recognize the reports against the Chilean bishops, denouncing the letters as "calumny." Every instance of a national breakthrough on sexual abuse was precisely a recognition of the politics of neglecting the claims of vulnerable relatives wanting to protect their children. [28]

---

[26] Isabel Wilkerson, *Caste: The Origins of Our Discontent* (New York: Random House, 2020), 17–18.

[27] James F. Keenan, "The Gallant Rule: A Feminist Proposal," in *Feminist Catholic Theological Ethics: Conversations in the World Church*, ed. Linda Hogan and Agbonkh-ianmeghe Orobator (Maryknoll, NY: Orbis Books, 2014), 219–31.

[28] James F. Keenan, "Vulnerability and Hierarchicalism," *Melita Teologica* 68, no. 2 (2018): 129–42.

The work of university ethics argues that though universities teach the professional ethics of every corporate field but its own, its disinterest in ethics only appears when a scandal erupts. Yet even then, the university engages a politics of overlooking the claims. For instance, Megan McCabe begins her essay on campus rape culture with these words: "Despite pervasive sexual violence against women, especially the extensive problem of rape on college campuses, there is virtually no Catholic response."[29] More recently I have argued that contingent faculty and community colleges are grossly neglected by tenured faculty who conveniently overlook the situations of both.[30] Remarkably, with the help of its siloed context, the university has consistently promoted a culture of diverting recognition.

"Black Lives Matter" is effectively a clarion call that white America has politically neglected the physical and often deadly assault on Black lives by police and by white supremacists. The protests are shocking precisely because they want to awaken in others a recognition of the situation. Thus, in Rochester, NY, naked protesters seated and shackled with spit hoods called attention to the vulnerability of Daniel Prude, who was naked and only wearing a spit hood when he asphyxiated after being held face-down on pavement for more than two minutes by those charged with protecting us.

Katie Walker Grimes wants us to recognize not only that Black Lives Matter but also the consistent and pervasive violence of unrecognized white supremacy. She insists that we recognize it in the churches where we pray: "Since the racially segregated space of the United States operates as a habitat of white supremacy, the vice of white supremacy pervades the church's corporate body and thereby permeates all of its practices, including those of baptism and the Eucharist."[31]

My last example is personal, from when I was among twenty Catholic ethicists invited by Mark McGreevy, the founder of the Institute for Global

---

[29] Megan K. McCabe, "A Feminist Catholic Response to the Social Sin of Rape Culture," *Journal of Religious Ethics* 46, no. 4 (2018): 635–57, at 635.

[30] James F. Keenan, *University Ethics: How Colleges Can Build and Benefit from a Culture of Ethics* (New York: Rowman and Littlefield, 2015); Keenan, "Vulnerable to Contingency," *Journal of the Society of Christian Ethics* 40, no. 2 (2020): 221–36; Keenan, "The Community Colleges: Giving Them the Ethical Recognition They Deserve," *Journal of Moral Theology*, 9, no. 2 (Special Issue, 2020): 143–64.

[31] Katie Walker Grimes, "Breaking the Body of Christ: The Sacraments of Initiation in a Habitat of White Supremacy," *Journal of Political Theology* 18, no. 1 (2017): 22–43, at 22; see also her *Christ Divided: Antiblackness as Corporate Vice* (Minneapolis: Fortress Press, 2017); "Antiblackness," *Theological Studies* 81, no. 1 (2020): 169–80.

Homelessness, to a conference in Rome in 2017 on street homelessness. He initiated the conference by informing us that not one ethicist had ever bothered to recognize in her or his writings the plight of the homeless. The conference was a call to consider whence the politics of overlooking the homeless, a fairly universal practice even by those dedicated to recognizing those on the margins.[32]

Ultimately, I believe that educators must attend to the constraints of the politics of negligence and aim to bring students experientially to the insight of mutual recognition, time and again. Whether it is through art, immersion programs, accompanied learning, tutorials, informal sharing, or simply exploring in class what it means to see a dead boy's body washed up on a beach, we need to not miss those moments where we help students cross the threshold and understand that it is only by recognizing that we capture the vulnerability or answerability that is within us and the other.

I turn to Thomas, again, who argues that the life of perfection is three stages: to resist the vice, to develop the virtue, and to perfect the habitual practice. These are not separate stages; as we struggle to perfect the practice, we recognize yet again the vice within. So, as I sat in Rome, I realized yet again that I failed to recognize, in that instance, the homeless. As Niebuhr, Grimes, and Wilkerson warn us, we will never have an unflinching gaze. But, then, the Scriptures taught us that as well.

We need to explore much more often the multitudinous ways that our students and we get accustomed to the normal where those "beneath" us go unnoticed, because we think that we are "above" them. In a way, we need to teach them and one another lessons for the practice of recognizing a new virtue of vigilance, or what the wonderful, late Johann Baptist Metz called "a culture of sensitivity and a mysticism of painfully-opened eyes that must not only focus on the closest neighbor, but also especially on the strange others."[33] In his book on recognition, *The Mysticism of Open Eyes: When Spirituality Breaks Out,* Metz reminds us that recognition can be unsettling but brings us closer to Christ, a point to close this essay.[34]

In the gospels, recognition is always connected to the Christological. For Matthew, because the sheep recognized the hungry, they were saved for feeding Christ. As Augustine and others taught, the parable of the Good

---

[32] James Keenan and Mark McGreevy, eds., *Street Homelessness and Catholic Theological Ethics* (Maryknoll: Orbis Books, July 2019).

[33] https://www.katholisch.de/artikel/2549-jesu-blick-gilt-dem-leid.

[34] Johann Baptist Metz, *Mystik der offenen Augen: Wenn Spiritualität aufbricht* (Freiburgh, Germany: Herder, 2011).

Samaritan is really the Gospel of Christ saving wounded Adam. That some of the most important parables in the gospels are on recognition is not a surprise. Indeed, that is what the gospels ask of us: to recognize in Jesus the Christ. Recognition is, in our tradition, the way we find in him ourselves.

Once we allow ourselves to be vulnerable to the other, we begin the work and life of conscience. Conscience finds its foundation by being first vulnerable, open and responsive to the other, capacious to the variety of ways that we are called to be human. In that vulnerability we become, like the Good Samaritan, able to hear the cry for help, or like the father who sees his prodigal son on the horizon. The birth of Christian conscience is in the vulnerability of being human.

But conscience needs to be activated, and recognition gives conscience both its path and its legs. By recognition, the conscience is first awakened to the other. In that awakening, conscience recognizes the other as sharing in the very vulnerability of humanity and in that moment identifies with the other. That identification, intimately linked to the early experience of "mutual recognition," becomes then the prompt for conscience to respond to others in all their need and fragility, as well as in their capacity and promise.

In the story of the Good Samaritan, we get a glimpse of his vulnerability and his conscientious recognition of the wounded man. Still the details of the narrative need to be filled out. Those details, about the cleansing and the bandaging of the wounds, the search for a place for the wounded man to mend, the even more difficult investigation for an innkeeper capable of trust, care, and prudence, the finding of the funds to return to the inn, the resolution to bring the wounded man to the Samaritan's homeland, and the eventual incorporation of the wounded man into the land of Samaria, all these meticulous details are the stuff of conscience, the working out of human vulnerability wherein we recognize and live out our shared humanity.[35] And, therein is the work of moral education.

---

[35] While I am very sympathetic to those who are burdened by the manipulative impositions of others who try to force those with less power due to gender, class, race, or caste to respond to those in need (see Valerie Saiving Goldstein, "Human Situation: A Feminine View," *Journal of Religion*, 40, no. 2 (April 1960): 100–112), I share the feminist presuppositions of Butler, Benjamin, Gilson, and Wilkerson and their awareness of human vulnerability, its mutuality, its aim of inclusiveness, and its recognition of human fragility and finitude. These presuppositions assist us in educating others to their capacities for vulnerability, recognition, and conscience. Hopefully, as lessons from the pandemic have taught us, those so burdened are among those to whom we learn to be vulnerable, to give due recognition, and to conscientiously respond.

Conscience and Academic Freedom in Catholic Higher Education

Darlene Fozard Weaver

Conscience is a critically important topic in Catholic education. Catholic education is a site for the formation of conscience, as students are introduced to Catholic teaching on faith and morals and are shaped within its culture, which includes communal practices of service to those in need and advocacy on behalf of the dignity and equality of all persons. Conscience is exercised in matters of school governance, including decisions about budgets and investments, policy and personnel, curricular and cocurricular offerings, workplace and student culture, and diversity, equity, and inclusion. Dilemmas of conscience arise within Catholic educational institutions and between these institutions and their surrounding communities and governments.

Considering the pervasive importance of conscience, anyone involved in Catholic education will find much to enlighten and ponder in Catholic treatments of conscience. Catholic teaching about conscience shows development in significant ways, and disagreement that is sometimes quite strident. But an essential dynamic lies at the heart of otherwise divergent views of conscience, that of accountability. This emphasis on accountability is the great insight into conscience that Catholic thinking about conscience offers. It is also an ingredient in tensions that arises over the role of conscience in Catholic education. After exploring development in and disagreements about conscience in Catholic tradition, this essay explores their implications for academic freedom. Academic freedom illustrates Catholic disagreements about conscience, shows what is at stake in them, and is itself a source of moral dilemmas within Catholic education.

Conscience in Catholic Tradition

The development of conscience through Catholic tradition is highly instructive. In Scripture various tropes are used to express aspects of human life before God, which were later named under the concept of conscience.[1] The concept appears in the New Testament in the letters of Paul, who construed conscience variously as a capacity for knowledge or awareness of what God requires (1 Cor 8:7–13; Rom 2:14–15), as an antecedent experience of being convicted for one's sin (Rom 13:5), and in terms of deliberating about how to act (1 Cor 8:7–13). Importantly, Paul also links this operation of conscience to responsibility toward neighbors whose own consciences may be in error or weak (1 Cor 9:19–23). The meaning of conscience evolved in concert with early changes in the sacrament of reconciliation, as the practice of repeated and private confession of one's sins would come to shape practices for examining conscience and parsing moral actions or omissions.[2]

Medieval theologians developed the concept of conscience through debates regarding the differences between the terminology of *synderesis* and *conscientia*, further contributing to a multidimensional notion of conscience as both a capacity for the knowledge of right and wrong and a faculty for decision-making.[3] Thomas Aquinas described conscience in terms of the human person's apprehension of first principles for practical reasoning, such as "Seek good and avoid evil." He also developed Catholic teaching regarding the erroneous conscience and the culpability of an agent whose conscience is erroneous or ignorant.[4] In doing so, Aquinas further clarified that conscience has objective and subjective dimensions. Conscience is accountable to a moral reality that is established by God and knowable, at least in part, by human reason. The subjective dimension of conscience refers to the person's awareness that they are answerable to God.

Manuals of moral theology developed Thomistic thinking about conscience. Manuals were used in seminary instruction to prepare priests for administering the sacrament of confession. The manualist tradition maintains

---

[1] Linda Hogan, *Confronting the Truth: Conscience in the Catholic Tradition* (New York: Paulist Press, 2001), 46–47. See also Kathryn Lilla Cox, *Water Shaping Stone: Faith, Relationships, and Conscience Formation* (Collegeville, MN: Liturgical Press, 2015).

[2] John Mahoney, *The Making of Moral Theology: A Study of the Roman Catholic Tradition* (Oxford: Clarendon Press, 1987).

[3] Hogan, *Confronting the Truth*, 66–77.

[4] Ibid., 81–85.

the link between conscience and natural law but emphasizes the objective dimension of conscience. The manuals construe conscience as the intellect's capacity to apprehend first principles of morality and deduce proximate norms for moral action. As James Keenan argues, the manuals situate conscience in an approach to moral theology that focuses on actions not persons, on the authoritative teaching of the magisterium rather than the "personal judgments of conscience," and on an extrinsic notion of moral truth.[5]

In *Gaudium et Spes*, the Second Vatican Council described conscience as "the most secret core and sanctuary" of the person.[6] While conscience so understood is a singular and innermost encounter between the individual person and God, the phenomenon of conscience joins human persons "in the search for truth, and for the genuine solution to the numerous problems which arise in the life of individuals from social relationships."[7] Vatican II affirms the objective dimension of conscience, stating that "in the depths of his conscience, man detects a law which he does not impose upon himself, but which holds him to obedience."[8] Indeed, "right" conscience means a conscience "guided by the objective norms of morality" and caring for "truth and goodness."[9] This objective moral order can be summed up as the love of God and neighbor. Importantly, *Gaudium et Spes* also states that "conscience frequently errs from invincible ignorance without losing its dignity."[10] This contrasts with the impact "habitual sin" has on conscience by dimming its vision.

The reception of Vatican II can be understood in part by subsequent disagreements over the meaning and role of conscience. In his encyclical *Veritatis Splendor* Pope John Paul II argued, among other things, that some moral theologians at the time were advocating for a creative notion of conscience as a source of moral norms.[11] He argued instead that conscience is only free when it adheres to the truth. A free conscience is one that apprehends the objective moral order. Conscience *discerns* what is right, it does not *decide* what is

---

[5] James F. Keenan, "From Teaching Confessors to Guiding Lay People: The Development of Catholic Moral Theologians from 1900–1965," *Journal of the Society of Christian Ethics* 28, no. 2 (2008): 141–57.

[6] Pope John XXIII, *Gaudium et Spes: Pastoral Constitution on the Church in the Modern World,* in *Vatican Council II: The Conciliar and Postconciliar Documents*, ed. Flannery, Austin (Northport, NY: Costello Publishing, 1975), no. 16. Hereinafter *GS*.

[7] *GS* no. 16.

[8] Ibid.

[9] Ibid.

[10] Ibid.

[11] Pope John Paul II, *Veritatis Splendor*—"The Splendor of Truth" (1993).

right. Conscience consists in a rightly ordered rational judgment. Notice that this account of conscience presumes more than abstract rules or principles. It presumes a vision of the created world and the human person, in which moral meaning is inscribed. This vision of a morally freighted creation appears, for example, in Catholic sexual ethics, in which human sexual differentiation is read as gender complementarity and the procreative capacity of heterosexual coitus inspires a sexual ethics built about the conjugal act.

While arguments over the role of conscience persist, recent work in Catholic ethics argues that concepts of conscience need to reckon with the reality of social sin, which refers to the disruption of proper relation to God and neighbors in social systems and institutions.[12] Elizabeth Sweeny Block argues that Catholic concepts of conscience are inadequate to the complexity of systems problems such as racism.[13] Katie Grimes developed an examination of conscience that reflects on complicity in relation to structural sin, framing it as a supplement to traditional practices that fail to reckon with social sin.[14] Considering conscience in light of social sin means acknowledging the moral agent is profoundly influenced by and in turn influences the social organizations, customs, and structures that situate and mediate her life with others and before God. It thereby includes this mutual influence within the scope of her moral responsibility. Revisions of conscience in light of social sin comprise a way of reasoning about our accountability before God and to others.

Pope Francis and Conscience

Pope Francis brings a distinctive stamp to Catholic treatments of conscience. His understanding of conscience can be called personalist, developmental, and dialogical. For Francis, the operation of conscience is deeply personal, unfolding in the unique circumstances of an individual's life. While his encyclical *Amoris Laetitia*[15] focuses on the family, the document has broader implications for morality as it endeavors to help families "navigate the tension between the gospel's high ideal for daily life and the inevitable imperfec-

---

[12] Matthew Levering, *Conscience and Ethics: A Century of Catholic Moral Theology* (Grand Rapids: Eerdmans, 2021).

[13] Elizabeth Sweeny Block, "A Call to Action: Global Moral Crises and the Inadequacy of Inherited Approaches to Conscience," *Journal of the Society of Christian Ethics* 37, no. 2 (2017): 79–96.

[14] Katie Grimes, "Examining Our Consciences in Light of Structural Sin," April 8, 2011, Women in Theology, https://womenintheology.org/.

[15] Pope Francis, *Amoris Laetitia*—"The Joy of Love" (2016). Hereinafter *AL*.

tions of reality."[16] This is particularly true of its account of conscience and of moral discernment. As Conor Kelly puts it, "This is not the straightforward notion of conscience as an act or 'event,' nor is it the juridical conception of an important application of the law to specific circumstances. It is a much more personalist account."[17] Conscience encompasses the person's whole navigation of moral life before God and in relation with others.

Francis's personalist view of conscience implies its developmental character. Conscience is not an isolated faculty rendering discrete judgments about how to act in discrete situations but the person's active moral engagement with their circumstances before God and within their many relationships. Conscience therefore unfolds over time, waxing and waning in terms of its sensitivity to good and evil, evolving as experience and knowledge impact it, and operating within dynamics of sin and grace. While Francis maintains that conscience must be formed in accordance with moral truth and that freedom of conscience should not be mistaken for a blank check for one's ego, he also objects to a vision of morality that is impersonal, legalistic, and cold toward the struggle and complexity of human life.[18] Similarly, James Keenan perceptively links conscience with the *sensus fidelium* with regard to morals. In this respect conscience refers to "judgments arrived at only by deep, prayerful, conscientious struggle" over time.[19]

Conscience is therefore properly understood as dialogical. Conscience names the person's response to God's invitation of love and mercy in and through her own life. While Francis affirms the objective moral order, he also argues that conscience is not first and foremost about rules. Indeed, Francis articulates profound humility and respect for the individual conscience and exhorts pastors to do the same. In *Amoris Laetitia* he laments, "We . . . find it hard to make room for the consciences of the faithful, who very often respond as best they can to the Gospel amid their limitations, and are capable of carrying out their own discernment in complex situations."[20] He goes on to say, "We have been called to form consciences, not to replace them."[21]

---

[16] Conor M. Kelly, "The Role of the Moral Theologian in the Church: A Proposal in Light of *Amoris Laetitia*," *Theological Studies* 77, no. 4 (2016): 922–48, 924.

[17] Ibid., 927.

[18] Pope Francis, Statement accompanying the *Angelus*, June 30, 2013, www.vatican.va.

[19] James F. Keenan, "Redeeming Conscience," *Theological Studies* 76, no. 1 (2015): 129–47, 131.

[20] *AL,* no. 37.

[21] Ibid.

Accordingly, the most palpable aspect of Francis's approach to conscience is his profound respect for it. The inviolability of conscience has long been respected in Catholic tradition. Minimally, it means refusing to coerce another to violate a deeply held moral conviction such as not drafting those who claim a conscientious objection to war. The notion that individual persons should not be coerced into acting against their conscience is also reflected in contemporary appeals to conscience protections in relation to equal protection laws, as when pharmacists refuse to dispense the "morning-after pill" or a baker refuses to make a wedding cake for a same-sex marriage ceremony. More fully, respect for conscience means active regard for the moral competence of another.[22] While one's conscience may err, Catholic teaching about conscience recognizes both that this error may not be culpable, thereby mitigating the agent's guilt, and that even a culpably erroneous conscience must be followed, albeit with the understanding that the agent must endeavor to form conscience in accordance with moral truths.

Catholic theologies of conscience reflect internal theological, moral, and ecclesiological differences. Critics argue that the views of conscience offered by Pope Francis and revisionist moral theologians tend to undercut objective moral norms, permit wrongdoing in the name of pastoral exemptions, encourage moral subjectivism or relativism, sow confusion about church teaching on faith and morals, and cause scandal, which in Catholic ethics means occasioning others' sin.

I argue that conscience in Catholic theology can be described as a dynamic process of accountability. In doing so I build on Anne Patrick's description of her important work on conscience as "one's personal sense of obligation . . . reached and held in the presence of a community of accountability."[23]

Academic Freedom and Catholic Education

As we noted at the outset, academic freedom illustrates Catholic disagreements about conscience, shows what is at stake in them, and is also itself a source of moral dilemmas within Catholic education. Richard Hofstadter points out that the case for academic freedom stretches back to Socrates's

---

[22] Diane M. Yeager and Stewart Herman, "The Virtue of 'Selling Out': Compromise as a Moral Transaction," *Journal of the Society of Christian Ethics* 37, no. 1 (2017): 3–23.

[23] Anne E. Patrick, *Conscience and Calling: Ethical Reflections on Catholic Women's Church Vocations* (New York: Bloomsbury, 2014), 17.

apology.[24] Hofstadter charts the evolution of academic freedom in the medieval universities of the twelfth and thirteenth centuries through the Civil War. His account demonstrates that notions of academic freedom reflect and influence a mix of cultural, economic, political, and historical factors. These include the economic autonomy or dependence of universities, their cultural prestige, degrees of power wielded or sought by the political and ecclesiastical leaders, supply and demand for faculty and students, and of course significant cultural developments, such as the McCarthyism to which Hofstadter was responding.

In the United States, contemporary concepts of academic freedom in higher education typically use the 1940 Statement of Principles on Academic Freedom and Academic Tenure by the American Association of University Professors (AAUP) as their touchstone.[25] According to the statement, faculty have latitude to conduct research and publish their results and speak freely in the classroom when discussing their subject. The statement also states that faculty should be free from censorship or reprisal on account of their speech as citizens. In each of its three sections the statement concedes some limitations on academic freedom. In section 1, it acknowledges "adequate performance" of "other academic duties" as a relevant consideration to academic freedom in research, as well as implicit concerns related to compensation for scholarship. In section 2, it makes provisions for limitations on academic freedom related to an institution's mission (religious or otherwise), provided these are stated in writing upon appointment, and encourages faculty to refrain from controversial extramural topics in the classroom. Finally, in section 3, the statement encourages faculty to take care to distinguish their civic speech from the views of their institution and to exercise other civic behaviors. Notably the statement itself does not address the freedom to determine curriculum, decide admission standards, dissent from administrative policies, or due process in adjudicating disciplinary measures involving faculty, all of which are typically included within contemporary American standards of academic freedom and shared governance.

The key essential claims in notions of academic freedom are that faculty should enjoy discretion in decision-making about their scholarship and teaching, in speech about their institution and extramural matters related to

---

[24] Richard Hofstadter, *Academic Freedom in the Age of the College* (New Brunswick, NJ: Transaction Publishers, 1996), 3.

[25] American Association of University Professors, "1940 Statement of Principles on Academic Freedom and Academic Tenure by the American Association of University Professors," https://www.aaup.org.

their expertise, and in academic decision-making for their institution, and to exercise these free from institutional reprisal. Academic freedom includes faculty speech regarding issues of shared governance, such that faculty should not be sanctioned for disagreeing with administration officials or policies, provided that the manner of disagreement does not violate institutional policies regarding matters such as confidentiality and civility. Academic freedom also includes extramural faculty speech regarding public matters of import, as when faculty author editorials, give expert testimony in legal matters, or engage in professional consulting work. In American higher education academic freedom is closely associated with tenure. Tenure largely protects faculty from dismissal.

Does it follow that any activity ostensibly undertaken in the name of research or teaching is therefore permitted in the name academic freedom? Research, which fails to respect ethics and laws governing human subjects, is subject to sanctions, and faculty who violate these norms are subject to disciplinary action. So, too, are faculty who claim the mantle of pedagogy as a justification while creating instructional environments marked by sexually suggestive or racist language. Such activity undermines students' access to educational opportunities.[26] This dimension of academic freedom raises questions about offensive speech outside the university. Is a faculty member protected from institutional sanction because of such speech? Stanley Fish criticizes a notion of academic freedom that overreaches beyond disciplinary expertise, arguing against interpretations that inflate the role of faculty as cultural saviors and advocating for a view more tightly yoked to core faculty functions of teaching and research.[27]

Fish's point is worth noting, since the AAUP's Statement of Academic Freedom makes no claims about the nature of education or goals of research. There are some moral values implicit in the statement, but it largely floats free of substantive claims about the moral character of education or the role of faculty or higher education relative to the common good. Even so, the statement's counsel regarding extramural speech suggests that academic freedom is rightly exercised within a set of relational responsibilities, and that academic freedom is not a blank check to say or do whatever one likes with impunity.

---

[26] U.S. Department of Education, Title IX of the Education Amendments of 1972, U.S.C. §1681 et seq.

[27] Stanley Fish, *Versions of Academic Freedom: From Professionalism to Revolution* (Chicago: University of Chicago Press, 2014).

Academic Freedom and
Catholic Higher Education

Academic freedom is important in and compatible with Catholic higher education. It is integral to the pursuit of knowledge and love for the truth. It protects research and teaching from censorship, and it protects faculty who express unpopular or unorthodox views from retaliation on account of those views, thereby contributing importantly to the conditions necessary for inquiry to unfold and innovation to occur. Academic freedom does not threaten Catholic teaching on faith and morals. The authors of the 1967 "Statement on the Nature of the Contemporary Catholic University," better known as the *Land O'Lakes Statement,* argued that "institutional autonomy and academic freedom are essential conditions of life and growth and indeed of survival for Catholic universities as for all universities."[28] The authors envisioned a university "in which Catholicism is perceptibly present and effectively operative," and the disciplines and professions taught therein are free from ecclesiastical and political control, and adhere to their respective academic standards and best practices. Activities such as bishops prohibiting the publication of faculty research, banning books from course syllabi, or intervening in decisions regarding faculty hiring or dismissals are inconsistent with the autonomy Catholic universities enjoy. At the time *Land O'Lakes* was published, many Catholic institutions of higher education were appointing boards comprised of laypeople, seeking accreditation, and seeking to comply with state and federal regulations regarding government funding. To the mind of supporters, asserting institutional autonomy and academic freedom was necessary for the long-term institutional viability.

Still, there are some who decry the *Land O'Lakes Statement* as a source of many ills in Catholic colleges and universities. From their perspective, the emphasis on institutional autonomy and academic freedom has led to a steady deterioration of the Catholic identity of these institutions. Rather than preserve a distinctive cultural identity, critics argue, *Land O'Lakes* represents "a moral struggle with the temptation to pride and prestige at the expense of Catholic identity."[29]

---

[28] *Land O'Lakes Statement: The Idea of the Catholic University* (Land O'Lakes, WI: privately printed, 1967). Reprinted by University of Notre Dame. https://cushwa. nd.edu/assets/245340/landolakesstatement.pdf.

[29] Patrick Reilly, "The Land O'Lakes Statement Has Caused Devastation for 50 Years," The Cardinal Newman Society, July 20, 2017, https://newmansociety.org/.

For critics of *Land O'Lakes*, the Apostolic Exhortation *Ex Corde Ecclesiae: On Catholic Universities* was a welcome correction. In addition to "a Christian inspiration" and "an institutional commitment to service," *Ex Corde* requires Catholic colleges and universities to reflect upon human knowledge "in light of the Catholic faith" and contribute to that store through their own research and display "fidelity to the Christian message as it comes to us from the Church."[30] *Ex Corde* was met by some concerns over academic freedom. Not only does the requirement of fidelity raise questions regarding how such fidelity is to be demonstrated and by whom, *Ex Corde* also states plainly that Catholic colleges and universities should strive to maintain a majority of Catholic faculty members and that "All professors are expected to be aware of and committed to the Catholic mission and identity of their institutions" and "exhibit not only academic competence and good character but also respect for Catholic doctrine." *Ex Corde* further requires that faculty who teach theology obtain a mandatum from the local bishop. The mandatum signifies that faculty member's communion with the church.

In hindsight, concerns about *Ex Corde*'s impact on academic freedom seem overdrawn. Catholic colleges and universities have sought to leverage their identity to distinguish themselves in the marketplace of American higher education. Mission offices and officers have increased in numbers as professionals who collaborate with faculty and administrators to articulate the Catholic intellectual tradition and translate their institution's particular charism for its constituents and the wider public.

Rather than specifically ecclesiastical threats to academic freedom, what has emerged instead are self-appointed guardians of orthodoxy who police Catholic institutions of higher education, weaponize social media, and exploit internal moments of disagreement and dialogue for their own ends. As I have described elsewhere, "the fight for institutional sustainability, contested questions about Catholic identity on campuses, and intra-Catholic polarization can make fidelity to mission fraught."[31] We will explore these tensions further in the next section. For the moment we can note that from the perspective of Catholic intellectual tradition, research and teaching are not value-free under-

---

[30] Pope John Paul II, *Ex Corde Ecclesiae: Apostolic Constitution on Catholic Universities* (Washington, DC: Office for Pub. and Promotion Services, United States Catholic Conference, 1990), 13. Hereinafter *ECE*.

[31] Darlene Fozard Weaver, "Doing Ethics and Advocacy in Catholic Higher Education," in *Ethics and Advocacy*, ed. Harlan Beckley et al. (Eugene, OR: Cascade Books, forthcoming).

takings, exercises of some pure intellectual activity untouched by bias, error, the personal foibles of the faculty member or student, or social structures. The human realities of research and teaching do not mitigate the importance of academic freedom, but they do clarify that the research and teaching being protected are unavoidably muddled, as all human undertakings are.

That said, academic freedom should not amount to immunity from performance appraisal, including mandatory improvement plans or sanctions by their institution, publisher retractions of one's published work or other sanctions responding to violations of academic norms like plagiarism. Faculty who are incapable of or unwilling to perform essential professional functions are reasonably subject to institutional policies and procedures regarding disciplinary action up to and including separation. Peer review is an essential ingredient for genuine academic freedom. Practices of peer review locate the exercise of academic freedom within a community of accountability, subjecting scholarship and pedagogy to critical scrutiny by fellow experts. This statement presumes faculty and students are acting in good faith. Academic freedom does not protect a faculty member from sanctions when they have falsified their data, for example, or in instances of incompetence or malpractice. The next section considers some instances in which academic freedom and the mission of Catholic higher education need to be navigated.

Academic Freedom and Living the Mission

Academic freedom is a crucial good in higher education. It is a condition for open inquiry, critical thinking, and innovation. It is the freedom to pursue ideas, challenge received thinking and conventional practices, and forward arguments without fear of censorship or retaliation. Many practical issues and tensions surround academic freedom in American higher education. A professor at the University of Iowa, for instance, recently included a syllabus policy stating expectations that students would refrain from behavior that is "othering," such as racism, but she would not accept assignments in which students argued for any position that "takes at its base that one side doesn't deserve the same basic human rights as you do (i.e., no arguments against gay marriage abortion, Black Lives Matter, etc.)."[32] The University required the faculty member to change the syllabus.

---

[32] Alaa Elassar, "University Forces Professor to Change Syllabus That Threatened to Dismiss Sudents Who Argue against BLM, Abortion or Same-Sex Marriage," *CNN*, August 23, 2020, www.cnn.com.

This is an interesting example especially because it points to the importance of thinking of conscience in terms of a community of accountability.
While academic freedom certainly includes individual faculty discretion in
syllabus design and in setting expectations for assessing student learning,
faculty exercise that freedom within overlapping relationships, structures,
forces, goods, and responsibilities. For example, for some stakeholders and
observers, the syllabus statement exemplifies the narrative that universities
are bastions of liberal politics that are inhospitable to conservative perspectives. Here the issue of academic freedom lies in the threat of sanctions against
students who express conservative positions on the issues identified in the
syllabus. For others, the academic freedom issue concerns the University's
decision to mandate a change to the syllabus. While the syllabus statement
raises concerns about students' constitutional rights to freedom of speech, the
faculty member appears to have been trying to create an educational environment that would be free from discrimination. Clearly, faculty are accountable
in several directions—accountable to their own conscience, professional
integrity and disciplinary standards; accountable to students, their access to an
educational environment that is safe for exploration and learning, respectful
of their individual conscience and right to free speech; and accountable to
their institution's mission and policies.

This last form of accountability strikes to central issues for academic
freedom vis-à-vis the mission of Catholic higher education, such as considering topics and claims in tension with Catholic faith and morals, as well as
critically engaging Catholic teaching or practice, or the institution's interpretation and manifestation of its Catholic identity. An instructive resource can
be found in David DeCosse's consideration of the Danish cartoon controversy of 2005–2006 as a test case for Catholic social teaching on free speech.[33]
DeCosse notes that Catholic responses "were critical of a concept of free
speech in which a notion of freedom was detached from respect, and especially from respect for religion," and "evinced a keen concern for how speech
can disrupt communal peace."[34] While responses from the Vatican acknowledge freedom of speech, they yoke freedom of speech to moral obligations of
respect for others and, particularly, for others' rights to freedom of religion.[35]

---

[33] David E. DeCosse, "The Danish Cartoons Reconsidered: Catholic Social
Teaching and the Contemporary Challenge of Free Speech," *Theological Studies* 71, no.
1 (2010): 101–32.

[34] Ibid., 109.

[35] Ibid., 110–11.

Freedom of speech is not absolute. It is not equivalent to the right to give offense.[36] Rather, there are moral constraints upon free speech, related to the well-being of the community. DeCosse argues that the Vatican's response to the controversy focused on giving offense. It places perhaps undue confidence in the prospect of rational consensus, underestimates the degree and depth of disagreement, and assumes a negative view of conflict.[37] DeCosse is not arguing that the cartoons were morally good or even neutral. They fail a test of respect for others.[38] But he does argue that over-concern for giving offense or scandalizing others comes at a cost.

Catholic teaching about conscience illustrates these tensions. On the one hand, accountability to the consciences of others constrains us from coercing or tempting them to act against conscience and from carelessly offending their conscience. On the other hand, Catholic educational communities sit within diverse communities and include various forms of diversity in their own make-up. They also face increasing pressure to attract students and employees in order to remain sustainable and to navigate internal polarization within Catholicism. The latter can manifest itself in divergent interpretations of an institution's mission, for example, when a group of faculty and students argue that respect for human dignity requires visible and robust support for LGBTQIA+ members and other faculty or board members or alumni view manifestations of that support as contrary to Catholic teaching. The mix of religious and moral diversity among stakeholders, tuition-driven dependence, compliance requirements with government and accreditors, and ecclesial relationships is ripe for conflicts over academic freedom and mission.

There is no simple formula for navigating these. Indeed, they must be lived through in their complexity as an exercise of communal conscience. Doing so, however, does require understanding and respecting the distinctive character of Catholic higher education. Catholic colleges and universities have cultures, norms, and structures that differentiate them from other workplaces or organizations and are not easily understood beyond academe. Sara Gross Methner notes that universities too often "imbalance or compromise essential values in haphazard fashion without explanation, rather than holding them in tension in a way that stakeholders can understand."[39] She argues that "inclusive

---

[36] Ibid., 111.

[37] Ibid., 114–15.

[38] Ibid., 116–17.

[39] Sara E. Gross Methner, "A Catholic University Approach to Campus Speech: Using Constitutional Academic Freedom to Hold the Tension of Free Speech, Inclusive

diversity," which includes the values of "diversity, civility, and safety,"[40] are critical to universities' mission, as is "the institutional autonomy that is necessary to manage the tension between them."[41] These values express the relationships of accountability that are essential for being an academic community that respects individual dignity and freedom of conscience, protects academic freedom, provides students' access to a safe and equitable educational environment, reflects on and contributes to human knowledge in light of Catholic faith, and lives out "fidelity to the Christian message as it comes to us through the Church."[42]

Conclusion

Catholic treatments of conscience, particularly as developed since Vatican II and by Pope Francis, have much to contribute to reflection on and practice within Catholic education. Internal debates about conscience reflect tensions that also operate in Catholic education surrounding academic freedom and fidelity to the mission of Catholic institutions. These tensions can be enervating or generative as academic communities negotiate them. While concerns about giving offense and causing scandal are legitimate, they jostle alongside other significant concerns and can sometimes be subordinated to the latter. Leaders in Catholic education need to work assiduously to articulate the distinctive space of Catholic education with its diverse and tensive purposes, goods, principles, and stakeholders, and strike tirelessly to cultivate relationships of mutual accountability that bring this vision of Catholic education to life. Reimagining conscience in terms of a community of accountability is an essential part of this needed work.

Diversity, and University Identity," *University of St. Thomas Law Journal* 15 (2019): 358–418, at 413.
[40] Ibid., 358.
[41] Ibid., 361.
[42] *ECE* 13.

Embodied Cognition, Embodied Formation

What Neuroscientific Research Reveals
about Conscience Formation

Elizabeth Sweeny Block

The question of how we form consciences—our own and those of others—is more urgent in an era in which a global pandemic has turned a spotlight on vast inequalities and numerous injustices, including profound racial disparities. Alongside COVID-19, this second insidious pandemic of racism spreads, brought to the surface by recent police killings of unarmed Black people, including George Floyd and Breonna Taylor. The rate of fatal police shootings of unarmed Black people in the United States is more than twice that of White people.[1] How do we form consciences in this context?

Recent scholarship has turned its attention to the sin of racism as more than intentional, deliberate acts or conscious thoughts. In her book *Raising White Kids: Bringing Up Children in a Racially Unjust America*, Jennifer Harvey observes, "We feel race. Race is in our bodies."[2] She is referring not only to the way a BIPOC (Black, Indigenous, and People of Color) individual feels walking into a room full of White people but also the way White people embody their Whiteness. Drawing on the work of philosopher Shannon Sullivan, Harvey asserts that White privilege is not only a way of thinking but a "way of 'bodying.'"[3] It is not enough to "have all our ideas, beliefs, and thoughts correct [because], as white people, our bodies will give us away every time."[4] Racism operates physiologically and biologically, as a gut reaction in

---

[1] "Fatal Force," database in the *Washington Post*. https://www.washingtonpost.com/graphics/investigations/police-shootings-database/.

[2] Jennifer Harvey, *Raising White Kids: Bringing Up Children in a Racially Unjust America* (Nashville, TN: Abingdon Press, 2017), 195.

[3] Ibid., 199.

[4] Ibid., 200.

addition to, or perhaps even more strongly than, a mental belief.[5] The case of Amy Cooper illustrates the way racism can operate as a reflex.

On May 25, 2020, in New York's Central Park, Amy Cooper, a White woman, impulsively called the police on Christian Cooper, a Black man, unrelated to her, who had requested that she abide by the park rules and leash her dog. Bryan Massingale observes that she "knew," in a noncognitive way, that being White makes life easier and that a White person can make life harder for a Black person. She did not learn this; she absorbed it, as do we all, "just by living. Just by taking in subtle clues such as what the people in charge look like. Whose history you learned in school. What the bad guys look like on TV. The kind of jokes you heard. How your parents, grandparents and friends talked about people that didn't look like you."[6] This culturally cultivated assumption about Black people was evident in Cooper's reflexive response. This kind of assumption is apparent when one's heart races and stomach tenses as one passes a Black man on the street. These examples illuminate why Massingale understands racism not merely as an act, where one person, usually White, consciously and deliberately does something harmful to a BIPOC, but as a culture, "a set of meanings and values that inform the way of life of a community."[7] A culture of racism is constituted by the assumptions, meanings, and values we embody. "Culture is not principally a way of acting, but a way of being . . . that informs a people's attitude and stance toward life."[8]

These observations about racism as more than action and belief, as an embodied culture and a way of being in the world, are particularly poignant at the time of this writing, at the close of a year (2020) in which too many Black people in America died needlessly at the hands of police. The scholars above draw our attention to the depths of racism and to the noncognitive, unconscious dimensions of morality. If racism is embodied, a so-called gut reaction, embedded in our culture and camouflaged in our assumptions, meanings, and values, then surely we need more than reason and alternative ways of thinking to overcome it. What these observations about embodied and unconscious racism reveal is the inadequacy of conceptions of conscience

---

[5] Shannon Sullivan, "The Hearts and Guts of White People: Ethics, Ignorance, and the Physiology of White Racism," *Journal of Religious Ethics* 42, no. 4 (2014): 592–93.

[6] Bryan N. Massingale, "The Assumptions of White Privilege and What We Can Do about It," *National Catholic Reporter*, June 1, 2020, https://www.ncronline.org.

[7] Bryan N. Massingale, *Racial Justice and the Catholic Church* (Maryknoll, NY: Orbis Books, 2010), 16.

[8] Ibid., 18–19.

in the Catholic tradition that prioritize reason, knowledge, and overt action while neglecting agents' unconscious formation by cultures of sin, including not only racism but also, for example, the social sins of rape culture and hostility toward immigrants.[9]

This essay considers what recent neuroscientific research on embodied cognition can contribute to fleshing out conscience formation. First, I begin with the traditional Roman Catholic understanding of conscience and conscience formation, which prioritizes conscious reasoning and deliberate decision-making and is inadequate in the face of the embodied, unconscious racism described above. Second, I turn to developments in neuroscience, which reveal the inadequacies of this approach to conscience that understands the person solely as intentional, conscious decision-maker. I address the reasons to proceed with caution in mixing the fields of moral theology and neuroscience but conclude that neuroscience can provide us with indispensable insights into the human person, the very subject of moral theology. Third, I turn specifically to research on embodied cognition, which argues that thinking, reasoning, and remembering depend on and are carried out through the whole body and in partnership with the culture, environment, and relationships in which we participate. Embodied cognition points to the need for Catholic educators to think outside the box if education is going to be truly formative. I conclude with three suggestions for how Catholic educators ought to practice conscience formation in light of the centrality of the body: through creative, bodily formation; through ritual and practice; and through an embodied solidarity with others. Formation cannot simply be the transfer of knowledge and values but must be active, sensory, and tactile in order to be transformative.

Conscience and Conscience Formation in the Catholic Tradition

The quintessential Catholic statement on conscience is found in the Second Vatican Council's *Pastoral Constitution on the Church in the Modern World,*

---

[9] See Megan McCabe, "A Feminist Catholic Response to the Social Sin of Rape Culture," *Journal of Religious Ethics* 46, no. 4 (2018). Kristin Heyer, *Kinship Across Borders: A Christian Ethic of Immigration* (Washington, DC: Georgetown University Press, 2012). See also Lisa Fullam, "Joan of Arc, Holy Resistance, and Conscience Formation in the Face of Social Sin," in *Conscience and Catholicism: Rights, Responsibilities, and Duties,* ed. David E. DeCosse and Kristin E. Heyer (Maryknoll, NY: Orbis Books, 2015).

Gaudium et Spes.[10] Conscience is described as "the most secret core and sanctuary" of a person where one is "alone with God, Whose voice echoes in [one's] depths." Conscience is a law—one that is not self-imposed, but rather written on our hearts by God—that holds persons "to obedience." The "voice of conscience," explains *Gaudium et Spes*, speaks to the human heart: "Do this, shun that." At this point, conscience sounds notably individual and personal, characterized by one's relationship to and with God. However, the pastoral constitution continues,

> In fidelity to conscience, Christians are joined with the rest of men in the search for truth, and for the genuine solution to the numerous problems which arise in the life of individuals from social relationships. Hence the more right conscience holds sway, the more persons and groups turn aside from blind choice and strive to be guided by the objective norms of morality.

Together, Christians search for the truth, for the objective norms of morality that we do not invent or construct but that we must discover and discern in relationships with each other.

However helpful this definition is in pushing away from a purely individual understanding of conscience and toward a recognition of the social nature of conscience and morality, most official Catholic descriptions continue to characterize the moral agent as deliberate, intentional, and conscious of all factors at play in any discrete moral decision. The *Catechism of the Catholic Church* describes the human person as a rational being created by God with "the dignity of a person who can initiate and control his own actions,"[11] and defines moral freedom as "the power, rooted in reason and will, to act or not to act, to do this or that, and so to perform deliberate actions on one's own responsibility."[12] Additionally, the *Catechism* calls conscience "a judgment of reason whereby the human person recognizes the moral quality of a concrete act that he is going to perform, is in the process of performing, or has already completed. In all he says and does, man is obliged to follow faithfully what he knows to be just and right."[13]

---

[10] Pope John XXIII, *Gaudium et Spes: Pastoral Constitution on the Church in the Modern World* (1965), no. 16, www.vatican.va. All subsequent quotes from *Gaudium et Spes* are from no. 16.

[11] *Catechism of the Catholic Church*, 2nd ed. (1992), para. 1730.

[12] Ibid., para. 1731.

[13] Ibid., para. 1778.

The U.S. Catholic Bishops' guide to voting, *Forming Consciences for Faithful Citizenship*, similarly emphasizes human control over conscious, deliberate decision-making: "Prudence shapes and informs our ability to deliberate over available alternatives, to determine what is most fitting to a specific context, and to act decisively."[14] Roman Catholic understandings of conscience formation are narrow and inadequate for preparing moral agents to confront, acknowledge, and alter their own complicity in sins such as racism, sexism, homophobia, xenophobia, and climate violence. Undoubtedly, people do frequently make deliberate moral decisions, but it is clear that conscience cannot only be driven by reason and knowledge.

Massingale has called attention to the inadequacies of the two ways the Catholic Church conceives of conscience formation.[15] One approach treats conscience formation as "information gathering," while the other views it as a "process of character development" or moral maturation. The "information gathering" approach to conscience formation prepares conscience to confront a particular moral dilemma by collecting information relevant to the situation at hand. This approach considers a number of sources of moral wisdom, especially the hierarchical magisterium, in order to illuminate and guide conscience in its decision-making. The second approach to conscience formation focuses not on a particular action or judgment but on cultivating a person's moral maturity and integrity. One creates an "upright moral character," the other a "well-rounded decision maker." Neither approach has been well explained or given much substance, other than the clear directive that conscience formation requires consulting church teaching. Moreover, these dominant typologies of conscious, deliberate, cognitively driven conscience formation fail to account for the ways that cultures of sin are formative, not only of our thoughts and worldviews but also our bodies. For example, our senses are impacted by our formation in these cultures of sin: what we see or fail to see, what we hear and how we listen, what we feel. Our culture and our community shape our senses, our emotions, and our intuitions, such that what we sense and notice arises within our bodies, influenced by sins such as

---

[14] United States Conference of Catholic Bishops, *Forming Conscience for Faithful Citizenship: A Call to Political Responsibility from the Catholic Bishops of the United States* (2019), no. 19, www.usccb.org.

[15] Bryan N. Massingale, "Conscience Formation and the Challenge of Unconscious Racial Bias," in *Conscience and Catholicism: Rights, Responsibilities, and Institutional Responses*, ed. David E. DeCosse and Kristin E. Heyer (Maryknoll, NY: Orbis Books, 2015), 61–63.

racism, sexism, and xenophobia. We embody cultures of sin. Neuroscientific research on embodied cognition illuminates the centrality of the body, so to this I now turn.

Moral Theology and Neuroscience

If neuroscience and theology seem an unlikely pair, neuroscience and conscience are perhaps a bit less so, given that everything humans experience, feel, and know is processed through (but not only through) the brain. Questions commonly associated with and asked of a person's conscience are strikingly similar to those questions of identity associated with the brain's processing responsibilities: "Who are you? What are your aspirations, values, and goals? What do you know? How do you know what you know? What are you currently feeling and sensing? How aware of all of this are you?"[16] Moreover, it is not uncommon for people to associate the conscience with the brain and to want to locate the region of the brain responsible for moral behavior. The ways that the brain is understood to adapt to and interact with its surrounding environment mirror descriptions of a person's conscience in formation and action.

Approximately 90 billion neurons and 100 billion connections form the elaborate neural network that is the brain, which has long been the subject of research, dating back to the ancient Egyptians in 3000 BCE. In 400 BCE, Hippocrates famously acknowledged the brain as the center of human thinking and emotions. In the 1990s, with widespread access to magnetic resonance imaging (MRI), scientists began mapping structures of the brain and studying its functional architecture. What has emerged in recent neuroscientific research is that identifying neuronal pathways, that is, the connections between and within brain structures, is more fruitful than associating specific regions of the brain with single functions.[17] Neural connections that lie between and within regions of the brain are more determinative of behavior than isolated structures in the brain. While it is unlikely that we can locate the conscience in a precise region of the brain, we can at least acknowledge that the brain makes possible the existence and practice of conscience. We will

---

[16] Matthew R. Evrard, Jacopo Annese, and Marilee J. Bresciani Ludvik, "Basic Brain Parts and Their Functions," in *The Neuroscience of Learning and Development*, ed. Marilee J. Bresciani Ludvik (Sterling, VA: Stylus Publishing, 2016), 30.

[17] Ibid., 37. See also Sebastian Seung, *Connectome: How the Brain's Wiring Makes Us Who We Are* (New York: Houghton Mifflin Harcourt Publishing, 2012).

see, however, that the brain is not doing this alone. Before we can proceed, we must attend, however briefly, to some complexities and words of caution regarding placing moral theology and neuroscience into dialogue.

Theological engagement with neuroscience must proceed with care. First, the extent to which we should derive prescriptive judgments from the descriptive claims of neuroscience is debatable.[18] Moral norms cannot simply be lifted from neuroscientific findings. Neuroscience provides insights into the way our brains and bodies work, but it cannot be the sole arbiter of what is moral. Descriptions—in this case, scientific descriptions—of human beings are morally significant, but they are not static or unassailable. These descriptions change as new discoveries are made and must be interpreted in dialogue with other disciplines. Second, scientific research is never objective and unbiased. What research scientists undertake and their interpretation of scientific data are influenced by their surroundings and culture. Hille Haker warns of the supposed objectivity of brain research, noting that the interpretation of neurobiological findings is steered more by social assumptions than empirical data.[19] Third, the exaggerated association of the human person with her brain, reducing all intellectual and cultural achievements to the work of the brain, is problematic. Mind and consciousness cannot be entirely explained by physical and chemical processes. Neuroscience overreaches when it implies that all mental phenomena can be traced to measurable data in regions of the brain and their activities.[20]

The frequently cited example of Phineas Gage illustrates the narrow understanding of moral agency that results when human behavior is explained solely by the brain. A railroad worker injured in 1848 by an iron rod that pierced his skull and damaged parts of his brain, Gage's injury became the defining feature of his life and the only explanation for his subsequent behavior. While the physical trauma undoubtedly caused his drastic personality change, this narrow focus eclipses his humanity and overlooks that not only was his brain damaged but also "his prospects, . . . his faith, [and] his

---

[18] See, for example, Craig Boyd, "Neuroscience, the Trolley Problem, and Moral Virtue," in *Theology and the Science of Moral Action*, ed. James A. Van Slyke et al. (New York: Routledge, 2013).

[19] Hille Haker, "Gender Identity, Brain and Body," in Thierry-Marie Courau, Regina Ammicht Quinn, Hille Haker, and Marie-Theres Wacker, eds., *Theology, Anthropology, and Neuroscience* (*Concilium: International Journal of Theology* 2015/4).

[20] Klaus Muller, "The Dulcet Tones of a New Doctrine of Salvation?: On the Achievements and Limits of Neurosciences," in Courau et al., *Theology, Anthropology, and Neuroscience*, 43.

self-love," all of which surely impacted him.[21] "Assumptions of scientific naturalism produce a kind of blindness to the larger human story, a blindness that prevents both an adequate account of morality and an adequate view of the moral actor himself."[22] Recent research in cognitive neuroscience, which I introduce below, will return us to this physicalist problem and offer an alternative perspective.

And yet, theology—and therefore discussions of conscience and morality—benefits from neuroscience.[23] "A consideration of neuroscientific data doubtless seems called for, if the human being represents a biologically constituted being whose existence, action, feeling and thinking would not be possible without a brain."[24] Moreover, attending to neuroscientific research about the human person prevents moral theology from being mere abstraction and grounds it in the lived realities of the human body. It is well-documented that moral theology draws its wisdom from numerous sources, including Scripture, tradition, reason, and human experience, which includes the experience of disciplines outside of theology, such as science. Neuroscience may not be equipped to offer normative claims in response to particular moral quandaries, but it has the potential to broaden our knowledge about the very subject of moral theology: the human person. Neuroscience can help us unpack the "how" of morality—how humans operate as moral agents—but not necessarily the "what" of specific moral norms or even moral theories more broadly. Neuroscience cannot provide the content of morality, but it can contribute to our understanding of the human person.

There are several developments in the vast field of neuroscience that have the potential to offer important contributions to understanding what the work of conscience formation requires.[25] In this essay, I focus on cognitive

---

[21] Marilynne Robinson, *Absence of Mind: The Dispelling of Inwardness from the Modern Myth of the Self* (New Haven, CT: Yale University Press, 2011), 49–50.

[22] Christina Bieber Lake, *Prophets of the Posthuman: American Fiction, Biotechnology, and the Ethics of Personhood* (Notre Dame, IN: University of Notre Dame Press, 2013), 32.

[23] It is undoubtedly worthwhile to explore the ways neuroscience benefits from theological and ethical discourse also, but that is beyond the scope of this essay.

[24] Elisabeth Hildt, "Brain, Morals and Ethics: What Is the Connection?," in Courau et al., *Theology, Anthropology, and Neuroscience*, 64.

[25] Research on neuroplasticity, for example, suggests that the brain's ability to modify neural connections means that humans are particularly open to being formed by life experiences. The human prefrontal cortex does not reach full adult maturity until the second decade of life. Even after that, the adult brain remains malleable, capable of

neuroscience's recognition that cognition is not only an activity of the brain but also involves the body, what is called "embodied cognition." In contrast to traditional cognitivist views, embodied cognition recognizes "the body as an actual participant in moral judgment"[26] and, therefore, calls attention to the centrality of the body in conscience formation.

Embodied Cognition

"Physicalism," "naturalism," and "reductionism" are all terms that capture, with some variation, the claim that everything we need to know about human beings is located in their physical nature. With respect to cognitive neuroscience, physicalism assumes that cognition—conscious intellectual activity such as thinking, reasoning, or remembering—depends entirely on the physical brain. Traditional cognitivist views assume that "anything outside the brain has little theoretical interest other than as providing sensory input and motor output,"[27] and "mental life is treated as formal, disembodied, computational processes, governed by universal natural rules of various kinds."[28] On this view, the mind is abstract, and thinking is the manipulation of abstract, disembodied information.

Embodied cognition has emerged as an approach that emphasizes the physical context of cognition but does not understand cognition to be grounded in the physical brain, emergent from the brain, or entirely explicable in terms of the brain. "Embodied cognition is actually a broad and quite diverse set of theories which agree about what they are rejecting more than about what they are asserting."[29] Embodied cognition understands cognition

being shaped by interactions with the environment. There is a widely cited study of the expansion of London taxi drivers' spatial memory and posterior hippocampus of the brain over time due to the complex maze of streets they navigate daily. See Matthew R. Edvard and Marilee J. Bresciani Ludvik, "Unpacking Neuroplasticity and Neurogenesis," in Ludvik, *The Neuroscience of Learning and Developmentn*; Warren S. Brown and Kevin S. Reimer, "Embodied Cognition, Character Formation, and Virtue," *Zygon* 48, no. 3 (2013): 838–39.

[26] Katie Grimes, "Elusive Intentions: Just War Theory and the Fragmented Nation State," *Journal of Religious Ethics* 47, no. 4 (2019).

[27] John A. Teske, "From Embodied to Extended Cognition," *Zygon* 48, no. 3 (2013): 761.

[28] Leon Turner, "Individuality in Theological Anthropology and Theories of Embodied Cognition," in ibid., 819.

[29] Fraser Watts, "Embodied Cognition and Religion," in ibid., 748. More expansive theories of embodied cognition are referred to as "grounded cognition" and "contextual

to involve the body as a whole and assumes brain/mind continuity. To try to understand how mental functioning arises from the brain is "to take the brain out of the context of the body of which it is part."[30] Fraser Watts describes embodied cognition this way: "Our minds don't make decisions or take actions; neither do our physical brains; nor even an integration of our brains and minds. It is people that make decisions and act in the world. We do so as creatures who are physically embodied and socially embedded."[31]

Thomas Aquinas insisted that we know everything in and through our senses, therefore in some respects this turn to the body's role in cognition is not new. Aquinas understood that apprehending intelligible truth requires cooperation between the intellect and the senses, calling the body "the organ of sense."[32] The human soul is not naturally gifted with the knowledge of truth but must gather knowledge from individual things through the senses, and it is those humans with the best sense of touch that have the best intelligence, according to Aquinas. "Those who are refined in body are well endowed in mind."[33] Although "we must not expect the entire truth from the senses," it is the case that for Aquinas the senses are the gateway to knowledge.[34] Our sense experiences work together with our reason to discern what is good.

Examples of embodied cognition bring this theory to life. Our perception is intertwined with our bodily states. Studies have shown that "being tired from a run makes a hill look steeper; carrying a heavy back pack makes a path look longer."[35] Additionally, "perception is frequently associated with activation of the motor system; so, when you are observing someone else perform an action, there are often subtle signs that people are simulating that action themselves."[36] Those signs include the activation of mirror neurons in the brain, evidence that we simulate not only the actions of others but their

---

cognition," both of which suggest that the context of cognition is wider than the human body and includes social context (ibid., 751). Yet another theory, "extended cognition," asserts that "cognition not only requires a brain, but is grounded more fully, not only in the body, but in the marriage of a whole person with the world." See Teske, "From Embodied to Extended Cognition," 760.

[30] Watts, "Embodied Cognition and Religion," 749.

[31] Ibid., 751.

[32] Thomas Aquinas, *Summa Theologica*, trans. Fathers of the English Dominican Province, 5 vols. (Notre Dame, IN: Ave Maria Press, 1981), I 76.5.

[33] Ibid.

[34] Ibid., I 84.6.

[35] Teske, "From Embodied to Extended Cognition," 764.

[36] Watts, "Embodied Cognition and Religion," 748–49.

mental states as well. Research also suggests that "Social and moral cognition may be guided or constrained by specific bodily and affective reactions, and states of bodily excitation readily transferable across situations."[37] We integrate our bodily states, feeling, and knowledge, and our knowledge comes to us through our bodily states such that "missing an embodied state, like a galvanic skin response [a change in the skin's sweat gland activity that reflects intensity of emotion] in anticipation of possible loss," as patients with damage to the ventro-medial cortex do, means they "miss information essential to making a less risky choice."[38]

Memory is also not limited to the brain but works in accord with the whole body:

> Remembering an event inevitably triggers memories of what our bodies were doing in that narrative, or are doing, as we recall that event; placing our bodies in familiar places or positions may draw us into vivid memories of previous events, a form of déjà vu. Events repeated over time, or even once, form new "facts" about the world. New events confirm or challenge our known facts about the world and fill in the blanks in our recalled stories.[39]

There is evidence that gestures that accompany speech have cognitive functions, helping the speaker to recall words, listeners to understand the speaker, and children to learn words.[40] According to embodied cognition theory, what is outside the brain is part of a person's mental life, including the body, other people, and elements of our physical and cultural environments. "Our cognitive processes are, at their core, sensorimotor, situated, and action-relevant."[41]

John A. Teske argues in favor of extended cognition, the theory that the extension of cognition does not stop at body boundaries but expands into the cognitive agent's environment, even including other human agents. Externalism is one type of extended cognition that understands the mind to be "constituted by the mechanisms and resources that we use to think."[42] The theory of externalism contends that "the constitution of thoughts, beliefs,

---

[37] Teske, "From Embodied to Extended Cognition," 772.

[38] Ibid.

[39] David A. Hogue, "Re-membering Our Body of Work," *Journal of Pastoral Theology* 29, no. 1 (2019): 38.

[40] Teske, "From Embodied to Extended Cognition," 765.

[41] Brown and Reimer, "Embodied Cognition, Character Formation, and Virtue."

[42] Teske, "From Embodied to Extended Cognition," 776.

and desires often includes, even requires, states and processes external to our biological organism."[43] However, this "does not mean that the mind's location is separate from heads and bodies, as these are proper parts of a mind . . . Mental phenomena are hybrids that couple events in the world to physical processes in the nervous system."[44] Teske recognizes the externalization of human memory—the offloading of memories onto other persons or into journals, for example—as an instance of human beings displaying evidence of extended cognition. External resources, such as the journal, not only duplicate internal cognitive functions but also shape and develop our own capacities in ways that impact future cognition. Computation is another example; it may include counting on fingers, doing multidigit addition on paper, or addition with a calculator. These "cognitive artifacts" with which the brain is coupled can actually change the brain, as when manipulating objects improves reading comprehension in school children.[45] Teske goes so far as to include relationships in our extended cognition: "Preeminent among the externalities from which our selves are composed are our relationships with other human beings, particularly those with whom we have deep and lengthy intimacies, but necessarily, and also, with those we do not, but with whom we share an increasingly interdependent planetary ecology."[46] Extended cognition suggests that "mental life is both embodied and embedded in the world, not just located within the nervous system: the nervous system is a necessary part, but it is only a part, not the whole construction."[47]

Related to extended cognition is the theory of the extended mind, which recognizes that culture is also drawn into human cognition. Léon Turner cites as examples, or cultural artifacts, notebooks and computer hard drives, which are potentially as important to cognition as anything inside our head:[48]

Much of culture . . . "is encoded in the body and perpetuated that way—hidden in plain sight by ways of talking, walking, standing, sitting, eating, and so on that often come to seem "natural" to us. These

---

[43] Ibid.

[44] Ibid.

[45] Arthur M. Glenberg, Megan Brown, and Joel R. Levin, "Enhancing Comprehension in Small Reading Groups Using a Manipulation Strategy," *Contemporary Educational Psychology* 32, no. 3 (2007): 389–99.

[46] Teske, "From Embodied to Extended Cognition," 781.

[47] Ibid., 779.

[48] Turner, "Individuality in Theological Anthropology and Theories of Embodied Cognition," 821.

"natural" ways of being in the world are often not consciously reflected on, but they push us invisibly (and without argument) toward certain psychological mindsets and a certain outlook on the world.[49]

Laboratory studies on racial bias, such as the Implicit Association Test, which is used to identify attitudes and beliefs that people do not necessarily self-report, exemplify these claims about the interrelationship of culture and cognition.[50] These studies have shown that racism has in some sense shaped our brains, such that people more quickly associate negative words or images with BIPOC than with positive words or images, even when participants report themselves as rejecting such negative, racist associations. These same studies show that these rapid, racist associations arise out of the region of the brain called the amygdala but can be overridden or interrupted by signals in the anterior cingulate cortex, even to the point that this interruption happens unconsciously. Indeed, our cognitive states are influenced by bodily actions, which in turn are shaped by cultural artifacts and scripts.

Implications of Embodied Cognition
for Conscience Formation

The interplay of bodily actions, relationships, and culture in human cognition illuminates the discussion of social sin with which this essay began. Cultures of sin are ways of being in the world that are encoded in our bodies and yet largely invisible to us. The frequency with which people consciously engage in intentional, overtly racist acts of hatred and violence cannot be ignored. However, the theory of embodied cognition also suggests that we decide with our bodies, sometimes before we are even conscious of what we are doing, and our bodies—and some argue the extended context outside of our bodies— are integral to our perception, memory, and conscious intellectual activity. In other words, we think, reason, and perceive in, with, and through our bodies, and it is possible that our bodies are a step ahead of our conscious thinking.

---

[49] Ibid., 823. Turner is quoting Dov Cohen and Angela Leung, "The Hard Embodiment of Culture," *European Journal of Social Psychology* 39 (2009): 1279.

[50] My discussion of this study is indebted to David A. Hogue, "Imaging the Other: Neuroscientific Insights into Human Experiences of Culture and Race," in *Complex Identities in a Shifting World: Practical Theological Perspectives*, ed. Pamela Couture et al. (Zurich: International Academy of Practical Theology, 2015). See also T. Ito and B. Bartholow, "The Neural Correlates of Race," *Trends in Cognitive Sciences* 13, no. 12 (2009).

Embodied cognition carries with it implications for the moral life and conscience in particular. Although many Catholic scholars since Vatican II have been arguing that conscience is not simply a decision-making faculty, embodied cognition further demonstrates how treating conscience as cognitive decision-maker misses the mark. Furthermore, embodied cognition tells us we are mistaken if we think about conscience formation as only instilling distinctions between right and wrong. Conscience cannot be a decision-making tool that precedes bodily actions. It is, rather, our moral agency formed by and lived through our bodies and bodily experiences. Conscience formation, therefore, must be the formation of *whole bodies*, including emotion, intuition, perception, and movement.

This insight has implications for the way that Catholic educators approach conscience formation that I can only begin to unpack here. These suggestions will benefit from the experiences of those in the educational trenches who can more fully flesh them out. First and foremost, conscience formation must be more robust than the mere transfer of knowledge or the articulation of beliefs and principles. Describing for our students what it means to be people of conscience is necessary but not sufficient. Formation of conscience "is not the accumulation of a rich bank of abstract ideas which one can manipulate off-line to understand the world and act appropriately."[51] If moral agency is impacted by forces outside of our consciousness, and if moral cognition is processed not only through the brain but also the body, then formation of conscience must be holistic and bodily, active and tactile.

In some sense, this is not new. Virtue theorists have always told us that we become virtuous by doing virtuous actions, and the more we do certain actions, the more we become a certain sort of person. Aristotle and Aquinas both recognized that virtues are not truly virtues unless they are *lived*. This implies the need for certain traditional sorts of activities, to be sure, such as field trips, service learning, and community engagement. It also reaffirms the importance of the development and formation that occurs outside the classroom and when students are not seated at desks or in front of computers. Music, art, meditation, yoga, outdoor education, and exercise are all as significantly formative as mathematics and reading. But embodied cognition also means as educators we must think outside the box to help students to do the same. Higher education research shows that integrating creativity— "representative of something different, new, or innovative"—into campus

---

[51] Brown and Reimer, "Embodied Cognition, Character Formation, and Virtue," 841.

environments results in transformative learning and, more importantly, trades a segmented, linear approach to teaching and learning with a focus on developing the whole student.[52] Experiential learning also helps students to learn to make connections across disciplines and experiences, and make meaning out of their experiences.

Second, rituals, religious and otherwise, and communal practices are indispensable for the formation of conscience. "In an increasingly virtual world," writes Hogue, "physical bodies, in the same place, at the same time, still matter."[53] This insight hits close to home as the world navigates the COVID-19 pandemic, and most of our lives have gone virtual, including online worship and remote education. Lest we think that remote learning could ever replace being physically together, embodied cognition reminds us that "our care for each other, for the world, and our response to trauma and suffering are full-body practices."[54] Massingale recognizes the importance of the practices of Baptism and Eucharist, among others, in the work of racial justice. These practices call us to an alternate way of life, shape us by a narrative other than the dominant cultural one, and empower us to take risks of racial transformation.[55] Eucharist evokes Jesus's vision of radical human equality before God. But what is crucial for embodied formation is that these require bodily engagement and so form us in ways that simply hearing about racial transformation does not. Moreover, Eucharist does not only transform our thinking, valuing, and deciding; participation in Eucharist and Liturgy touches our senses and has the power to evoke feelings, through our bodies, that form us to embody radical equality.

Third, embodied conscience formation requires physical solidarity with those from whom we differ. Solidarity is the recognition that we are responsible for one another because we are one human family and so we must strive for the good of all. Genuine solidarity is more than words; it must be embodied. This means that schools, from elementary through university, must be diverse and inclusive. We simply cannot overcome our embodied, unconscious culture of racism without confronting it with our very bodies. As Jennifer Harvey asserts, "If having and ensuring our children have the right ideas about difference were all it took to raise healthy white kids, racial

---

[52] Shaila Mulholland, "Enhancing Creativity," in Ludvik, *The Neuroscience of Learning and Development*, 177–193.

[53] Hogue, "Re-membering Our Body of Work," 38.

[54] Ibid.

[55] Massingale, *Racial Justice and the Catholic Church*, 126.

tensions and division in the United States would have been long gone by now."[56] This is not just making space in predominantly White schools for BIPOC. Here Pope Francis's newest encyclical, *Fratelli Tutti*, is instructive. Francis challenges us to be open to being changed by encounters with those from whom we differ: "We find that our hearts expand as we step out of ourselves and embrace others."[57] Solidarity requires cultivating an openness to being changed by encounters with others, which educators must model and facilitate for students.

  Forming people of conscience necessitates embodied formation. We must form not only minds, values, and characters, but whole selves, which requires more than simply knowledge transfer. Because our bodies are the vehicle for morality, and because our bodily actions often precede conscious thinking, the future of conscience formation amidst cultures of sin requires us to think creatively about how to shape embodied consciences.

---

[56] Harvey, *Raising White Kids*, 174.

[57] Pope Francis, *Fratelli Tutti*—"On Fraternity and Social Friendship" (2020), no. 89, www.vatican.va.

Conscience, Law, and Catholic Schools

What Every Catholic School Administrator Needs to Know

Mary Angela Shaughnessy, SCN

Catholic school administrators across the globe will not easily forget the spring of 2020. Planning for reception of sacraments, graduation, and other ceremonies stopped. Schools closed and transitions to online learning were made. As of this writing in the spring of 2021, administrators continue to deal with the realities and collateral damage of COVID-19, even as they prepare for a new school year.

In the United States, deaths of people of color such as Breonna Taylor and George Floyd laid bare the reality that Martin Luther King Jr.'s dream of a country where Black children are judged on character content, rather than skin color, has not yet been realized. Protests and riots occurred throughout the country and the world. In a very real sense, a twin pandemic tore through the world, one a very real disease of body and the other, one of soul and conscience.

Possibly no cause of action has caused greater pain than sex abuse, which remains a continuing, festering wound in the life of the Catholic Church. The first cases burst upon national consciousness in the 1990s, and more cases continue to emerge even today. The reticence that once precluded an individual suing the Catholic Church began to crumble, until today there is seemingly little reluctance. For many years, civil authorities considered churches and their internal governance matters "off-limits." If Father were stopped for running a red light, he might be let off with a verbal warning. If he were driving drunk, the officer might drive him home. The collar was both a statement of authority and virtual unassailability. More than a few cases began to break through into that "off-limits" realm.

The *Boston Globe* investigation in 2002 and more recently in 2018, the Pennsylvania Attorney General Report, brought most remaining vestiges of supporting clergy at all costs to a screeching halt. No longer was what Father or Sister said enough for parents, students, lawyers, or judges. The oft-quoted principle that no man (or woman) is above the law emerged as the rule, rather than an absolute pass, for members of the clergy. Although sending Father to a rehabilitation facility and back to parish ministry may have once been acceptable, it certainly no longer is. However, it must be observed that in earlier times, the prevailing wisdom of psychiatrists and others in the medical community was that pedophilia, if not curable, could at least be arrested, much like alcoholism. This author has heard more than one bishop state over the years, "But I did what the doctors told me to do. They said it was safe for Father to return to ministry." That return all too often had tragic consequences.

In the midst of such continuing angst, the first word administrators speak may not be "conscience." Yet conscience understood basically as our awareness of good and evil, right and wrong, informs everything one does. School administrators often appeal to conscience as they continue to ask when confronted with a variety of situations, "What is the right action to take for everyone concerned?" Sometimes our judgments of conscience are clear: a law or precept manifests what we need to do. Perhaps more often our consciences struggle to make moral judgments amid the inevitably complex, as well as concrete, circumstances of Catholic schools.

Conscience, Law, and Catholic Schools

In this essay, I would like to focus on one aspect of conscience in Catholic schools: those places where concerns of conscience intersect with civil law. Such concerns have always been part of Catholic education in a pluralistic society such as the United States. Indeed, in the nineteenth century, the emergence of networks of Catholic schools in America raised questions about whether the conscience of a Catholic owed more allegiance to the laws of the church than to American law. A century later in the presidential election of 1960, the nation's first Catholic president, John F. Kennedy, was often asked which had a greater claim to his loyalty—the Catholic Church or the United States of America. His response was "[I]f the time should ever come . . . when my office would require me to either violate my conscience or violate the national interest, then I would resign the office."[1]

---

[1] John F. Kennedy, "Address of Senator John F. Kennedy to the Greater Houston Ministerial Association," September 12, 1960. John F. Kennedy Presidential Library and Museum Archives.

More recently, these challenges of conscience, law, and Catholic education have grown. On the one hand, Catholic schools may now admit and employ non-Catholic students and staff; the convictions of conscience of some such individuals may clash with the Catholic doctrines that inform the rules of a school. On the other hand, some Catholics who now work at Catholic schools have made conscientious decisions about matters like identity and family that may clash with established Catholic teaching.

Such individuals may ask, "What legal or Constitutional concepts can help Catholic school administrators think respectfully through these difficult decisions?" I intend in this essay to identify some of the challenges and to provide a type of roadmap for Catholic school administrators. In doing so, I hope also to assist administrators in the exercise of their own consciences as they wrestle with these challenging situations. Of course, ethics codes and mission statements guide the decision-making of most Catholic schools. The strong affirmation of the primacy of conscience in Catholic teaching underscores the great weight that such teaching puts on the personal responsibility of Catholic school administrators and of everyone else. Codes, mission statements, and church teaching can point the way. In the end, however, each administrator has to make such decisions as a matter of conscience.

The Catholic Church teaches that each person has a duty to have an informed conscience. Administrators have legal and moral duties to ensure that those they supervise demonstrate ethical behavior, giving evidence that conscience is the guiding factor in decision-making. And teachers, regardless of the level of students or subject taught, have a responsibility to help students develop their consciences.

All who serve in the educational ministries of the Catholic Church must avoid the appearance of impropriety. In 1984, the author was a high school principal when a male teacher said, "I would never stay alone in a room with a student unless the door was open or people could see in through a window." That observation is as true today as it was thirty-seven years ago.

There must be boundaries in relationships. Sometimes, well-meaning persons get "too close" to others, tell all, and answer any questions, no matter how personal or salacious the details. Boundaries are destroyed. As an attorney who has represented victims, religious orders, schools, and alleged perpetrators, I suggest that good intentions, if not regularly examined, can lead to the proverbial road to hell. Every educator must scrutinize personal behavior and understand that the safety of students is primary.

One must be careful about keeping confidences. There are only two legal privileges protecting communication left in the United States: priest-penitent, which is absolute (although some states have passed or are attempting to pass laws that would overturn any priest-penitent privilege); and attorney-client, which is not absolute as only past, not future, acts are covered. All others, including counselors, psychologists, and psychiatrists who receive information that may indicate actual or potential danger or injury to individuals, must report that information to the appropriate parties.

Civil Law and Catholic Education:
Historical Perspective in the United States

Although Boston Latin School, established in 1635, is the first public school in the United States,[2] various forms of private education were present from the earliest days of the colonies, though some are undoubtedly lost to history. The first Catholic school in the United States is considered to have officially opened in Philadelphia in 1783.[3] A history of Catholic education in this country is beyond the scope of this essay, but as one who attended Catholic grade and high school in the 1950s and '60s, I understand the belief that what Father or Sister said was absolute, unless Father disagreed with Sister in which case Father prevailed. By the mid-1960s, many sisters were leaving religious life or leaving their convents for small community living; more than a few priests were leaving the priesthood. The certainty that one had in what Sister or Father said was shaken and may well have helped to set the stage for the many sex abuse cases that followed.

Decades and even centuries ago, Catholic schools were rarely sued. The reluctance to sue the church and its institutions may have been due to a number of factors: (1) the Catholic Church's patriarchal stance, which could be found in society at large; (2) the view that the Catholic Church's authority was absolute and should not be challenged; and (3) the cost of attorneys and litigation. It must be noted that the same reluctance existed in other religious communities of the day.

---

[2] *This Day in Geographic History, April 23, 1635, C.E.*. National Geographic Resource Library.

[3] "A History of Catholic Schools," Catholic Schools Center of Excellence, https://www.cscoe-mn.org/history-catholic-schools.

Catholic School Administrators:
Rights and Responsibilities in the Exercise of Conscience

Administrators can be held responsible for injuries occurring in Catholic institutions, and the court system offers one way to hold institutions accountable. One decision in particular ensured the rights of Catholics to operate schools and parents to choose those schools.

In the 1925 case, *Pierce v. the Society of Sisters*, the U.S. Supreme Court recognized the right of Catholic schools to exist. Oregon lawmakers, fearing the influence of foreigners on the "American way of life," had enacted a law requiring children ages eight to sixteen to attend public schools. A religious community, the Sisters of the Holy Names of Jesus and Mary, who operated a parochial school, challenged the law. The Supreme Court held that religious institutions have a right to exist and offer both religious and secular education.

The case is noteworthy for a number of reasons. The least understood is the legal principle underlying the decision. Many thought the case was decided in terms of a matter of conscience—the right of parents to choose their children's schools; for that to have been the deciding factor, parents would have had to be the litigants bringing the case. The sisters were not parents. To be heard in court, a litigant must have *standing to sue* or what is sometimes properly described as "having a dog in the fight." The sisters made a Fourteenth Amendment due process property argument: the Oregon law, if enforced, would cause the sisters to close their schools; they could not then support themselves and would lose property. Oregon had to show a compelling interest before it could enforce the law, if the enforcement would result in property loss. The state's argument, based in prejudices of the day, including the belief that the way to assimilate foreigners into culture was to force them into public schools, failed. Perhaps unknowingly, the court made a judgment about the conscience formation of children when it wrote, "Young children do not discriminate. That is a function of maturity."[4] The court stated in a *dictum* (not strictly speaking part of the decision, but something the court nevertheless wanted to say) that parents had the right to choose their children's schools. After the Pierce decision, Catholic schools were assured a place in the United States. Legislation could not abolish a Catholic school's right to exist, and parents would have the right to choose the education for their children.

---

[4] Pierce v. the Society of Sisters, 268 U.S. 10 (1925).

Individual Constitutional Rights in Catholic Schools

While the Catholic Church, a private institution, has constitutional rights guaranteed by the government, it is not required to recognize and protect the constitutional rights of those in its institutions. Many of the most vexing concerns of conscience on the part of students and staff pertain to constitutional matters—or at least to the usually incorrect assumption that the Constitution protects Catholic school actions made based on individual conscience considerations. The lack of constitutional protections in the private sector is a reality not always well understood. For over thirty-five years, the author has used a *true/false* test in education law seminars and lectures. The first statement is, "Students and teachers in Catholic schools do not have the same rights they would have if in public schools." Employees and parents encountering this statement for the first time generally answer *false*. The statement is *true*. When persons step into any private institution, they surrender constitutional protections, because the Constitution is concerned with what the government may do.[5] For example, if a Catholic school principal sees a student wearing a button, "Abortion is a woman's right," the principal can require removal of the button as it offends Catholic teaching. A student in a public school could wear such a button. Why? First Amendment freedom of expression exists and is protected in the public sector but does not exist in the private setting. The Constitution dictates what the government must do, *not* what private persons or institutions must do. Indeed, the Constitution does not protect the rights of individuals with constitutional protections when they are not in the public sector. A Catholic school is not a public place or business; therefore, those in the school cannot claim protections of the Constitution. It does appear problematic: the Catholic institution has constitutional rights, but the persons within the institution have no such rights that the institution must protect.

The main source of the law for those alleging wrongs in the private sector is contract law; judges, juries, and other fact-finders must examine the existing contract in such settings or try to ascertain what the implied contract is. Therefore, each person in a Catholic school or other setting has constitutional protections, but they apply only to actions in the public sector. For example, all automobile manufacturers in the United States are privately owned and

---

[5] See generally Mary Angela Shaughnessy, *The Law and Catholic Schools: A Guide to Legal Issues for the Third Millennium* (Washington, DC: National Catholic Education Association, 2005).

operated. Persons in those institutions must rely on the provisions of the union contract and state law for any rights and protections they have in the workplace.[6]

Catholic school administrators can prohibit behaviors that public institutions cannot. In early rulings, the doctrine of separation of church and state protected church-sponsored institutions from being sued successfully. This doctrine protects the rights of churches and church sponsored institutions to exist. Arguably, any action a Catholic school administrator takes can be viewed through the lens of religion. The last fifty years have seen the number of cases brought against the Catholic Church rise; as the primary law governing church relations with members and employees is contract law, it is on that basis that such cases are decided.

No court to date has ruled that religious institutions must grant constitutional protections; for this to happen, the substantial presence of the state, called *state action*, must be demonstrated: the court must determine that the state is significantly involved in a specific, contested private action to such an extent that the action can fairly be said to be that of the state.

In 1969, the U.S. Supreme Court ruled in *Tinker v. Des Moines Independent School System* that "It can hardly be argued that either [public school] students or teachers shed their Constitutional rights . . . at the schoolhouse gate."[7] Shortly thereafter, Catholic school students began bringing cases alleging violation of constitutional rights. These cases were largely discipline cases, and any attempts to make constitutional arguments were squashed, as we will see in the next section.

Contract Issues

Private school discipline cases alleging constitutional deprivations have resulted in findings for the school. Even if one prevails in the first court approached, to this author's knowledge, every case to date has been overturned on appeal or subsequently settled outside court.

As constitutional arguments have not been successfully advanced in Catholic school cases, persons often raise breach of contract issues. In Catholic school expulsion cases, the plaintiff's argument is generally that the

---

[6] M. A. Shaughnessy, *School Handbooks: Some Legal Considerations,* 3rd ed. (Washington, DC: National Catholic Education Association, 2017).

[7] *Tinker v. DesMoines Independent Community School District et al.,* 393 U.S. 503 (1989).

school breached its contract with the student and parents. Aggrieved students, parents, and employees often appeal to the decision-maker's conscience by citing instances of persons in similar situations who were disciplined less severely. Catholic educators should carefully examine their consciences when making decisions regarding those they supervise. Because one *can do* something is not always a good reason *to do* it.

Cases involving student discipline in Catholic schools are generally heard in lower courts and may progress to state courts. However, most such decisions are not found in state court reports because the judge has labeled them "not for precedential use," so Catholic schools do not have the plethora of precedents that public schools have.

When administrators discipline students, particularly when expulsion is imposed, the school may be sued. While a Catholic school cannot do anything it wishes and/or disregard its own policies, the doctrine of *judicial restraint* means that a court will not substitute its opinion for the opinions of professionals. While there have been a few instances of judges ordering a student returned to school pending trial, I know of no case in which a Catholic school student has been ultimately successful in challenging an expulsion. Similarly, no teacher in a Catholic school has been able to win continuing employment in a Catholic school after having been dismissed, as will be discussed below.

Courts do not decide matters of conscience. The court does not ask if administrators chose the *right* thing to do. Rather, a court determines whether administrators appropriately applied existing rules. So, what is an aggrieved teacher, parent, or student to do? Courts apply the "exhaustion of administrative remedies" theory. If the school handbook or other document outlines a step-by-step process of appeal and litigants have not followed the process, a court will apply the theory and send the litigant back to follow existing processes.

Issues of Lifestyle and Belief

A specific area of concern in discipline of employees is that of lifestyle and belief. Indeed, these are the cases that most often involve what we could call claims of conscience about things like sexual identity or dissent from church teaching. Catholic parish and school employees can be said to represent the church twenty-four hours a day, seven days a week. Their actions can and do affect the reputation of the institution in particular and the Catholic Church in general. It is not uncommon for a news story to lead off with, "Catholic school teacher [or principal] accused of. . . ." rather than "John Doe accused of. . . ." The Catholic Church has the right, both constitutionally and as a matter of contract law, to set behavioral standards for its students, employees, volunteers, etc. This right is not absolute, however; courts will hold private institutions to their stated policies and procedures, to their contractual responsibilities, and to statutory law.

An old case illustrates. While a state and not a federal case, this case is important because it demonstrates the restraint with which a court views an allegation of breach of employment contract for religious reasons. In the 1973 Michigan case of *Weithoff v. St. Veronica School*, a teacher married her pastor, a priest who had not been laicized, and the teacher was subsequently dismissed from her position. She sued. The teacher's contract bound her to the *promulgated policies* of the parish.[8] Generally, the parish council in a parish with a school will have final approval over actions affecting the school, even if there is a separate school board. At this time in the school, the parish board governing the school passed a policy requiring that all teachers be practicing Catholics, but that policy was not promulgated; its passage had been noted in the board minutes that were filed with the board secretary, locked in a folder in a file drawer, but never promulgated. The court found that the parish breached its contract with the teacher because it had failed to promulgate the policy it was holding her responsible for not obeying. For a policy to be in effect, it needed to be both passed and promulgated. The teacher was not reinstated; but she was able to avail herself of the remedy for breach of contract: damages, in this case a year's salary. This case illustrates the theory that one cannot hold one to a written rule that has never been promulgated. Although one could argue (and I have often said) that anyone teaching in a Catholic school has to know that you are not supposed to marry the priest/pastor, this case still stands as an example of the rule of promulgation.

In 1991, a Pennsylvania court decided the case of *Little v. St. Mary Magdalene Parish*.[9] Because it is almost impossible to find any court decisions in which a litigant won a breach of contract case against a Catholic school, the Weithoff case cited above is important. The Little case demonstrates that even non-Catholics can be held to the teachings of the Catholic Church. Ms. Little, a non-Catholic teaching in a Catholic school, had signed the standard contract containing a provision popularly called the "Cardinal's Clause" which required persons to live according to the teachings of the Catholic Church.

---

[8] Weithoff v. St. Veronica School, 210 N.W.2d 108 (Mich. 1973).
[9] Little v. St. Mary Magdalene Parish, 739 F. Supp. 1003 (W.D. Pa. 1990).

Ms. Little entered into marriage with a divorced Catholic whose previous marriage had not been annulled (Catholic teaching prohibits divorced Catholics from remarrying until their previous marriage has been annulled in an official proceeding of the Catholic Church). Although the plaintiff was not Catholic, the court upheld the school's right to dismiss the teacher from her position because she violated a contract clause.

Prior to 2020, there were no U.S. Supreme Court cases dealing with student and/or teacher dismissal in Catholic schools, so we must look to state cases for any sort of historical precedent or comparison. If an attorney does not have a case in his or her state to cite, the attorney will go to other states. In 2004, for example, a Delaware Catholic schoolteacher signed a pro-choice newspaper ad. The school administrator dismissed her. The teacher sued, stating that she believed in her conscience that women have the right to have an abortion.[10] The court upheld the termination and ruled that a religious organization can terminate the employment of one who acts in a manner inconsistent with the teachings of the sponsoring religion.

The Brebeuf and
Cathedral Catholic High Schools' Dilemma

Two relatively recent and closely related cases from the Archdiocese of Indianapolis further illustrate the conscience struggles within Catholic schools: in these cases, similarly situated employees were treated very differently by the two schools in question. How was that possible as a legal and canonical matter? One case involves a longtime Brebeuf Jesuit Preparatory School male employee. The other involves the husband of the male Brebeuf Prep employee; the husband worked at Cathedral High, another Catholic school in the archdiocese. In 2019, the Archbishop of Indianapolis instructed both schools to terminate the teachers' employment; Cathedral terminated, Brebeuf did not. The archbishop moved to impose penalties on Brebeuf, including not being able to be called a "Catholic" school. As a Jesuit-owned institution, Brebeuf appealed this penalty to the Vatican.

The facts of this case illustrate that two same-sex individuals teaching in different Catholic schools in the same archdiocese can be treated differently when they marry each other. This case also illustrates that Catholic schools exist under two sets of laws, the civil law of the United States and the Canon

---

[10] Curay-Cramer v. Ursuline Academy of Wilmington, Delaware, Inc., 344 F. Supp. 2d 923, 934 (D. Del. 2004).

Law of the Catholic Church. This reality is what can result in the seemingly diametrically opposed results for the two men, married to each other, being treated differently in their respective schools.[11]

How can two schools, each employing one member of the same-sex couple, end up with such seemingly divergent decisions? Cathedral High school can call itself Catholic only with the approval of the local bishop. Indeed, Canon 803 of the Code of Canon Law states, "Even if it is in fact Catholic, no school is to bear the name Catholic school without the consent of competent ecclesiastical authority."[12] Normally, the competent ecclesiastical authority is the bishop or archbishop. When Cathedral High School administrators indicated that they wished to keep the teacher they employed, the archbishop said the penalty would be the inability to use the name Catholic, to call itself a Catholic school, and to have Catholic religious services in the school. Cathedral then terminated the employment of the teacher. As a canonical matter, the Catholic identity of Cathedral flows from the archdiocese, led by the archbishop.

Brebeuf is a Jesuit-founded and operated institution, and the Jesuits constitute a separate juridic person under Canon Law. Therefore, its identity flows from the Jesuits. A discussion of canon law is beyond the scope of this essay; however, readers should be aware that the principle of *judicial restraint* would apply to the Cathedral-Brebeuf controversy, which holds that civil courts will not substitute their opinions for that of the experts, in this case religious and canonical ones.

Identification as Gay or Transgender: The U.S. Supreme Court Speaks

In their decision regarding the 2020 case *Bostock v. Clayton County, Georgia*,[13] the U.S. Supreme Court ruled that employers who did not deny that termination of employees was at least partly based on the employees' status as gay or transgender had violated Title VII of the Civil Rights Act, which prohibits discrimination based on sex. What does this mean for Catholic educators and administrators? At the time of the writing of this essay, what is called the ministerial exception, which will be discussed at greater length below, would seem to allow administrators to make a decision on, for instance, terminating

---

[11] See the related essay in this volume by Cathleen Kaveny.
[12] Code of Canon Law, Book III, Can. 803 S1.
[13] Bostock v. Clayton County, Georgia, 590 U.S. __, 140 S. Ct. 1731 (2020).

a gay or transgender employee by appealing to religious beliefs and thus framing such a decision to terminate as one based on religious doctrine and not on sex *per se*. Gay and transgender persons may certainly find this exception troubling and unfair.

Does the ministerial exception mean that we act in a certain manner simply because we can? That is a philosophical and theological question, as well as a legal one. Currently, American law may seem to protect Catholic education administrators who terminate employment based on sex or gender.

In terms of morality, a person may make a claim of conscience about sexual identity or personal conviction, which then is opposed by a Catholic school to the point of dismissal or to the imposition of some other disciplinary measure. In turn, in terms of the law, the person with such a moral claim of conscience may turn to civil antidiscrimination law as a way to seek redress from the action of the school. For a successful claim of discrimination, a litigant must make a *prima facie* (on the face of it) case. Practically, this means that a reasonable person would agree that what is alleged, if proven, could constitute discrimination. For example, the mere existence of a disability in a student applicant who is denied admission might not be enough to make a *prima facie* case of discrimination. However, if witnesses heard the admissions officer say, "We can't keep taking kids with disabilities," a *prima facie* case could be established.

However, just because the decision-maker can do something doesn't mean it is the right thing to do. A wise woman in my religious community, who recently died at ninety-six, used to state, "What's legal and what's right could get married tomorrow because they usually aren't related." Her words have resonated in my mind for forty years. They seem as apt today as they did when first uttered.

What Does It Mean to Be a Religious Employee?

In the last decade, employees of Catholic institutions have questioned a Catholic school's ability to terminate the employment of an individual who becomes pregnant outside marriage and/or becomes pregnant by artificial insemination. At the time of any litigation of such cases, there was no clear national or state precedent. Historically, a religious institution has the right to give hiring preference to members in good standing of that particular religion and to hold employees, volunteers, and students to its precepts. Catholic schools, like all private schools, are not free, however, to discriminate against persons on other federally protected grounds such as race, national origin, gender, age, and disability. The Bostock decision held that LGBQT persons cannot be discriminated against on the basis of sexual orientation and was hailed as a victory for gay and transgender rights. The opinion holds that everyone is protected in this manner but concedes that some religious institutions probably will and can discriminate on that basis because of the ministerial exception, if an employee exhibits behaviors that violate the sexual codes of the sponsoring religion. However, merely being LGBQT is not and cannot be a reason for adverse employment actions, according to this decision.

As the Our Lady of Guadalupe School case discussed below indicates, one's status as being older does not automatically trigger such protections in Catholic schools. It appears that, absent a clear statement that a person's contract is not being renewed for a federally protected reason, the court will presume that the school or parish is simply exercising its right to employ and dismiss at will any employee who can be considered a religious or ministerial employee.

In 2020, two major cases[14] were decided by the U.S. Supreme Court with significant implications for the meaning of the term "religious employee." These two cases involved teachers in parish schools in the Archdiocese of Los Angeles, and the U.S. Supreme Court combined these cases on appeal. In one case, Ms. Morrissey-Berru claimed age discrimination when her contract was not renewed, and a younger teacher was hired. In the second case, Ms. Biel held that her contract was not renewed because she was ill and took time off for breast cancer surgery and recovery, in violation of the Americans with Disabilities Act and other antidiscrimination laws. The main argument of the two plaintiffs was that they were not ministers, but rather lay employees. The plaintiffs were attempting to distinguish their case from the Hosanna-Tabor[15] case in which the Court held in a unanimous ruling that federal antidiscrimination laws do not protect religious ministers in a school operated by a religion. In the Hosanna-Tabor decision, the U.S. Supreme Court officially recognized the applicability of the ministerial exception.

More specifically, both plaintiffs sought to distinguish themselves from the plaintiff in Hosanna-Tabor who was found to be a ministerial employee by her contract as a "called" teacher. The plaintiffs stated that they were not ministers, did not hold the title minister, and therefore were able to claim

---

[14] Our Lady of Guadalupe School v. Agnes Morrissey-Berru and St. James School v. Darryl Biel, As Personal Representative of the Estate of Kristen Biel, 591 U.S. __ (2020).

[15] Hosanna-Tabor Evangelical Lutheran Church and School v. Equal Employment Opportunity Commission, 565 U.S. 171 (2012).

the protection of federal law. However, the Court accepted the schools' arguments that the teachers were religious employees. Both were teachers in Catholic schools that held that teachers teach religion by their actions every day. The Court found that the dismissal of the two plaintiffs, though in different schools in the Archdiocese of Los Angeles, but employed under "nearly identical" agreements, was not discriminatory.

Negligence

Legal cases alleging negligence are the most common cases brought against educators. Negligence involves an absence of intent. These are less about claims of conscience by staff and students and more about the creation of a culture of attentive conscience in a Catholic school. Here clearly established and enforced rules within a school can help administrators avoid having claims of negligence lodged against them. But nothing defeats such claims more than administrators who take it upon themselves as a matter of conscience to pay attention to the staff and students under their care. As a legal matter, four elements are necessary for the success of a claim of negligence lodged against a Catholic school: (1) duty, (2) violation of duty, (3) proximate cause, and (4) injury. If one is missing, there is no negligence.[16] Administrators should try and imagine the worst that could occur, and discuss how those events could be handled; the time to develop a plan is not when one is needed, but before a situation arises. Merely saying "I didn't think about that" will not help one avoid legal responsibility. Administrators have moral and legal obligations to examine, exercise, and use conscience when developing rules and responding to violations.

In the 2007 case *Dwyer v. Diocese of Rockville Centre*,[17] the diocese won summary judgment in the claim of a high school athlete who was injured when he ran into a pane of glass. Since the glass met applicable building codes when installed, the court gave the diocese summary judgment as a matter of law. In *McCollin Jr. v. Roman Catholic Archdiocese of New York*,[18] a student sustained injuries when another student kicked him in the face; the court held that the student's action was not reasonably foreseeable, and the school was not liable. Students and parents accept risks involved in playing a sport.

---

[16] M. A. Shaughnessy, *Policy Formation in Catholic Education* (Washington, DC: National Catholic Education Association, 2004).

[17] Dwyer v. Rockville Center, 45 AD3d 527 (NJ App. Div. 2d 2007).

[18] McCollin v. Roman Catholic Archdiocese of New York, 45 AD3d 478 (NY 2007).

In the past, injured students often stated, "I got hurt and no teacher was present," but now students may allege, "I was hurt, and you were there, but you weren't paying any attention." One must be *mentally*, as well as *physically*, present. A court will generally ask, "Did the supervisor act as a reasonable person?" Supervising adults are expected to be mentally present. How can administrators ensure mental presence? By talking about it and by supervising the supervisors. Administrators must pay attention to those they supervise. This is a matter of conscience. Employees agree to follow rules; paying attention is one of these. Regular examination of conscience should include, "Have I kept my attention on my class as I should have? Have I tried to cut corners?"

Conclusion

Legal issues can be both challenging and frightening for educators. One question that arises is, "Do I do what the law says I can do or what my conscience tells me?" A related question is, "What do I do if I believe one course of action is right, but my pastor, superintendent, religious superior, or bishop thinks another is?" Another is, "Why can't I have a gay teacher of a secular subject on the faculty who is married to a person of the same sex?" Is civil law stretching us to pray more intensely and ponder more deeply what our faith demands and why it demands it? And how can we live those demands out in our everyday ministry?

Cases against Catholic institutions and programs are increasing. The majority of educators were not thinking about laws and litigation when they became teachers and/or administrators. Yet, civil law weaves a boundary around everything that is done in society. Stay within the boundary and one should be safe. Move outside it and one puts everything inside, including one's ministry, at risk. Is our faith a boundary around conscience or is conscience a boundary around faith? And what does that mean?

When in doubt, seek competent advice. It is far better to ask a question than to guess at the answer and find oneself in a quagmire. The Master Teacher Himself, Jesus, perhaps said it best, "Render unto Caesar the things that are Caesar's and unto God the things that are God's."[19] Sometimes determining what are conscience issues and therefore, ones we believe are inspired by God, and what are simply civil issues can be difficult. History is replete with examples of those who stood against civil law for the sake of conscience and suffered severe penalties, even death. Educators need to challenge what they

---

[19] Mk 12:17.

believe is wrong in civil law and society and thus add richness to the educational experience. A thorough discussion of all that this might entail is beyond the scope of this essay. The gay Catholic school teacher marrying a same-sex partner may well lose employment if that information becomes known. The discussions concerning the rightness or wrongness of those in the Brebeuf and Cathedral High School cases will in all likelihood continue for a long time and undoubtedly will be part of the discussion of conscience. If educators are respectful of legal boundaries, they will be better able to perform their roles. Reflective administrators who regularly examine their own consciences and encourage others to do the same will be faithful to the demands of both civil law and the gospel.

Conscience, Role, and Sphere

A Reflection on the Brebeuf Controversy

Cathleen Kaveny

In a canonical decree effective June 21, 2019, Archbishop Charles C. Thompson declared that "The institution known as Brebeuf Jesuit Preparatory School . . . can no longer use the name Catholic and will no longer be identified or recognized as a Catholic institution by the Archdiocese of Indianapolis."[1] What caused the archbishop to cut ties with Brebeuf, one of the most distinguished Catholic high schools in the United States? The school's leadership refused to terminate the employment of an openly gay teacher who had entered into a civil marriage with a person of the same sex.

How did this impasse come about? After the United States Supreme Court handed down its decision in the *Hosanna-Tabor* case,[2] many religious institutions took the opportunity to declare that a wide range of school employees, including laypersons, were "ministers" of the faith, thereby allowing their employment to be terminated without regard to the prevailing antidiscrimination laws. In 2015, the Archdiocese of Indianapolis ordered every Catholic school in its jurisdiction "to clearly state in its contracts and ministerial job descriptions that all ministers must convey and be supportive of all teachings of the Catholic Church." In the Archdiocese's view, all teachers, guidance counselors, and administrators count as "ministers." The contractual requirements are pervasive: according to the Archdiocese, they require that "in all their professional and private lives [ministers] must convey and be supportive of Catholic Church teaching."[3]

---

[1] Katie Cox, "Archdiocese of Indianapolis to Cut Ties with Brebeuf Jesuit After School Refuses to Fire Gay Teacher," *WRTV News*, June 20, 2019, www.wrtv.com/news.

[2] HosannaTabor Evangelical Lutheran Church and School v. Equal Employment Opportunity Commission, 565 U.S. 171 (2012).

[3] John Shaughnessy and Natalie Hoefer, "Archbishop Thompson, Archdiocesan

In 2017, the Archdiocese became aware that both members of a civilly married same-sex couple were teaching at different Catholic schools within its purview. It ordered both schools to refuse to renew the teachers' employment contracts. While one school, Cathedral High School, complied with the order, the other, Brebeuf Jesuit Preparatory High School, declined to do so.[4] Two years of negotiations resulted in an impasse. In its statement to the Brebeuf Jesuit community, the school administration raised two key points about the separation from the Archdiocese.[5] The first defended the Jesuits's legitimate sphere of authority over the internal life of the school. The second asserted a claim of conscience in exercising that authority. While conceptually distinct, the Jesuits viewed these two key points as intertwined. The statement noted, "After long and prayerful consideration, we determined that following the Archdiocese's directive would not only violate our informed conscience on this particular matter, but also set a concerning precedent for future interference in the school's operations and other governance matters that Brebeuf Jesuit leadership has historically had the sole right and privilege to address and decide."[6]

But the Archdiocese also invoked a combination of conscientious decision-making and role-related responsibilities in justifying the decision to strip Brebeuf of its official Catholic identity. Archbishop Charles Thompson clearly viewed his decision as entailed by his fiduciary duty to the diocese: "I'm a sinner, too. I don't have all the perfect answers. My goal is not to carry out Chuck Thompson's vision or Chuck Thompson's teachings. I've been entrusted with the care of souls in central and southern Indiana, and

School Superintendent Address Issues Involving Brebeuf and Cathedral High Schools," *Criterion Online Edition*, July 5, 2019, www.archindy.org.

[4] Cathedral High School is affiliated with the Brothers of the Holy Cross. It is far more dependent on the Archdiocese than Brebeuf, both for its not-for-profit status and for its funding. Arika Herron, "Cathedral High School Terminates Gay Teacher to Stay in Indianapolis Archdiocese," *Indianapolis Star*, June 23, 2019, www.indystar.com.

[5] Brebeuf Jesuit Preparatory School, "Statement to the Brebeuf Jesuit Community," June 20, 2019, www.brebeuf.org.

[6] The Jesuit provincial involved in the case also clearly recognized the two prongs of the problem: "I recognize this request by Archbishop Charles Thompson to be his prudential judgment of the application of canon law recognizing his responsibility for oversight of faith and morals as well as Catholic education in his archdiocese. I disagree with the necessity and prudence of this decision. This is a disagreement between two church leaders of goodwill with related, but distinct responsibilities." Jesuits Midwest, "Statement of Provincial Brian Paulson SJ Concerning Brebeuf Jesuit Preparatory School," June 20, 2019, https://www.jesuitsmidwest.org.

I've been entrusted to do that, and to use as my markers the teachings of the Church."[7]

The Midwest Province of the Society of Jesus appealed Archbishop Thompson's canonical decree to the Vatican's Congregation for Catholic Education, which suspended the application of the decree during the course of the appeal.[8]

In this essay, I will suggest the ongoing controversy between the Archdiocese of Indianapolis and the Jesuits offers an illuminating case study in the social dimensions of "conscience." More specifically, understanding the claims of conscience in the context of the life of an educational institution—indeed, in the life of any institution—first requires moving beyond a "quandary ethics" approach to conscientious decision-making. Second, it entails untangling the knotty relationship between conscience and role. Finally, it invites us to attend carefully to the social spheres in which moral agents can legitimately expect their conscientious decisions to be honored by others. These three steps will not avoid clashes of conscience. But they may well help us negotiate a responsible and workable solution to those clashes.

The Limits of Quandary Ethics

Fifty years ago, the philosopher Edmund Pincoffs published a now-classic article that critiqued the moral myopia created by the dominance of "quandary ethics" in academic reflection on the moral life.[9] Pincoffs helped us see that the overwhelming fascination with difficult moral problems, often framed as hypothetical cases featuring extreme circumstances, tends to occlude the moral challenges of ordinary life.

Until quite recently, most analyses of the claims of conscience have proceeded in a manner that corresponds to the type of quandary ethics criticized by Pincoffs. They usually focus upon a solitary individual making

---

[7] John Shaughnessey, "Archbishop Encourages ChristCentered Approach to Move Forward in Unity," *Criterion Online Edition*, July 12, 2019, www.archindy.org/criterion. In a press conference held a couple of weeks after the event, the archbishop noted, "While stressing that 'one's [sexual] orientation is not a sin,' the issue involving the two schools 'is about public witness of Church teaching on the dignity of marriage as one man and one woman. That is our Church teaching.'"

[8] Brebeuf Jesuit Preparatory School, "Update from Brebeuf Jesuit President, Fr. Bill Verbryke, S.J.," September 23, 2019, https://brebeuf.org.

[9] Edmund Pincoffs, "Quandary Ethics," *Mind* (New Series), 80, no. 320 (Oct. 1971): 552–71.

a momentous moral decision. That decision itself is isolated, in three senses. First, it takes place in the lonely interior of the decision-maker's psyche. Second, it is framed as a choice of individual integrity against the illegitimate encroachments of a larger and more powerful group. Third, it is sacrosanct, and as such it is untouchable by anyone else. The individual's exercise of conscience occurs in a holy place where God and a human encounter one another; it must not be breached by other mortals.[10]

Moreover, in this dominant picture, the conscientious decision-maker decides to act or refrain from acting in a situation framed as an urgent binary choice. The stakes are clear. There is no factual uncertainty or moral ambiguity. Paradigmatic instances include moral agents who say, "I must not kill another human being, even during war," or "I must go to worship, even if my religion is prohibited by the state." The conscientious decision-maker is represented as a romantic, heroic figure standing up to overbearing powers, saying, "No, I will not," or "Yes, I must." Images come to mind of Thomas More resisting the demands of Henry VIII, Martin Luther nailing a copy of his Ninety-five Theses to the cathedral door, or Rosa Parks deciding to sit all alone in the front of the segregated bus.

This dominant picture does convey important truths. Certain people are indeed confronted with extreme tests of conscience. At the same time, however, the focus of the dominant picture on extreme cases distorts our picture of conscience in several key ways. First, it fails to recognize that the exercise of conscience is an ordinary occurrence in the life of every morally reflective human being—it is not always the raw material for Oscar-winning movies. In a less dramatic passage, the *Catechism of the Catholic Church* recognizes that conscience "is a judgment of reason whereby the human person recognizes the moral quality of a concrete act that he is going to perform, is in the process of performing."[11]

Second, and relatedly, the dominant picture obscures the fact that in the Catholic tradition, the exercise of conscience is not limited to situations that

---

[10] The definition of "conscience" in the *Catechism of the Catholic Church* reinforces this dominant view: See para. 776: "Deep within his conscience man discovers a law which he has not laid upon himself but which he must obey. Its voice, ever calling him to love and to do what is good and to avoid evil, sounds in his heart at the right moment. . . . For man has in his heart a law inscribed by God. . . . His conscience is man's most secret core and his sanctuary. There he is alone with God whose voice echoes in his depths." The *Catechism* is quoting *Gaudium et Spes* (1965), para. 47. Pope John Paul II, *Catechism of the Catholic Church* (1992). Hereinafter *CCC*.

[11] *CCC* para. 1778.

call for the applications of a categorical imperative, whether that imperative is framed in the terms of Immanuel Kant or Pope John Paul II. The word "conscience" does not apply only to a refusal to commit an intrinsically evil act or to an insistence upon performing a required act of piety. Conscientious moral judgments involve any reflective assessment about what to do or not to do in a particular situation. Consequently, they involve prudential assessments of facts, including the circumstances of an act and its likely consequences. According to St. Thomas Aquinas, every fully human act is a moral act.[12]

Third, the dominant picture fails to grapple with the social and institutional context of conscience. Other scholars have perceptively talked about the social *formation* (or deformation) of conscience in important recent work.[13] What I think needs more attention is the socially conditioned nature of the *exercise* of conscience. Accordingly, my focus in this essay will be the reciprocal relationship between conscience and role. A role, in my view, is a socially created bundle of responsibilities, conferring power and authority tied to those responsibilities. Examples of roles include parent, teacher, employee, and manager. An agent's conscientious decisions are shaped by her sense of her role-related obligations, which include reflections on the nature and scope of those obligations. But social roles rarely exist in isolation from one another. An agent's decisions (including their implementation), in turn, affect and are affected by the conscientious decisions of other moral agents who serve in roles that are institutionally related to her own.

Fourth, the question of role naturally leads to the consideration of *spheres of influence*. A sphere is the realm in which a role operates, and over which it has rightful authority. No role confers unlimited influence and authority. Overriding a conscientious judgment is more likely to be perceived as a violation of conscience when it involves the invasion of a sphere of agency by someone who does not have authority within it. For example, suppose I am an "at will" employee working for a temperamental boss. From a legal perspective, the fact that I am an "at will" employee means that I can legally be fired for any reason or for no reason, except for those reasons that violate applicable civil rights laws. So, if my boss fires me because I have prominently installed a picture of "Velvet Elvis Flying over the Cosmos" over my desk, we can say

---

[12] See Thomas Aquinas, *Summa Theologica*, I-II, q. 18, art. 9.

[13] For a helpful history, see Linda Hogan, *Confronting the Truth: Conscience in the Catholic Tradition* (New York: Paulist Press, 2000). For a helpful overview of the necessary social formation and social orientation of conscience, see James F. Keenan, SJ, "Redeeming Conscience," *Theological Studies* 76, no. 1 (2015): 129–47.

she has overridden my conscientious decision about workplace aesthetics. She has not, however, *violated* (e.g., wrongfully overridden) my conscience because her role gives her full authority over the workplace. But if my boss fires me because the same picture is displayed over my fireplace at home, we would say she *violated* my conscience. She has no moral authority in the sphere of my home life, even though the law does not prevent her from firing me because she does not like my domestic interior decorating.

In my view, the notion of "protected spheres" allows us to refine the notion of "inviolability" of conscience by defining it more precisely. The notion of inviolability does not simply signal a moral prohibition against psychological coercion—it is not merely an injunction that no one should overwhelm the capacity of persons to reach a conscientious judgment in their own deliberations. It is also a signal that we need to be attentive to the spheres—the physical and social spaces—in which persons should be morally free to express those judgments, even if the law does not always protect their freedom. It follows, of course, that our disagreements about the claims of conscience very often turn on disagreements about the definition and justification of "protected spheres."

Rethinking the Brebeuf Controversy

Both the archbishop and the Jesuits made a conscientious judgment, rooted in their prudential concerns, about whether or not the school should renew the contract of a teacher who had entered into a same-sex marriage. Each resisted the judgment made by the other. How should we analyze the relationship of conscience and role in this controversy?

Looking at the situation from the archbishop's perspective, we can see that his conscientious exercise of episcopal leadership was *impeded* by the Jesuits at Brebeuf. He believes that it was *wrongfully* impeded—he thinks it was *thwarted*. From the perspective of the Jesuits, however, things look very different. The Jesuits believe that their staffing decisions at the Jesuit-sponsored high school were not only *overridden* by the archbishop, they were also *violated*—they were *wrongfully* overridden.

How do we assess not merely these clashing claims, but more fundamentally, these clashing perspectives on conscientious decision-making? I propose that we analyze them in terms of four factors: (1) the nature of the dispute, (2) the reasons each party puts forward for interfering with the conscientious judgment of the other party, (3) the role relations of the parties, and (4) the spheres in which each party to the controversy legitimately expects its conscientious decision to control.

The Nature of the Dispute

Viewed narrowly, the subject matter of the dispute is not the stuff of great drama. The stakes are not life and death on either side. At its core, this case concerns the renewal of a one-year employment contract. From the perspective of contract law, there is no breach of contract involved. The archbishop did not suddenly demand that the teacher be fired in the middle of the school year. He gave ample notice of his intention not to renew the teacher for an additional year. Moreover, it is highly unlikely the teacher in question would be left destitute even if he were fired; someone so talented would easily be able to find another job at a public or private school, likely for higher pay.

From the perspective of contract law, a decision not to renew a term contract is not generally viewed as different from a decision not to enter a contractual relationship in the first place. In real life, however, there are significant differences, because human beings make plans, build relationships, and invest in their communities over time. From a purely abstract point of view, for example, a landlord who refuses to offer an initial one-year lease to a family may be in the same situation as a landlord who refused to renew a lease for the fifth straight year. From an existential perspective, however, the difference to the tenants—and their neighbors—is enormous. In the former case, they can relocate without much loss to a different dwelling. In the latter case, the life they have made in that domicile will be snatched away from them.

In the same way, a hypothetical directive of the archbishop to refrain from hiring teachers whose public life violates official Catholic teaching is existentially if not legally different from a directive to terminate the employment of teachers already embedded within the community. For many high school students, good teachers are analogous to wise aunts and uncles. The teachers inspire them, they listen to them, they give them perspective on their parents and their family lives. Terminating the employment of teachers already well ensconced in the school community inevitably ruptures the lives of the students and other faculty members, as well as the lives of the teachers themselves.

In my view, therefore, this criterion suggests that the archbishop's case is strongest with regard to future hiring decisions. The Jesuits, however, have a far more persuasive argument with regard to terminating the employment of—and functionally ejecting from the community—teachers who are already on the faculty.

Clashing Conscientious Judgments

Before turning to the reasoning of the Jesuits and the srchbishop, we must recognize the first—and most basic—conscientious decision made in this saga: the decision of a Brebeuf teacher to marry another man in accordance with prevailing law.[14] While marriage is a public act in the United States, it also builds a protected sphere for the marital union. In our culture, the decision about who to marry and why is a matter for the parties themselves. Under some circumstances, that decision may be questioned by family members, close friends, and spiritual advisors. But most Americans do not believe that the sphere of marriage is a legitimate matter of concern for one's employer. For a boss to say to an employee, "Get a divorce or I will fire you," would be experienced by most people as a profound violation of their conscientious decision about whom to marry. In fact, in many states (although not in Indiana), discrimination on the basis of marital status is prohibited by law.

So, in resisting the decision to fire the teacher, the Jesuits were acting in accordance with their conscience as an employer. They took seriously their role-related obligations, which includes showing proper regard for the independent sphere of the employee's family life. But they also took seriously their obligations as educators. More positively, they were making a conscientious decision about what they believed best for the particular group over whom they were given authority: the Brebeuf school community, and how the members of that community would interpret the termination of employment of a well-known and well-respected teacher.

In response to the foregoing observations, the archbishop would doubtless reply that his reasons for calling for the termination of the Brebeuf

---

[14] While initially remaining anonymous, the identity of the teacher was eventually disclosed: see Arika Herron, "Cathedral Fired a Gay Teacher. Brebeuf Protected One. They Are Married to Each Other, Lawyer Says," *Indianapolis Star*, July 10, 2019, www.indystar.com. Layton Payne-Elliot continues to teach math at Brebeuf. Joshua Payne-Elliott was fired from Cathedral High School in Indianapolis in 2019; he sued the archdiocese for wrongful termination in Indiana trial court; his case was dismissed in 2021. Arika Herron, "Lawsuit from Indiana Teacher Over Same-Sex Marriage Is dismissed," *Indianapolis Star*, May 8, 2021, www.indystar.com. Joshua Payne-Elliott is appealing the dismissal.

teacher in question are programmatic, not personal. He has no particular animus against the teacher. But he believes that a primary task of a Catholic institution is to proclaim Catholic moral teaching in a clear and unambiguous way, particularly against the overwhelming counterwitness of a secular culture. His judgments in this matter are not idiosyncratic; they find their place within the vision of the church and the world promoted by Pope John Paul II, Pope Benedict XVI, and in recent years, the U.S. Conference of Catholic Bishops. In this view, a major task of the church is to promote a "culture of life," in opposition to the secular "culture of death," which entails taking a firm stand against abortion, same-sex marriage, and "gender ideology," because they all threaten the traditional family. The task of Catholic institutions, including Catholic schools, is to offer a courageous and prophetic stand on these matters. From this perspective, recent U.S. Supreme Court decisions protecting religious liberty make such a necessary stand possible.

Yet the Jesuits have a rejoinder to the archbishop's analysis. They can point out that other moral teachings are in play too, particularly the equal dignity of LGBTQ persons. They are not to be demeaned, shunned, or rejected. While not denying the tension with other Catholic teachings, the Jesuits can maintain that this teaching needs to take precedence in high schools, when young persons are at their most fragile. No LGBTQ person should be expelled from family or community. From the perspective of the students, terminating the employment of the teacher looks very much like such an expulsion. Like the archbishop, the Jesuits can also support their approach by situating it within a broader theological and ecclesial context. Pope Francis's theology of accompaniment prioritizes the nurturing of human connection and the exercise of compassion. In fact, Pope Francis has stated, "Homosexuals have a right to be a part of the family. . . . They're children of God and have a right to a family. Nobody should be thrown out, or be made miserable because of it."[15]

The archbishop might justly reply that the pope has called for the recognition of civil unions, *not* same-sex marriages. That is an important point. Yet the Jesuits might respond that that distinction, while theoretically important, is not currently applicable in the United States. Civil marriage law has been extended to cover both heterosexual and homosexual couples. In both cases, the purpose of the law is to regularize and stabilize affective sexual relation-

---

[15] Taylor Ardrey, "Pope Francis Said Same-Sex Couples Should Be Covered by a Civil Union Law," *Insider*, October 21, 2020, www.businessinsider.com.

ships, holding the partners accountable to each other, as well as to family and community. The law of domestic relations has a pedagogical function, which cannot be understood apart from its goals of minimizing conflict and creating order and stability. Given the nature and sexual mores of the United States in the twenty-first century, many people believe those functions are best served by legalizing same-sex marriage.

The archbishop would doubtless agree that law does indeed have a pedagogical function. The question is, "What should the law be teaching?" If he were being particularly candid, the archbishop might express the worry that any acquiescence or accommodation to the secular view of marriage will inevitably erode the plausibility of Catholic teaching that sexual behavior between persons of the same sex is immoral. More strongly, he might express the worry that liberal Catholics are hoping that widespread experience with LGBTQ people will lead to the inauthentic development of church teaching on same-sex relations.

Liberal Catholics might respond in one of two ways. Some might maintain that they are not trying to develop doctrine on same-sex relations but only attempting to implement the full teaching (including the dignity of LGBTQ persons) as it already exists. Other might say that yes, indeed, they are working for such a development, because they see themselves as responding to the promptings of the Holy Spirit. Just as John Courtney Murray drew upon the experience of Catholics in the United States to develop teaching on religious liberty, so they are drawing upon the experience of LGBTQ Catholics to develop teaching on same-sex relations.

The general relationship of conscientious prudential judgment to (authentic) development of the church's moral teaching is beyond the scope of this essay. But I will say that it is the Holy Spirit that guides the development of the church's doctrine through the magisterium and the *sensus fidelium*. Securing or forestalling development of doctrine is beyond the purview of most individual decision-makers—it is beyond the responsibilities of their roles. Consequently, I believe that both the archbishop and the Jesuits can and should focus upon the concrete needs of the communities in their charge in making their conscientious decisions. Strategic activism to force— or stay—the hand of the Holy Spirit in the life of the church is out of place here. Prudent prediction of the likely consequences of one's decisions is an important aspect of the exercise of conscience. But predicting, promoting, or preventing changes to church teaching is too speculative and remote to enter into the discernment process.

Roles and Relationships

Many people think the relationship between the Jesuits and the Archbishop is the same as that between a diocesan priest and the archbishop. They assume that the archbishop is the "boss" of everything Catholic that occurs within his diocese. Yet that assumption is incomplete, if not entirely incorrect. Their relationship is structured by the law of the church. The Jesuits are not a creature of the bishop; they an independent religious order. Consequently, canon law gives them freedom to establish their own schools.[16] At the same time, the bishop of the diocese in which such a school is located has responsibility of oversight.[17] But that oversight is not unlimited. For example, the bishop legally holds the specific right to appoint and remove teachers of religion—but the law says nothing about other teachers.[18] More generally, the bishop has the right and duty to "watch over and visit the Catholic schools in his territory," even those run by religious orders. At the same time, the bishop "issues precepts which pertain to the general regulation of Catholic schools; these prescripts are valid also for schools which these religious direct, without prejudice, however, to their autonomy regarding the internal direction of their schools."[19]

Note the way canon law invites us to frame the relationship between the archbishop and the Jesuits in terms of overlapping spheres of responsibility. Responsibility for overall Catholic life within his *territory* belongs to the archbishop. The Jesuits, however, are not his employees, subjects, or agents. They are not subject to his direction and control; they are not bound to do his bidding or to act to promote his view of the relationship of the church and the world. In their relationship to him, and in their own schools, canon law recognizes that they possess "internal autonomy." It would be fair, then, to say that both the Jesuits and the Archbishop exercise their conscientious judgments in overlapping spheres of authority. The task facing both is to negotiate the tension, not to find a way to trump the other.

---

[16] *Code of Canon Law*, canon 803 § 1.

[17] Canon 801 § 3 provides that "Even if it is in fact Catholic, no school is to bear the name Catholic school without the consent of competent ecclesiastical authority"—presumably the bishop. But this criterion is vague in three respects. First, does it apply only to institutions where the name "Catholic School" appears in the title? If so, Brebeuf is not affected. Second, who counts as "competent ecclesiastical authority"—only the local ordinary? Third, what are the criteria the appropriate authority ought to use in giving or withholding consent?

[18] Ibid., canon 805.

[19] Ibid., canon 806, § 1.

Spheres of Authority

In my view, the concept of overlapping spheres of authority for conscientious decision-making sheds helpful light on the controversy. A helpful analogy might be the status of embassies in foreign lands. In contrast to popular conception, the land that an embassy sits on *does* remain part of the territory of the host country under international law. Nonetheless, its walls define a protected sphere that cannot be entered by anyone without permission of the ambassador. What happens *within* those walls is under the authority of the visiting country, not that of the host country.[20]

The overarching purpose of the rules of diplomatic immunity is not to allow foreign diplomats to "get away" with violations of the law. As a State Department brochure states, "the purpose of these privileges and immunities is not to benefit individuals but to ensure the efficient and effective performance of their official missions on behalf of their governments."[21] A key aspect of that purpose is to maintain personal relationships, as well as to increase mutual understanding, despite significant differences. Without the strong and reciprocal rules of diplomatic law, relations between countries would need to be conducted at a safe distance for all parties. Because of those rules, representatives even of warring countries can build connections that facilitate better understanding and respect. Moreover, the diplomatic framework serves even friendly countries to preserve autonomy while building closer relations. Its overarching purpose is to foster unity within the human family, while taking due account of difference.

How can the diplomatic analogy be helpful here? I think that the archbishop might profitably view Jesuit high schools as analogous to an embassy from a different country in the Catholic world that is based in his jurisdiction. The analogy is not as farfetched as it might seem. International law in general, and diplomatic law in particular, owes a great deal to the traditions of the Roman Catholic Church.[22] So it may be both fitting and fruitful that Catholics draw upon these principles to address controversies within their

---

[20] For a helpful, practical account of diplomatic immunity, see United States Department of State, Office of Foreign Missions, *Diplomatic and Consular Immunity: Guidelines for Law Enforcement and Judicial Authorities* (2018), https://www.state.gov/wp-content/uploads/2019/07/2018-DipConImm_v5_Web.pdf.

[21] Ibid., 5.

[22] See, e.g., Jordok Troy, "The Catholic Church and International Relations," *Oxford Handbooks Online*, April 2016, https://ssrn.com/abstract=2627477.

own ecclesial context. The Jesuits may have a different, more liberal approach to the admittedly difficult problem of same-sex couples teaching in Catholic schools than the Archbishop of Indianapolis does. But their approach no more wrongfully impedes his conscientious judgment than would the different, more liberal approach of a neighboring archdiocese. By allowing the Jesuits some autonomy within their sphere, he maintains connections with them, and through them, with people the Catholic Church might not otherwise reach. In the realm of international law, maintaining relationships across difference is a goal of diplomacy. In the realm of theology, it is a prerequisite to evangelization.

But the archbishop might well ask, "Are not there *any* limits to what falls into the boundaries of Catholic world?" Yes, of course, there are. Fortunately, this case does not raise those hard questions. There is no strict obligation in Catholic moral theology to terminate the employment of a (math) teacher in a same-sex marriage.[23] The decision to do so is intelligible as part of a particular approach to ecclesiology and moral theology, which emphasizes the need for the church to confront the culture on disputed points of sexual morality. That approach may be legitimate, but it is not exhaustively legitimate. As we have seen, the pope, as well as other American prelates, operates out of a quite different ecclesiology of accompaniment.

How would viewing the controversy in terms of diplomatic law constructively reframe the problem? It could lead us to say that an archbishop rightly expects his ecclesiology to be implemented within schools under his direct control. But he ought not to insist that schools run by other entities in the church comply with his directives, provided that their approach is credibly represented by other constituencies within the broader church community. Let me emphasize that this approach is not liberal or conservative, nor tied to a particular outcome on this particular issue. It is a question of protected spheres of authority. If the shoe is on the other foot, more progressive bishops ought to strive to accommodate traditionalists in their midst on just the same grounds. So, for example, I would say that Cardinal Cupich ought to allow the same internal autonomy to an Opus Dei high school under his jurisdiction that Archbishop Thompson should allow to a Jesuit high school under his.

---

[23] A theology teacher would raise a different set of questions.

Closing Thoughts

According to some reports, many segments of the United States are in the process of breaking up. In both real and virtual spaces, we divide ourselves into groups according to race, socioeconomic status, and political conviction.[24] The same thing is happening in the church: there are liberal parishes and conservative parishes, liberal religious orders and conservative religious orders. But in recent years, this clustering of like-minded people has taken a disturbing turn, moving not only to avoid the other but also to exclude them from a broader communal life. Cancel culture, which is a tactic of the culture wars, operates on both the left and the right, in both the church and the country.

Whether liberal or conservative, a culture war approach to the church carries with it a significant danger of overriding the rightful independence of all spheres, in part because it tacitly conceives of the Catholic community as an army, rather than the body of Christ. It may be appropriate for an army to control virtually all aspects of soldiers' lives, from what they eat to how they make a bed. But it is not appropriate for church leaders to behave the same way. An approach that emphasizes uniformity can easily be extended to justify pervasive surveillance and control over the lives of Catholics associated with the church.

Someone might respond that the focus is only on public behavior, not private. But the line between private behavior and public behavior is very thin, in this age of Twitter, Instagram, and cancel culture. It is hard to see how, in the hands of weak and sinful people, efforts to enforce a laudable call to consistent evangelical witness will not devolve into some form of Catholic McCarthyism. The combination of social media and the totalizing tendencies of the culture war framework can easily push beyond promoting a legitimate Catholic perspective on the relationship between church and world, and fall into a kind of sectarianism on either the left or the right. A conservative bishop may find out that someone attended a same-sex wedding; a liberal bishop may discover that someone regularly attends an unapproved Latin Mass. Consequences may ensue for disloyalty.

Some people might respond that unless the bishop enforces a coherent strategic approach to controversial issues throughout the diocese, he is capitulating to relativism. I do not believe that is the case. In fact, the church's long

---

[24] Bill Bishop, *The Big Sort: Why the Clustering of Like-Minded America Is Tearing Us Apart* (Boston: Mariner Books, 2009).

history of diplomatic relations *ad extra* shows that it is possible to retain relationships, and to respect spheres of autonomy, without forfeiting one's own commitments. In these fractious times, a similar approach could be equally effective *ad intra*. We need to consider how Catholics might benefit from extending diplomatic privilege to one another.[25]

---

[25] For very helpful comments on an earlier draft, I would like to thank David DeCosse, as well as the members of the Boston College Seminar in Theological Ethics, particularly Ken Himes, who was tasked with being my respondent at the session presenting the essay.

Conscience and
the Lay Catholic School Superintendent

Kevin C. Baxter

When I started as superintendent in the Archdiocese of Los Angeles, a long-time employee told me to be vigilant because it was easy to lose your faith when you work for the church. I did not understand what he was referring to, partly because I had been working for the church for the previous twelve years as a teacher and a principal. But after I served ten years in the superintendent role, his warning made much more sense. Indeed, it has become a caution I offer to others who are starting out in diocesan leadership across the country. My faith in the church was challenged during my time in diocesan leadership, and I know from my discussions with colleagues across the country that my experience was not unique. This essay will delve into why that was the case with me, and perhaps others, and ideally prepare those who follow in such roles to deal with the challenges that await. Thankfully, my faith remained intact, but it was a struggle at times. In this essay, I hope to communicate my acknowledgment and embrace of that struggle as a matter of conscience.

Background in Catholic Schools

I began my role as the Superintendent for Elementary Schools in the Archdiocese of Los Angeles (ADLA) in July of 2009. The ADLA is the largest in the country, with between four and five million Catholics in Los Angeles, Ventura, and Santa Barbara Counties. The Catholic school system is also the largest in the country, with nearly 80,000 students when I began my role as superintendent. At that time there were approximately 53,000 students in the 220 PreK-8 elementary schools and 27,000 in the fifty high schools. The ADLA is also extremely diverse, with about 68 percent of the elementary student population coming from representative minority backgrounds. My approach to the role was to focus on leadership development and implementing innovative approaches to attract more students to Catholic schools. The ADLA, like other dioceses across the United States, had struggled with enrollment over the previous decade and I saw my task as collaborating with others to create structures and programs to change that trend.

I had been a principal at two different Catholic schools in the archdiocese prior to taking on this role, as well as a teacher and vice principal. Thus, I had ample experience being a faith leader in a school community, with the responsibility of formation of faculty and staff, in addition to students. I would often attend the 6:30 a.m. Mass in the morning, which would center me in the liturgy before the busyness of the school day began. As a principal, being the faith leader of a school community was a role I enjoyed, and I felt it was an area of strength for me.

My own educational experience was almost entirely within Catholic schools. I attended them from kindergarten through high school and then graduated from Villanova University, an Augustinian school outside of Philadelphia. After moving to Los Angeles and beginning my career in Catholic schools, I obtained a master's degree in secondary education from Loyola Marymount University, a Jesuit institution. The first time I studied at a non-Catholic school was when I began my doctoral studies at the University of Southern California. I have also been a part-time professor at Loyola Marymount University since 2002, where I have taught graduate classes to Catholic school educators (as well as public and charter school educators). At the time of this writing, I am completing two years working as the Chief Innovation Officer for the National Catholic Educational Association (NCEA) and preparing to transition to the University of Notre Dame, where I will teach in and direct the Mary Ann Remick Leadership Program, which prepares principals to lead Catholic schools across the country.

This background is to note that I have been well formed in my faith through my own educational experience as well as over the course of my professional life. Even in the world of Catholic school educators, my personal and professional connections to Catholic schools are extensive relative to others. Walking through the hallways of my Catholic school as a child, then educating and leading schools as a professional, gave me an understanding and a comfort level with the faith and my own conscience. And yet, when I began my position as superintendent in 2009, I found myself intimidated by the responsibility I was assuming. The diocesan office seemed imposing from an institutional church perspective—as a cradle Catholic the history, authority, and control were foremost in my mind—and I feared that the sense of community at the diocesan office was not as tangible or deemed as important as in a school setting. I also found that I was cognizant of saying something that could be perceived as "wrong" from a theological perspective more acutely than I had ever felt in a school setting. This reaction was partly due to the proximity to decision-making, but it was also due to some of the individuals in the building whom I felt were primarily focused on preserving tradition rather than on being open to new approaches that would lead to growth. While this was my personal perception more than anything made explicit, the result was that I often felt apprehensive about expressing my views, especially when it came to issues with church teaching.

As a Catholic school principal, I felt deeply connected to the community and was comfortable in my role as the faith leader of the school. There was great joy tangibly felt that resulted from working with young people. This joy is reflected in what Pope Francis wrote in *Evangelii Gaudium*: that the true mark of a Christian is joy, and that true evangelization is "full of fervor, joy, generosity, courage, boundless love and attraction!"[1] The vision for all schools, and indeed all organizations within the church, should be to have such a culture as the missionary core of the organization.

At the chancery office, it was harder to discover the joy, perhaps fairly because students are the source of much of the joy in a school setting. But joy also comes from the commitment to community, which schools naturally inculcate among faculty and families. It was difficult to build a sense of community across the various departments, and this often resulted in an absence of joy. The description I often used with my former school principal colleagues was that it was . . . an office. I used to jokingly ask the staff in the Catholic school department, most of whom had come from elementary school-level positions, "When does the bell ring for recess?" The office setting was clearly different than a school site. At a school there was a lot happening with a multitude of human interactions taking place daily. The chancery was quiet and cold. After my first days at the chancery, I knew I would have to adjust.

Clericalism

One of the first things that was evident was clericalism, which Pope Francis has warned about because it detaches priests and bishops from the people.[2]

---

[1] Pope Francis, *Evangelii Gaudium*—"The Joy of the Gospel" (2013), no. 261. Hereinafter *EG*.

[2] Christopher Lamb, "Pope to Priests: Clericalism Takes Root When You Seek Comfort Instead of the People," *The Tablet*, April 18, 2019, www.thetablet.co.uk.

Clericalism was reflected in policies that affected many schools that we worked with that were in dire straits. When new pastors would take over a parish, there was sometimes debt that had been accrued by the previous pastor. This would be waived for the new pastor, which was understandable because what occurred prior to their arrival was not their responsibility. The issue was that the same grace and understanding was not extended to principals who took over new schools. Thus, new principals in such a debt-ridden scenario would have to face a myriad of hard financial issues that new pastors often would not. Another issue that surfaced was that some priests who worked in ministry at the chancery did not think they should have to go through the performance review process that lay employees went through because the priests were not able to be terminated in the same way. This differential treatment meant in effect that priests evaded professional scrutiny for their work in the diocesan education office while lay employees faced a constant level of professional accountability. What these experiences communicated to me as a layperson—and who was often the only person in meetings who was not wearing a Roman collar—was that there were different rules for me than for clerics. This reinforced the sense that I should be wary of pushing too much against traditional approaches because of the potential consequences.

In the field of education, each progressive step up the leadership ladder involves trade-offs. I saw this in the choices I had to make at each stage of my career. As a teacher, you form very solid relationships with your class of students each year. You have an incredible opportunity to form and impact the kids you work with and have the potential to be a mentor they will remember for the rest of their lives. If you move to a principal position, you sacrifice those close student relationships to have a wider influence across the school community. That influence impacts faculty and staff and, if you do your job well, they will in turn influence the students in positive ways. A move to a diocesan office results in losing the sense of a school community, but you then have the capacity to influence an entire system. Each step is about increasing your capacity to influence a larger number of students and individuals, but each step involves the loss of the connectedness that is a driving factor for why people go into education in the first place. The issue for me was that the joy that was so evident at the school level, which came from the strong commitment to community, was absent from the wider realms of the chancery office. Approaching the sacred work of ministry in a bureaucratic fashion makes building community between departments much more difficult. In my mind, if such a culture of joy could be established in diocesan offices, the church would be more successful in retaining and developing lay disciples to serve. Researchers at Creighton University studied the attrition of ten Catholic superintendents and found that nine of them had left their positions earlier than expected. The study found that the "major reason for leaving early was related to negative experiences with church bureaucracy and politics at the head offices of their respective (arch)dioceses."[3]

The reason I did not initially grasp my colleague's warning about maintaining my faith was driven by my understanding that people are human, and that all organizations reflect this humanity, including church organizations. The nature of humanity was clearly on display in the chancery building, which was not a surprise. Politics is not the sole purview of Washington, D.C. Factions, gossip, and even backstabbing are all present in church work. There are also coalitions, strong relationships, and partnerships that all can yield fruitful results, but these can also cause frustration and pain. The art of politics is not inherently negative, and it is present in all organizations, including diocesan offices. In any case, the politics was not surprising to me, and I enjoyed certain aspects of that work. The larger challenge for me was seeing the Catholic faith, my faith, placed in a political frame. This was most clearly seen in the camps that would form between conservative/traditional and liberal/modern groups. I have had several conversations with other lay Catholic leaders, some in schools and some in other areas, which indicate that I am not alone in having this experience. Much of it has to do with different approaches to theology, which our modern society defines in political terms— conservative vs. liberal, or traditional vs. modern.

I recall a wonderful Catholic school educator who is a gifted administrator, although not yet a school principal. This person is a convert to the Catholic faith and has hesitations in becoming a principal because of the responsibility of being the spiritual leader of the school. Not having been raised in the Catholic Church, this person feels as if there are some basic understandings that they are lacking and they express concern about making a mistake that would be viewed negatively by the staff. This fear from lay leaders of making a "mistake" from a theological perspective is what the church has, perhaps inadvertently, instilled with its stronger focus on conscience being dictated by the magisterium, rather than by the individual. This, in the best case, acts as a barrier to people of good will and faith who are on a path seeking

---

[3] T. J. Cook, R. D. Fussell, and T. A. Simonds, "Turnover and Retention of Catholic School Superintendents in the United States: Averting a Crisis," *International Studies in Catholic Education* (forthcoming).

Christ to feel confident expressing their views in an authentic and transparent way. In the worst case, these individuals decide not to work for the church at all and may even end up having doubts about their faith.

Mercy and Truth

The terms "liberal" and "conservative" or "modern" and "traditional" are false constructs through which to view something as personal as our religious belief and practice. It separates the church into polarized camps and causes those within each camp to view issues through that particular lens. The value of different perspectives is that everyone can bring their own unique and unrepeatable experience to issues and discussions, which adds richness to whatever decision is reached. Trust needs to be present for this to occur and that is nurtured and developed when each person's conscience is respected as part of the decision-making process. There is "an inner core of Spirit-guided desire before we arrive at explicitly Christian interpretations of our experience. . . . There is a risk of rushing into the world of explicit religion without pausing on what is more fundamental in each of us—the experience of searching, of struggling to live genuinely, of being slowly transformed by the adventure of life."[4] Appreciating that many Catholics today, students and adults, are still working through this pre-Christian struggle to live a life of integrity allows us to approach and educate in a manner that will invite them in rather than push them away.

Julie Hanlon Rubio from Santa Clara University has written about these divisions within the Catholic Church in the context of *Amoris Laetitia* and its discussion of divorce and remarriage.[5] When we use terms like "conservative/liberal" or "traditional/modern," we put things into a political context, rather than a spiritual one. That creates factions within the church, which is not the purpose of our faith. When we reduce ourselves to such descriptions, we do damage to the body of Christ, which is meant to be one with many parts. The better description for how we view ourselves on a range of issues, according to Rubio, is in terms of mercy and truth.[6] Our faith and decisions

---

[4] Michael Paul Gallagher, SJ, *The Human Poetry of Faith: A Spiritual Guide to Life* (Mahwah, NJ: Paulist Press, 2003), 134.

[5] Julie Hanlon Rubio, "The Newness of *Amoris Laetitia*: Mercy and Truth, Truth and Mercy," in *Amoris Laetitia: A New Momentum for Moral Formation and Pastoral Practice,* ed. Grant Gallicho and James F. Keenan, SJ (New York: Paulist Press, 2018).

[6] Ibid.

about key issues that affect society and the church can best be addressed on a continuum of mercy and truth. If we proceed without mercy, we get the black-and-white harshness of truth; if we proceed without truth, we get mercy without accountability. While Rubio uses this construct in terms of divorce and remarriage, it also has relevance to how we work in the church with others who may have different worship practices but share the same faith. The environment would be much more constructive if we led with mercy, rather than judgment. The concept of mercy is best stated by Pope Francis, "No one can be condemned forever."[7]

Common Core State Standards

In terms of the chancery offices, the destructive effect of the contrasting poles of conservative and liberal was most evident when the Common Core State Standards (CCSS)[8] were rolled out in 2012. The CCSS were developed by the National Governors Association and the Council of Chief State School Officers to provide consistent academic standards for schools across the country. Prior to the development of the CCSS, each state had its own academic standards, which varied widely and led to inconsistent outcomes for students from different states. Most of the Catholic schools across the country, and all of them in the state of California, had plans to implement the Common Core but the standards soon became a lightning rod of controversy. This controversy was partly due to the political nature of the standards and how they were developed and implemented. But it was also centered on the Catholic faith, and those from more theologically conservative perspectives would use the CCSS to try and "delegitimize" Catholic schools that used them. The basis for this view was that Catholic schools would use the public school standards and then be more apt to be regulated by the state and lose the mission and Catholic identity that are central to their purpose. One conservative parish even took a full-page ad out in the diocesan newspaper, stressing that they were not implementing the standards and implying that those schools that were had substandard programs. Those who opposed the CCSS from this perspective were not looking at the issue on a continuum of belief, but rather from a fixed position. The view they held was the only view, and there was no way to see the possibility of a middle ground.

---

[7] Pope Francis, *Amoris Laetitia*—"On Love in the Family" (2016), no. 297. Hereinafter *AL*.

[8] Common Core Standards Initiative, http://www.corestandards.org/.

Significant effort was made by dioceses and the California Catholic Conference (the public policy arm of the Catholic bishops of California) to communicate the facts about the standards, but the pushback remained strong. Educators communicated the fact that standards in education are different from curriculum, so the CCSS could even be used as a framework to teach in a classically based education model, which would be of interest to those who had a more theologically conservative approach. This type of middle-ground approach did not resonate with most of those who opposed the CCSS. My interactions in person and online made it clear that many of those who opposed the CCSS were not looking at the issue in an objective fashion, but rather through a preestablished lens that was partially shaped through politics but was also clearly influenced by their understanding of Catholic teaching.

This is where I believe the view of conscience as an individual means to understanding and grace, as informed by study and prayer, best applies to the myriad issues that face society. When we fall into different camps within the church, we end up feeling isolated from each other and doubt arises about how "faithful" the other side is according to our own rules. Instead, conscience properly understood and properly formed can be a way by which we respect great difference and nevertheless find common ground. I know during the CCSS implementation that those who had concerns about the standards viewed those of us who supported them with suspicion, and they were not willing to consider arguments that pointed to the value of the standards. This happened on both sides of the debate because I found that I questioned those who opposed the standards in similar, reductive ways. If instead we understood and appreciated this spectrum of belief, we could recognize that we might fall at different ends of the spectrum on different issues, but that does not mean that one's belief is invalid or somehow operating against the church. This example demonstrates why I was sensitive about my approach on certain issues because of the potential for pushback and criticism if something I said was perceived as being detrimental to the faith.

There is room for debate and disagreement, but by seeing our faith as being part mercy and part truth we do not have to pigeonhole ourselves into a fixed mind-set of thinking. Rubio addresses this in her article on divorce and remarriage. Focusing only on truth leads to a lack of pastoral sensitivity for those who are struggling. But "focusing only on the mercy in *Amoris Laetitia* may result in too narrow an emphasis on whether an exception to the rules applies."[9] Through

---

[9] Rubio, "The Newness of *Amoris Laetitia*," 65.

prayer and study, we can be open to the Holy Spirit as a guide to what is the right path based on the reality of the situation. I must admit that in some very difficult moments I took comfort in the fact that the fear of saying something wrong is also found in the Gospel of Luke: "When Jesus left, the scribes and Pharisees began to act with hostility toward him and to interrogate him about many things, for they were plotting to catch him at something he might say."[10]

Engaging the "Nones"

No diocesan educational organization can be immune from the major concern that young people are disengaging and disaffiliating from the faith. This is something that is impacting all faiths, and the Catholic Church in particular. This disengagement also centrally raises the issue of conscience. The rise of the "nones," who are those who associate with no religious faith at all, has grown significantly over the past decade.[11] The disaffiliation of young people is exemplified in the study *Going, Going, Gone*,[12] which highlights the reasons why young people are leaving the faith. The study should be required reading for all members of the church, and especially those who work in Catholic schools, if it wants to address the challenges and issues in a constructive way. A startling statistic from *Going, Going, Gone* is that the median age that young people begin to feel separated from the Catholic Church is thirteen. The implications are clear for Catholic schools today in how they engage young students, but the results from the study also inform how best to nurture and grow lay leadership for diocesan offices over the longer term.

Soon after the study was published, I attended a gathering of Catholic educators to discuss the topic. At the table there were about eight other individuals, including a priest. The presenter showed a video of a young person who was struggling with her faith and was an example of the overall findings of the study. The young person spoke on several topics that would be familiar to those who are involved with the church today, such as feeling conflicted with organized religion but connected to a divine force, knowing her spiritual sense remained strong, and her disappointed sense that the focus of

---

[10] Lk 11:53–54.

[11] Frank Newport, "Millennials' Religiosity amidst the Rise of the Nones" (October 29, 2019), Gallup, https://news.gallup.com/opinion/polling-matters/267920/millennials-religiosity-amidst-rise-nones.aspx.

[12] Robert J. McCarty and John M. Vitek, *Going, Going, Gone: The Dynamics of Disaffiliation in Young Catholics* (Winona, MN: St. Mary's Press, 2018).

much organized religion centered on doctrine and rules rather than on the human connection with others. Here was the conscience of this young person speaking of spiritual longing, if not in an explicitly Catholic or Christian key.

After the video, the presenter asked us to have a conversation at our tables about how we would counsel this young woman if she came to us for guidance and shared the sentiments she expressed in the video. All of us at the table first looked to the priest who was sitting with us, thinking he must have experience with such conversations. His response was a bit terse and surprising and went something like, "I would tell her to let go of her Star Wars understanding of spirituality and understand the teachings of the church. It is hard to communicate with a person who is so off-base with the understanding of the faith and has not been properly formed." My immediate thought in hearing this was that the church is in big trouble if this is the approach of the clergy to young people struggling with their faith.

The concept of conscience provides us with a way to engage the sincerity of this young person and, indeed, of those who are disaffiliating with the church. Understanding and valuing the pre-Christian struggle with goodness and integrity allows us to invite them to conversation and deeper meaning. If conscience in the Catholic tradition is viewed only as a function of obedience to the magisterium, then we have left too little room for engaging the striving, sincere conscience of many young people today who are drawn to the Catholic faith and are also morally troubled by aspects of Catholic moral doctrine and practice. In his book on the possibilities and challenges to faith today, Jesuit Michael Paul Gallagher writes, "People are not hostile to the truth at the core of the gospel, but they are often unreachable by the usual church language."[13] Leading with a focus on doctrinal and dogmatic aspects of faith with young people threatens to alienate them from the beauty of the faith that develops over time. Gallagher describes the "risk of rushing into the world of explicit religion without pausing on what is more fundamental in each of us—the experience of searching, of struggling to live genuinely, of being slowly transformed by the adventure of life. Here in silence and even in secret we are being shaped as lovers: everyone, believer, unbeliever, Christian, Jew, Muslim, Buddhist, Hindu."[14]

Catholic school educators need to touch the core spirituality that exists in all people—a core deeply connected to conscience in its interaction with concrete experience. Every human being has an innate need to search for

---

[13] Gallagher, *The Human Poetry of Faith*, 162.
[14] Ibid., 134.

meaning in their life—this may take form from the start in formal religious practice, but it is also possible that it will not develop until later in life. The aim cannot be to start with formal doctrine with students if they have not already engaged in this innate spiritual seeking. The natural questioning that human beings possess can be nurtured in young people to touch their hearts and souls. As that is being further developed, we can begin to introduce the core tenets of the faith in a way that will more readily take hold.

LGBTQ Issues

The issue of LGBTQ individuals working in Catholic schools was another source of anxiety for me, primarily because it provided such a clear demarcation between the different attitudes within the church. There were approximately a half dozen principals (that were known to me) who were homosexual, and they were some of the strongest principals in the system. They all had to lead their communities without expressing this fundamental aspect of their humanity. They also lived with the understanding, and the fear, that they could be identified at any time and that being identified would put their careers at risk.

The situations that cause me pain and regret today are the ones where I had to address the issue with these principals because public comments about their sexual orientation were made known to me. This was usually done anonymously and would include social media posts and gossip about the individual's personal life. For many of those occasions, I chose to speak through the lens of church teaching rather than through a pastoral lens, primarily because of my role but also because of my concern that my own position would be put in jeopardy, if I openly advocated for them. This was a time ten to twelve years ago when the issue was particularly heated, and there were several factors that made the issue very sensitive. Some great leaders left Catholic school education all together, and I know that the schools are diminished because of their absence. I find myself sad and regretful about my approach because it centered more on the opposing poles rather than on the spectrum in between. The issue is that certain sins are viewed within the church as presenting greater obstacles to piety than other sins. In turn, a person is viewed in terms of such a sin. The rich, complex, faithful conscience of a person disappears from view behind the specification of their sin, a specification that determines their standing in the church and in the schools. But we are all are sinners and saints, and each of us at different times is blessed and broken.

As a superintendent, I wanted to draw the best out of the employees in both the diocesan office and the schools. If some are concerned that they will be viewed as less than worthy if they say or do something that is perceived as incorrect or inherently shameful, there will not be the honest, transparent risk-taking that leads to growth. I came to see the destructive power of what Rachel Held Evans identifies in *Searching for Sunday*, "There are always folks who fancy themselves bouncers to the heavenly banquet, charged with keeping the wrong people away from the table and out of the church . . . They strain out the gnats in everyone else's theology while swallowing their own camel-sized inconsistencies."[15] And I also came to see the necessity for the church, in its work in education, of what Pope Francis said in *Evangelii Gaudium:* "The Eucharist, although it is the fullness of sacramental life, is not a prize for the perfect but a powerful medicine and nourishment for the weak."[16]

Conclusion

Friedrich Nietzsche (and later, Viktor Frankl) said that "He who has a why to live for can bear almost any how." I view this as being central to a vocation versus a career. A vocation calls out to us to do it; it is not necessarily something we seek out and choose for ourselves. We are compelled to do the work because it is a cause that drives us. My vocational call to Catholic schools is based on my belief that they are vital pathways to a better life for students and their families, especially in underserved communities. That is what continues to motivate me to this day to do this important work for the church.

Guideposts are needed, and I do not believe that moral relativism is a strong framework by which to live one's life. Clear expectations and teachings that have been passed down for centuries direct us how to live so our lives are full of meaning, integrity, and grace. It is wonderful to know that I am loved by God no matter what I do, and there is nothing I can do to lose that love if I return asking for forgiveness. But I also want to know and remember that God is disappointed when I do not live up to the expectations that God has for me. Knowing you are loved unconditionally is peacefully satisfying, but knowing that you have caused God pain and sorrow compels your improvement moving forward. As Ann Garrido writes,

---

[15] Rachel Held Evans, *Searching for Sunday* (Nashville, TN: Nelson Books, 2015), 149.

[16] *EG* no. 47.

Everyone is obligated to follow their own conscience. Everyone must do what they judge to be best in any given situation. But conscience is not infallible. It needs to be formed by accurate knowledge about reality, awareness of the impact of our actions on others, and the wisdom of the Church accumulated over much time. Not all opinions are equal. Some are "truer" than others.[17]

The fact is that doubt has been a large part of my own faith journey, as it has been for much more saintly individuals than me throughout history. Certitude and the absence of doubt are the realms of both ardent dogmatists and atheists—they are the ones who express full confidence in things unseeeable and unprovable. Most of the faithful I know are in the middle of these two extremes, and it is where I find myself on most things with the church: in the space where questions are welcomed. Indeed, the seeking of answers is a part of the journey. Rachel Held Evans talks in her book about her struggle to belong but realizes that she could no more break up with Christianity than she could break up with her parents. "Sometimes we are closer to the truth in our vulnerability than in our safe certainties . . . Even when I don't believe in church, I believe in resurrection. I believe in the hope of Sunday morning."[18]

I believe firmly and truly that I will be a practicing Catholic for the rest of my life. It has been a source of support over the course of my life through times of both celebration and grief. But it also holds me to account for my behavior. The church is where I find peace and grace and where I feel at home. But the older I get, the more comfortable I become in expressing where I see fault in some of the approaches of the church. Not necessarily with what it believes but how it approaches the communication of belief, and how it prioritizes those aspects of faith and belief that are most relevant to our world today. This is the task for Catholic schools: how best to communicate the beauty and richness of our faith, while ensuring that students and families are engaged and active participants in parish life. The past few decades indicate that Catholic schools, and the church overall, have not been successful in that communication.

As with most adults, I find that my self-confidence has increased with age, largely due to the experiences I have had and due to the success I have been blessed to experience in my professional life. That lends some credibility and

---

[17] Ann Garrido, "Teaching about Truth in a Time of Doubt and Discord," *Catechist*, May 8, 2020, https://www.catechist.com/.

[18] Evans, *Searching for Sunday*, xvi.

weight to what I can say and write and is a large reason why I felt compelled to write this essay. I want to model the importance of being vulnerable and honest about my experiences so that others who are newer to the work in diocesan offices understand that they are not alone in what they may experience. I also am now of an age where I more fully understand that asking questions and seeking answers is something we all must go through to experience a fully lived faith life. That is part of everyone's faith journey, and those who work for the church in ways that center on evangelization and passing on the faith should be encouraged to embrace doubt and questioning as vital parts of that journey. The conscience of a Catholic educator requires nothing less.

"Can't Turn Around!"

The Road to Equity in Catholic School Leadership

Brandi Odom Lucas

If I close my eyes, I can hear the choir, in perfect harmony, singing,

> We've come this far by faith, leaning on the Lord,
> Trusting in his Holy Word, He's never failed me yet.
> Oooooooh, can't turn around, we've come this far by faith.[1]

We've Come This Far by Faith was most often sung in February, as my church near my home in Los Angeles, California, celebrated Black History Month. Those services were always my favorite because they were intentional, righteous, and relevant. The Black History Month celebrations at the church were completely different from anything I experienced in my private elementary school and Catholic high school. The elementary school I attended was a predominantly white private school in a small suburb outside of Los Angeles, and it served as a feeder school to my Catholic high school. As a child, walking into the Macedonia Baptist Church sanctuary made me feel like I was walking into a parallel universe from the one I experienced at my schools. Here, everyone was celebrated. There were no prerequisites for receiving love, support, or high expectations. Men and women who looked like me, sounded like me, and acted like me were leaders in this sacred space and, because of that, I was free to be myself. Macedonia Baptist was far from a perfect church. As a daughter of this sacred institution, I cannot overlook the impact sexism, homophobia, and capitalism, among other human sins, have had on our community. But for the purposes of this essay, I assert that Macedonia Baptist, as well as other African American churches, offered me

---

[1] Albert A. Godson, *We've Come This Far by Faith* (Illinois: Manna Music III, 1963).

and other students skills and lessons that benefited us in school and in the larger society.

I begin with my experience at Macedonia Baptist as a way to respond to the challenge articulated by African American Catholic theologian Bryan Massingale about formation of conscience and Catholic education. Massingale argues that the traditional methods of conscience formation—for instance, teaching from the *Catechism*[2] or focusing on the development of virtue—have their place but are inadequate in the face of the way that racism distorts the conscience of so many. In place of relying solely on those traditional methods, Massingale argues on behalf of what he calls "authentic interracial solidarity": a mode of formation that involves conversations, often hard ones, in which conversants share their vulnerabilities across racial lines. Among the essential requirements of such solidarity, he says, would be "an ability to hear and be present to black anger; the interior space to welcome perspectives that significantly differ from one's own; and the cultivation of genuinely affective relationships with persons of color."[3] From the perspective of my experience as a leader of Catholic schooling and as a woman of color, I consider this essay to be my own interpretation of Massingale's idea of authentic interracial solidarity as an indispensable mode of conscience formation. We can't turn around and remain only with the older modes of conscience formation. We must be creative and courageous. The church in which I was reared made that clear to me in so many spoken and unspoken ways.

Macedonia Baptist supported me in understanding myself as an empowered, historical being, which aided my engagement in school and other mainstream institutions. At a very early age, I understood that my school's culture was very different than my home culture and that, to achieve, I would need to become proficient in both cultures. In *Culture and Power in the Classroom,* Antonia Darder discusses bicultural students and their experiences in the classroom, distinguishing between dominant and subordinate cultures. Dominant cultures are ones where "ideologies, social practices, and structures affirm the central values, interests, and concerns of those who are in control of material and symbolic wealth."[4] Subordinate cultures

---

[2] Pope John Paul II, *Catechism of the Catholic Church* (1992).

[3] Bryan Massingale, "Conscience Formation and the Challenge of Unconscious Racial Bias," in *Conscience and Catholicism: Rights, Responsibilities, and Institutional Responses,* ed. David E. DeCosse and Kristin E. Heyer (Maryknoll, NY: Orbis Books, 2015), 65.

[4] Antonia Darder, *Culture and Power in the Classroom: Educational Foundations for the Schooling of Bicultural Students* (Boulder, CO: Paradigm Publishers, 1991), 28.

are those that exist in social and material subordination to the dominant culture. A bicultural student, then, is one whose home culture is different than the dominant culture. I am thus, by definition, a bicultural student. My African American culture is different than the dominant culture found in my school where I was educated as a child and teenager. This dominant culture was conveyed by my predominantly white teachers, who used a curriculum that centered white experiences while teaching and assessing in ways more congruent to white cultural traditions. Many cultural difference theorists argue that a deeper understanding of the cultural conflict experienced by bicultural students can help explain differences in achievement.[5] In order to succeed, I had to master the rules, moral preferences, desires, and feelings of the dominant culture. My church helped me navigate this requirement without losing myself in the process.

The Black History Month celebrations at Macedonia Baptist Church provide a clear example of the differences between my church and school cultures. During this time, the church took time to reflect on our history and show gratitude to God for the progress made thus far. At school, we acknowledged the contributions of a selective group of African Americans. These acknowledgments were often oversimplified and involved a weakened description of the context in which these contributions occurred or the impact of these persons on society. At church, there would be a critique of current examples of racism and dehumanization followed by ways, as a faith community, we would address them. At school, there was rarely, if any, discussion around current issues of racism. Often, efforts to bring up racial issues in history or religion classes were dismissed. In church, there would be a recommitment to our goal of freedom. In school, compliance was the goal, not freedom. The Black church has been proven to help bicultural students navigate the school setting. Through helping students critically understand their identities, teaching dialectical thought, and providing consistent access to critical teachings through relationships, the Black church provides a sacred community of refuge, renewal, and transformation for its congregants.[6]

I am both a daughter of Macedonia Baptist Church and the Catholic school system. I attended Catholic school for both high school and graduate

[5] Lisa D. Delpit, *Other People's Children: Cultural Conflict in the Classroom* (New York: New Press, 1998).

[6] Brandi Odom Lucas, "Sweet Spirit: The Pedagogical Relevance of the Black Church for African-American Males" (Ed.D. diss., Loyola Marymount University, 2014), 130.

school. In Los Angeles during the late 1990s, Catholic schools provided a safe, faith-based alternative to the segregated public schools where our parents had attended and that left them unprepared for many postsecondary options. My mother recalls her guidance counselor's admonishment to forgo college because she was not "college material." Because of their own experiences, my parents were very clear about what they did *not* want in an educational experience for their children. They did not want a lower quality education. They did not want our intellect and talents to go unnoticed. They did not want any postsecondary options to be withheld or discouraged because of racism or discrimination. My parents were willing to sacrifice time and money to ensure my siblings and I obtained a quality education. They believed success in college was achievable, and they desired schools for us that held that same belief.

My parents found a partner in a nearby Catholic high school. My Catholic high school was predominantly African American and Latino and experienced many issues common in low resourced schools serving students of color. I had four principals in the four years I was there. There were no Advanced Placement (AP) courses, very few highly experienced teachers, and little to no college guidance. Despite this, my school delivered on my parents' expectations. But at what cost? My high school, like many others, ignored issues of racism, and in doing so, reproduced them. My school taught me that color blindness was acceptable. Through their policies and processes, I learned that meritocracy was a better explanation for the lack of advancement in communities of color than racism. I learned that the more I subscribed to the dispositions and ideologies of the dominant culture, the more I would succeed. I learned that my future success was dependent on my ability to deny those aspects of myself viewed negatively by mainstream society. This impacted me greatly, well into adulthood. I became proficient at hiding aspects of my culture to assimilate in academic and professional spaces. The fractionalization of my humanity continues to impact me today.

Today I work to continue unifying the fractured pieces of myself in order to live out my vocation. As my consciousness as a bicultural student evolved to that of a bicultural professional, I grew more comfortable identifying those areas that required healing. I assert that Catholic schools must also learn to recognize those areas that prevent us from creating and maintaining spaces of freedom for our students, their families, and our colleagues.

Our Current Context

As we stand in the very real emotional and spiritual trauma caused by the aftermath of the killings of Breonna Taylor, Ma'Khia Bryant, and others, the rise in anti-Black, anti-Asian, anti-Muslim, anti-Semitic, and anti-LGBTQ+A speech and violence in our country, the physical, mental, and financial impact of a global pandemic, and the division and discord in our own families caused by a (now former) president whose actions and policies demonstrated a preference for self-preservation rather than service, most of us are saddened, scared, and exhausted. How did we get here? Have the past struggles been in vain?

The racial reckoning, coupled with the global pandemic, refocused society's attention on the inequities of our educational system. Statewide stay-at-home orders brought about an awareness of the vast differences in resources between and within schools. Many schools serving predominantly low-income students of color lacked the technological and curricular resources needed to facilitate online learning. Many students found themselves dealing with the responsibilities of virtual school as well as new, pandemic-related family responsibilities. And many educators had faith that this would be the beginning of an educational reformation that would reimagine our approach to school funding and student achievement. Unfortunately, we quickly found ourselves disappointed. Almost immediately, calls for equity were replaced with discussions around learning loss and mandated standardized testing.

Addressing issues of equity in this current context has been extremely hard. Many of us are experiencing the numbing pain from colleagues whom Dr. Martin Luther King Jr. referred to as negative peacemakers. In *A Letter from Birmingham Jail,* Dr. King describes negative peace as "the absence of tension." He distinguishes this from positive peace, which is "the presence of justice."[7] In our Catholic schools, many of our colleagues seem to share a commitment to maintaining the status quo. The tension between negative and positive peacemakers translates to countless battles over our faith, curriculum, student experience, and school policy. Over the past eighteen months going back from June 2021, I have heard about or experienced the following tensions:

- A school president engaged in battles with parents on the validity and importance of equity initiatives;

---

[7] Martin Luther King, Jr., *Letter from Birmingham Jail* (Penguin Modern, 2018).

- Principals receiving pushback from teachers who are confronted about their outdated curriculum, pedagogy, and instruction that prevent students from marginalized groups from experiencing academic success in their classrooms;
- Teachers feeling isolated and ignored by colleagues and administration due to the teacher's reluctance to uphold school policies that are producing inequitable outcomes for students of color;
- Parents and students feeling shut out of their school's culture because their experiences are not valued or acknowledged.

Schools also are faced with addressing structural inequalities that continue to impact students. This fact was made blatantly clear during the pandemic. In discussing the inequalities in educational outcomes found in America, Linda Darling-Hammond identified five factors that directly contribute to educational inequalities:

1. High levels of poverty and low levels of social supports for low-income children.
2. The unequal allocation of school resources.
3. Inadequate systems for providing high-quality teachers to all communities.
4. Rationing of high-quality curriculum through tracking and other interschool disparities.
5. Factory-model school designs that have created dysfunctional learning environments for students and unsupportive settings for strong teaching.[8]

These factors, Darling-Hammond asserts, allow children to leave school communities underprepared for the world that awaits them. These structural issues are very much present in our Catholic schools along with racial predictability in student achievement, inequitable school policies, and the growing disparities in resources between inner-city and affluent Catholic schools. Ignoring these issues ensures that we will fail to achieve the goal of Catholic education.

---

[8] Linda Darling-Hammond, *The Flat World and Education* (New York: Teachers College Press, 2010), 30.

The Goal of Catholic Education

Speaking to the *Gravissimum Educationis* Foundation in 2018, Pope Francis asserted, "Catholic education gives soul to our globalized world and radiates the promise of Christian salvation."[9] Catholic schools must provide more than rigorous coursework, safety, and structure. We are educating our students to be transformative agents of our world. To accomplish this, we must be courageous in our commitment to educate for freedom. Of course, "freedom" is a much-used and much-abused word. Today amid a pandemic we've seen legions of Americans invoke freedom as justification for why they're not going to wear a mask to prevent transmission of the virus to themselves and to others. That selfish, reckless freedom is not at all what I have in mind. By freedom, I mean the emergence of the idea in persons who are oppressed in any way that things should not and do not have to be what they are. By freedom, I mean the belief in their God-given right to *breathe*, *be*, and *become* without hindrance or restraint. By freedom, I mean the development of the agency to make changes for justice and love in oneself and in oppressive social conditions. Educating for freedom finds its roots in the early schooling of African Americans in native schools. Native schools were schools founded and funded by former slaves to support goals of literacy and freedom for African Americans. In these schools, learning was a direct response to oppression and an active pursuit of liberation and freedom.[10] Catholic schools will never satisfy the goal of giving soul to the world if we remain imitators of public education reforms and initiatives, such as standardized testing, which provide ineffective solutions to deep-rooted inequalities. Instead, we must lead this work of healing, transformation, and freedom for every student given to our care.

Healing, transformation, and freedom are outcomes specific to educating in faith contexts because this work requires shifts in two distinct areas. First, there must be a shift in each student's relationship with God. This involves a move from a cultural spirituality to one that is more personal in nature. For many students, culture and faith are interwoven. As in my case, to be Baptist was to be African American and to be African American was to be Baptist.

---

    [9] Devin Watkins, "Pope: 'Catholic Education Gives Soul to World', *Vatican News* (June 25, 2018), https://www.vaticannews.va/en/pope/news/2018-06/pope-francis-gravissimum-educationis-foundation.html.

    [10] James D. Anderson, *Education of Blacks in the South, 1860–1935* (Chapel Hill: University of North Carolina Press, 1988), 17.

But a critical shift to a relationship with a more personal God was needed for me to understand how I should move through society as an African American woman. Paulo Freire termed this critical consciousness *conscientization*, which can only occur when "men's consciousness, although conditioned, can recognize it's conditioned."[11] The Christian church holds an important role in promoting *conscientization* by recognizing and redefining the humanity of its congregants in a world that works to demean them. This first shift of consciousness can heal students from the trauma and pain inflicted by our society while helping to begin the process of transformation.

The second shift of consciousness found in faith contexts involves positioning students to understand themselves as historical beings actively engaged in the secular world. By "historical," I mean that students would come to understand themselves as capable of changing their own lives and the world around them: Their lives are not fixed in time but disposed to the possibility of change—of making history. This positions all students to respond to issues of racism and other forms of discrimination for themselves and others. This second shift continues transforming the student because it moves students from passive beings to active beings who can change the world. It also can transform the world around the student. Only when the student grows to understand themselves both as children of God and as historical beings with the power and intellect to actively engage their world, can they be free to be all that God intends for them to be.

As we look more closely at our current educational context, it becomes clear that school leaders need to recommit to equity practices and outcomes. School leaders are committing to equity when they educate for freedom understood in the way I have articulated it here: as the development of the awareness and capacity to make change for the sake of justice and love. Educating for freedom requires a reexamination of the ways school leaders engage with their stakeholders. I contend that through courageous companionship, truth-telling, and restoration, the school leader is better positioned to engage in equity work and ensure fidelity to the goal of Catholic education.

Encountering Companionship

The story in Luke's Gospel of the Road to Emmaus (24:13–35) begins rather simply with two men first encountering each other and then encountering a

---

[11] Paulo Freire, *The Politics of Education: Culture, Power, and Liberation*, trans. Donaldo Macedo (South Hadley, MA: Bergin & Garvey Publishers, 1985), 69.

stranger, Jesus. The reader meets the two men as they are discussing the events surrounding the crucifixion. I can imagine both men sharing their individual accounts and opinions of the day's events, as they travel on the same road to the same destination. After joining them, Jesus remains with the men until they reach their home.

This journey of companionship provides lessons for Catholic schools. Ensuring our schools are places of freedom for our faculty, staff, and students is impossible without a commitment to encountering each other along the journey. The Christian believes that it is through our encounters with each other that we encounter Christ. Far too often our encounters fall short in accomplishing true companionship. Instead, we settle for collegiality, but collegiality is not sufficient to do this work. Companionship requires us to push past the niceties that exist in our schools and to have the courage to listen to experiences of our marginalized brothers and sisters.

In our Catholic schools, we have been reluctant to listen to the experiences of all stakeholders, particularly the students, faculty, staff, and administrators of color. During the summer of 2020, many Catholic school students and alumni of color used social media to express their experiences of isolation, harm, and trauma inflicted by school personnel or policy. Many principals refused this invitation of companionship by explaining away students' experiences with comments like, "That was before my tenure," or "That teacher is no longer with us," or "I disagree with some of their memories of particular events." The compulsion to silence the experiences of those given to our care is antithetical to our faith.

Some Catholic school leaders found the courage for companionship. Through focus groups with past alumni and current students, meetings with faculty and staff, book studies and collaborations, leaders found the strength to begin the process of addressing issues of silence and invisibility that manifest themselves in the school curriculum, discipline policies, hiring practices, and relationships. These leaders were courageous enough to work past their own feelings of discomfort and guilt to address ways in which the systems we have created or maintained have produced outcomes that contradict our faith.

Courageous companionship can begin the process of *conscientization* for all stakeholders. As the school leader engages in companionship, they are invited to see issues they were once blind to or have avoided. Through the process of sharing their experiences and connecting those experiences to broader societal issues like racism, stakeholders can strengthen their critical consciousness. With shifts in consciousness experienced by the school leader and stakeholders, the community is positioned to undergo transformation. A commitment to companionship is thus the first step to achieving the goal of Catholic education.

Encountering Vulnerability through Truth-Telling

It is interesting to think about how vulnerable the two men on The Road to Emmaus felt given the events of the day. Jesus Christ was crucified despite being innocent of the charges against him, and now no one can find his body. The men meet the stranger, Jesus, on the road and again display vulnerability through their openness and eagerness to share with him their confusion and anxieties. Their final display of vulnerability is seen in their willingness to invite Jesus to stay with them overnight instead of continuing his journey.

Educating for freedom requires a form of truth-telling that has been absent from our American experience for centuries. Our country's narrative surrounding its origins has intentionally excluded the impact that centuries of genocide, abuse, and systematic exclusion have had on the Indigenous and African American communities. Moreover, communities of color learned, through our educational systems, that our histories were footnotes in the history of America, while our white brothers and sisters were raised seeing and hearing their histories and experiences centered in the classroom. Today many adults still have not learned the full contribution of people of color to this country's success.

Truth-telling requires vulnerability, which can be extremely difficult for most of us. Social scientist Brené Brown shares that vulnerability is "the core of shame and fear and our struggle for worthiness."[12] Decades of allowing society to define who I am made me feel unworthy to speak my truth in academic and professional settings. Withholding my truth protected me from potential psychological and social backlash like being labeled argumentative or contentious, but I quickly discovered that the consequence of withholding truth was guilt. I felt guilty for not advocating for all students. I felt guilty for allowing a program or policy to disproportionately impact a subgroup of my student population. I felt guilty that I did not demand the school prioritize justice over charity.

---

[12] Brené Brown, "The Power of Vulnerability," talk given at *TEDxHouston* (June 2010), www.ted.com.

If guilt is the consequence of truth-withholding, then transformation is the result of truth-telling. Providing the disaggregated data of student achievement (not simply grades or test scores but a broader set of measurements that are essential to students' development toward freedom) to faculty means we can begin improving the curriculum and instruction to meet all students' needs. Sharing data around students' feelings of belongingness and physical and psychological safety means we can begin having truthful conversations with teachers about our mission. Speaking freely about my experience as an African American woman in a school where leadership has traditionally been white or male opens the door for individuals to confront their own biases and educate themselves about how those biases appear in the organization.

To educate for freedom requires all companions to be truth-tellers of their experiences of the systems that impact them. To speak one's truth requires both vulnerability and a willingness to be transformed. This vulnerability has been my work for the past two years. Six years ago, when I stepped into the role of principal, I felt confident that I could improve student outcomes using the traditional approaches I learned in my graduate leadership courses. I focused on building trust with stakeholders, shifting my school to being more data-informed, implementing rigorous and relevant curriculum, and fostering growth mind-sets, just to name a few. I began to recognize that success on any improvement initiative was dependent on teachers' commitment to equity and justice. Did educators in this inner-city high school believe *all* students could learn? (equity). Did the educators believe that their policies, processes, and programs reflected God's love? (justice). Were the educators open to critically analyzing the spaces where their lack of equity and justice was causing harm?

I needed to be vulnerable in order to name these truths. I also had to be honest with the entire community about the impact this was having on our students. I am learning to be committed to offering my experiences and leadership in spaces that may not be welcoming. I am learning to be comfortable acknowledging issues that have gone unnoticed by others in my organization. I am learning to ask for forgiveness for times I have silenced or overlooked the needs of others. Working through each of the aforementioned areas liberates me. The more I am free, the more I can commit to freedom for students. As it is with our school communities, the more we liberate ourselves, the better we are positioned to support student liberation.

Encountering Restoration

While eating with the men who were traveling to Emmaus, the gospel notes that Jesus broke the bread, blessed it, and shared it. It was then that the men recognized Jesus. The reader can appreciate the transformation from the companions' sad or anxious hearts at the beginning of the journey to the burning, enthusiastic hearts at the end. The result of true companionship and truth-telling is transformation. This transformation marks the beginning of a new encounter or experience. Through restoration the individual is healed and returned to wholeness. Educating for freedom requires school leaders to create spaces where transformation and healing can occur.

Catholic school leaders encounter many obstacles in their pursuit to address issues of racism and equity. These obstacles prevent school leaders from encountering restoration. Often, in failing to encounter restoration, the leaders resign themselves to the work of charity. We create financial aid scholarships that allow the school to provide support for inner-city students. Upon discovering that students are experiencing racism and discrimination at our school, we settle for creating affinity groups. Here, we choose charity over companionship. We have a teacher who fails a high number of students each year but instead of supporting the teacher in improving their practice, we offer that teacher another position. Here, we choose charity over truth-telling. Instead of rewriting the hairstyle policy in a way that acknowledges all cultures and backgrounds, we add addendums to policies, which only adds to the scrutiny and feeling of otherness a subset of students already experience. Here, we choose charity over restoration.

Because true restoration involves transformation and healing, it requires that we interact with our previous environments and relationships in completely new ways. School leaders suddenly find themselves in search of liberatory practices to ensure all students succeed. The compromises and accommodations offered in response to issues of oppression and dehumanization are no longer sufficient, because we realize that to ignore the experiences of our students and colleagues, or to respond to them in a manner that does not restore their wholeness, is to contribute directly to their trauma.

Encountering restoration means acknowledging the mistakes of our past and actively working to ensure those mistakes never happen again. It means rethinking the traditional leaderships theories, models, and ways of knowing that have silenced our colleagues of color. Encountering restoration means focusing on impact over intent in our relationships with all stakeholders, especially our students, and committing to accompanying them on their journey. Finally, encountering restoration means listening to those voices often ignored, omitted, and patronized in school settings and doing our part to support healing.

"We've Come This Far by Faith"

In many ways this journey seems all too familiar. Our history is filled with examples of the dehumanization of Black and Indigenous bodies. We have seen the outcomes of separate-but-equal school systems. We know the consequences associated with racist, divisive rhetoric paired with equally racist and divisive policies and laws. Racism distorts the conscience of both those who practice it and those who experience it. But we are different from past generations because we have seen the results of ill-conceived solutions and broken promises. The time is now for courageous companionship that recognizes the dignity in every human experience. The time is now to own our vulnerability and speak our truth as we name issues of dehumanization occurring in our school community. The time is now for total and complete restoration that transforms our hearts, minds, and souls. We've come this far by faith. The time is now to journey to freedom.

Educating toward Difference

Diversity and Conscience Formation
in the Catholic High School Classroom

Paul Kuczynski

Imagine a typical morning in a Catholic high school classroom. As the first bell rings, the students begin to file in and find their seats, some chatting and laughing with friends, others furiously finishing a homework assignment, still others absentmindedly scrolling through their phones. As their teacher, you recognize the variety of perspectives that each student brings as they walk through the door. Charlie, whose parents are going through a divorce, grew up active in the Church of Latter Day Saints but has been increasingly antagonistic toward the faith of his parents. Amina, whose mother moved to the United States from Iran to finish medical school, wears a headscarf with her uniform every day. Francesco, whose father is a mechanic and a deacon at a Roman Catholic church, hasn't taken off his Kairos cross since he came back from a retreat a few months ago. Orange, who is an exchange student from China living with a host family, grew up without ever knowing anyone who actively practiced any Western religions. Constance, whose grandmother raises her and takes her to either a Catholic or nondenominational church every weekend, came to the United States two years ago as a refugee from Uganda and tends to sit quietly in the back unless she is with her friends.

In just a handful of students in a twenty-five-student class, of which you will teach several more over the course of the day, lies a myriad of life experiences, cultural traditions, religious narratives, and economic and social standings. Your task for the day is to instruct all of these students in the moral teachings of the Catholic tradition and to accompany them as they engage in the critical process of their own moral formation.

This is the daunting yet familiar task set before theology teachers and campus ministers in Catholic high schools every day. Catholic high school

119

classrooms in the United States are becoming increasingly diverse spaces. According to a 2020 report published by the National Catholic Education Association (NCEA), 21.8 percent of Catholic school students identify as racial minorities, while 18.5 percent identify as ethnically Hispanic/Latino, compared to a collective 10.8 percent of students identifying as "minority" students in 1970. Catholic schools are also more religiously diverse: 19.1 percent of Catholic school students identify as non-Catholic today, compared to a mere 2.7 percent of students in 1970.[1] While these statistics only express a few facets of the diversity within Catholic schools, the student bodies of Catholic high schools have started to reflect the globalized society around them.

Increased diversity in the Catholic high school classroom brings unique challenges and opportunities to the task of religious education, and it raises particular questions about conscience formation and moral education. Here, I would like to explore some approaches to helping students learn how to navigate these diverse spaces and the dilemmas that accompany them, while holding first and foremost that this diversity is a gift with the potential to open our hearts, expand our horizons, strengthen our convictions, and ultimately deepen our faith. In brief, we will find that entering into the challenges brought about by diversity in the supportive space of the classroom provides the greatest opportunity for learning lifelong practices central to conscience formation. Rather than a threat to faith and values that must be avoided or minimized, encountering diversity in our classrooms, and in our world, can become the source of moral conviction that guides students toward engaging difference instead of shying away from it.

Diversity and Conscience Formation

Unequivocally, the diversity present within Catholic schools is a gift. Having a variety of backgrounds and perspectives brings a richness to the shared life of the school community, reflective of God's own abundance. Yet it is also true that diversity brings with it a complexity that does not exist in more homogeneous spaces, and students' ability to coexist in diverse spaces or even celebrate diverse experiences does not always translate to their ability to navigate the conflicts caused by diverse perspectives. As religious educator Luigi Giussani notes, encountering a variety of perspectives on a consistent basis can

---

[1] Dale McDonald and Margaret Schultz, *U.S. Catholic Elementary and Secondary Schools 2019–2020* (Arlington, VA: National Catholic Educational Association, 2020).

be incredibly disorienting, especially for adolescents who are just beginning to develop the skills for navigating complex moral dilemmas. In response to perspectives that challenge their own, Giussani observes, students sometimes turn to "fanaticism for a particular position, bigotry against a certain position, or an 'anything goes' indifference" as a way of coping with this disorientation.[2] In a way that reflects contemporary social and political discourse, tolerance of diverse perspectives often breaks down when students' own perspectives, convictions, and values are directly challenged by the perspectives of others different than themselves.

While we hope to form students with strong moral convictions, we also hope that these convictions are coupled with an ability to engage with other perspectives productively. The challenge of diversity in the Catholic high school classroom mirrors the challenge of diversity in the world. How do we help young people develop mature consciences that remain open to encountering and learning from different perspectives? Diversity will remain a condition of life in today's world, and any attempt to articulate a vision of moral formation for today's world must address the impact of diversity on this formation.

The Catholic teaching on the universality of conscience and natural law provides a platform for exploring what moral formation might look like in the context of diversity. The Second Vatican Council recognized the emerging exigency of engaging with different perspectives, particularly in the areas of ethics and public life. As the conciliar document *Gaudium et Spes* asserts, "In fidelity to conscience, Christians are joined with the rest of men in the search for truth, and for the genuine solution to the numerous problems which arise in the life of individuals in social relationships."[3] Although rooted in the personal experience of conscience, the pursuit of moral truth and the common good is ultimately a common endeavor. In other words, the discernment proper to conscience, and the process of forming it, is not undergone merely within the individual or even within the Catholic community (in many ways a heterogeneous community itself), but rather with all people with whom Catholics are in relationship and who care to seek truth with them.

Moreover, engaging with people different from ourselves is a fundamental aspect of seeking truth. Catholic tradition suggests that the formation

---

[2] Luigi Giussani, *The Risk of Education* (New York: Crossroad Publishing, 1995), 62.

[3] Pope Paul VI, *Gaudium et Spes*—"The Pastoral Constitution on the Church in the Modern World" (1965), no. 16, www.vatican.va.

of conscience must first and foremost strive for an ever greater, more honest understanding of ourselves and the world, guided by the wisdom of tradition in tandem with reason.[4] However, it is also a deeply Christian notion that engaging with people different from ourselves is a critical component of coming to understand our own tradition in new and productive ways. David Hollenbach notes that the Christian intellectual tradition has been engaging productively with non-Christian perspectives since its beginning, and this tradition holds "a conviction that cultures holding different visions of the good life can get somewhere if they are willing to risk serious engagement with one another."[5] For this reason, Hollenbach promotes what he calls "intellectual solidarity," defined as "an orientation of mind that regards differences among traditions as stimuli to intellectual engagement across religious and cultural boundaries."[6] Rather than a guardedness against anything that might threaten our beliefs, intellectual solidarity promotes a posture of "hospitality," welcoming any "guest" that might help us understand ourselves, our tradition, and our world.[7] In fidelity to truth, dialogue with an outside perspective can give us new insight into our own tradition and its moral precepts.

Encountering diverse perspectives can also help us step outside of ourselves in order to see the biases and limitations of our own perspective more clearly. For example, Bryan Massingale notes that most Christians, and especially white Christians, have consciences that have been formed, or rather "blunted and twisted," by the insidious culture of structural racism.[8] In the recent events following the murder of George Floyd, Catholics in the United States and around the world responded in various ways. While some Catholics stepped up in explicit support of the movements against police brutality, often citing their faith as the primary reason for doing so, others condemned

---

[4] The *Catechism of the Catholic Church* states that "a well-formed conscience is upright and truthful. It formulates its judgments according to reason, in conformity with the true good willed by the wisdom of the Creator." Pope John Paul II, *Catechism of the Catholic Church* (1992), para. 1738.

[5] David Hollenbach, "The Life of the Human Community: How Can We Pursue a Ministry of Solidarity?", *America*, November 4, 2002, www.americamagazine.org.

[6] David Hollenbach, *The Common Good and Christian Ethics* (Cambridge: Cambridge University Press, 2002), 138.

[7] Ibid.

[8] Bryan N. Massingale, "Conscience Formation and the Challenges of Unconscious Racial Bias," in *Conscience and Catholicism: Rights, Responsibilities, and Institutional Responses*, ed. David E. DeCosse and Kristin E. Heyer (Maryknoll, NY: Orbis Books, 2015), 64.

the movements or continued to downplay the significance of racism in their communities. In light of these events, Massingale's question grows more urgent: How do white Christians, in particular, become conscious of a social sin that has malformed their consciences? How do we become aware of a bias that we have been conditioned not to notice? He suggests "interracial solidarity and transformative love" as a first step in combatting racism, and this suggestion indicates the broader importance of diverse, personal encounters as a part of conscience formation.[9] Our encounters and relationships with others provide the space to step out of our own experience into one different than our own, and therefore to see a facet of reality previously invisible to us.

Lastly, engaging with diverse perspectives can also mutually strengthen our moral convictions. In her work on human rights, Linda Hogan has found that the culturally embedded nature of human rights, which is sometimes used to invalidate them, can in fact be seen as the source of their strength. She argues for an "embedded universalism," asserting that "human rights discourse and politics will become more durable if the many and diverse forms of their justification can be harnessed."[10] Although we all think and act from our own embedded narratives, together "we can nonetheless strive to embody the virtues and excellences that we have come to believe reflect the best that human beings can be."[11] Importantly, Hogan ends on a pragmatic note that embedded universalism "cannot shy away from . . . areas of dissonance and ambiguity," and must "[acknowledge] the depth of difference" between diverse perspectives.[12] This is not finding common ground through glib, superficial comparisons, but rather a constructive, pluralistic dialogue built from a shared desire to live with integrity. From this space of integrity, we can honestly acknowledge and work through our differences. The discourse and dialogue between embedded perspectives, true to their particularity, offers the most truthful way forward. Rather than uprooting ourselves from our beliefs or values, honest encounters where each brings the entirety of their particular tradition can invite us deeper into our own.

These principles offer us a starting point for reimagining what Catholic education, and especially its role in moral formation, looks like in the midst of diversity. Rather than defending a singular vision of the good, perhaps our

---

[9] Ibid., 65.

[10] Linda Hogan, *Keeping Faith with Human Rights* (Washington, DC: Georgetown University Press, 2015), 103.

[11] Ibid., 108.

[12] Ibid., 129.

classrooms and hallways should aim to nurture a "culture of encounter."[13] Here, students would learn to be seekers of truth, encouraged to lean in to the "stimuli" of differences as opportunities to deepen their understanding of others, themselves, and their world. After all, religious education that fails to introduce the student to the diversity in the world beyond the walls of the school (or ignores this reality within the school) ultimately fails to help the student make sense of their world. This vision of moral education proposes an understanding of faithful conscience formation that moves beyond obedience toward agency. The students in Catholic schools, especially the students who are not themselves Catholic, cannot be seen as mere receptacles of magisterial teachings. In the words of Pope Francis, church leaders, including all Catholic educators, are called to "form consciences, not replace them."[14] Rather, our hope for all of our students, Catholic or otherwise, is that they become discerning members of their communities, able to respond creatively from the traditions they have received to the changing needs of their world.

Diversity and Adolescent Development[15]

Although there is theological support for engaging with diverse perspectives as a part of conscience formation and moral education, the reality is that this engagement is difficult work. This is particularly true for adolescents, who are just beginning to develop the capacities for navigating complex social and moral frameworks. Adolescence is a period of incredible growth and change, including neurological development within the brain. This is part of the reason adolescents often begin questioning simpler ways of making sense of the world, including their moral frameworks, that no longer prove sufficient for the new challenges they are encountering.

In fact, it is precisely challenging encounters with people different than themselves that trigger the possibility of growth toward more complex

---

[13] Although Pope Francis has used this phrase many times over the course of his papacy, I have in mind here his usage of the term in the papal exhortation *Christus Vivit*—"To Young People and to the Entire People of God" (2019), no. 169.

[14] Pope Francis, *Amoris Laetitia*—"On Love in the Family" (2016), no. 37.

[15] I am deeply indebted for many of the insights and resources in this section to Theresa O'Keefe, who introduced me to the work of Mezirow and Kegan. For her excellent overview of the neurological development of adolescence and its implications for religious education and youth ministry, see "Rigging a Larger Boat" and "Learning to Serve as Crew" in Theresa O'Keefe, *Navigating toward Adulthood: A Theology of Ministry with Adolescents* (New York: Paulist Press, 2018), 77–89, 90–103.

ways of thinking and relating to others. Educational theorist Jack Mezirow describes these triggering encounters as "disorienting dilemmas."[16] Essentially, these are experiences that are not easily dismissible and that directly challenge a person's worldview, causing them distress and "disorientation" as they wrestle with the implications of the fact that their worldview no longer quite "works." Although sometimes these "dilemmas" may seem trivial, these are crucial moments for moving us toward more complex systems of thought and behavior. As developmental theorist Robert Kegan notes, cognitive development is less a change in what we know or even how much we know, but rather a change in how we organize or make sense of what we know.[17]

According to Kegan's theory, the task of navigating environments with diverse perspectives requires a high-level cognitive framework that adolescents are still developing. In Kegan's schema, adolescent neurological development makes possible the shift from the second-order framework of "durable categories" to the third-order framework of "cross-categorical meaning-making."[18] The "durable categories" framework, typical of later childhood, recognizes that individual elements in the person's environment (such as objects, other people, and the self) possess properties that persist over time. This even includes recognizing that others have their own perspectives and ways of thinking distinct from our own. However, this framework is incapable of recognizing that the *relationships between these individual elements* are themselves persistent realities with their own properties. It is only by developing a "cross-categorical" framework that we become capable of recognizing others' unique points of view *and* of the relationships between these points of view. With a cross-categorical framework, we also become capable of "loyalty and devotion to a community of people or ideas larger than the self," for the sake of that community or idea itself.[19] In other words, we become capable of not only recognizing others' perspectives but actually cognizant of the implications of the relationships between these differing perspectives.

To illustrate, imagine a class discussion on antiracism and Black Lives Matter. The conversation turns to the violence sometimes present at protests.

---

[16] Jack Mezirow, *Transformative Dimensions of Adult Learning* (Hoboken, NJ: Wiley, 1991), 169, cited in O'Keefe, *Navigating toward Adulthood*, 91–92.

[17] Robert Kegan, *In Over Our Heads: The Mental Demands of Modern Life* (Cambridge, MA: Harvard University Press, 1994), 28–29.

[18] Ibid., 29–32.

[19] Ibid., 32.

One student, Gregory, raises the opinion that while everyone should have the right to free speech, no one has the right to use violence. The conversation gets heated for a while, and then the topic shifts to something else. Another student, Anita, comes to you frustrated after class, upset that one of her classmates could ever speak up against Black Lives Matter: "How can he not see that violence is sometimes the only way to get your voice heard?" From Anita's viewpoint, she and her classmate have directly opposing views that are irreconcilable. Working from a "durable categories" framework, Anita can recognize Gregory as an individual with his own set of ideas and values, but Gregory's ideas remain foreign to her. She cannot conceptualize the framework from which his ideas emerge. Therefore, either he is right, or she is right. There can be no middle ground. Meanwhile, an individual working out of a third-order framework can "zoom out" a bit more and place their own perspective in relationship to another's. If Anita and Gregory are encouraged to do so, perhaps they can begin to see the relationships between their perspectives. They both believe in promoting a fair society, but in this case, they hold different perspectives on what "fair" means and how "fair" society is to all people. The opposing views that seem irreconcilable at first begin to move toward a fruitful discussion, and students are challenged to use the "cross-categorical" ability to not only recognize another perspective but also bring it into conversation with their own.

In many ways, the work of engaging diverse perspectives directly corresponds to the development of higher-order cognitive frameworks. The actual tasks central to navigating diversity, such as recognizing the limitations of one's own perspective or critically comparing two distinct perspectives, require higher-level cognitive frameworks, and challenging encounters are what move us toward these more complex ways of making meaning. Religious educators interested in bringing diverse perspectives into the classroom must be aware that they are asking students to use a higher-level cognitive framework that they are still learning to comprehend.

However, the challenge inherent in encountering diverse perspectives is potentially a helpful thing, moving students to develop the "cross-categorical" moral frameworks demanded by the world and to become capable of discerning the responsibilities we hold in an interconnected world. In fact, the movement from second-order to third-order frameworks, though made possible because of the adolescent's physiological development, is not inevitable. If we are never challenged to move beyond a second-order framework, we can effectively operate from this framework our entire lives.

In order to develop higher-level cognitive frameworks, the movements between different frameworks must be practiced frequently in order to "stick." According to Kegan, they are best practiced in "holding environments," such as schools, families, and meaningful relationships, where adolescents "constantly experience an ingenious blend of support and challenge," pushing them toward more complex ways of understanding themselves and the world with the willing support and guidance of others.[20] As Kegan notes, our complex, interconnected culture already provides plenty of challenge.[21] It is almost inevitable that adolescents will experience "disorienting dilemmas" in the area of their moral convictions and ethical values. One only needs to look at the way youth have led and engaged in conversations around climate change and racial justice to recognize that adolescents are already navigating plurality, making judgments, and developing ways of making sense of the world. The question is whether or not we provide any intentional support as students engage these challenges and develop the capacities capable of handling this complexity. Catholic schools, as a community grounded in a common way of making meaning of the world, could be a fertile ground of challenge and support where students could practice engaging difference, developing increasingly complex perspectives, and pursuing more expansive ways of understanding their place and responsibilities in the world.

Diversity and Religious Education

The work of Luigi Giussani helps us envision what creating a holding environment of challenge and support might look like specifically in the setting of a Catholic high school theology classroom. A Catholic educator and priest, Giussani's method does not avoid the complexity of diversity. In fact, his method centers on having students practice the ability of critically assessing the traditions that are given to them and the complexities that arise from their engagement with traditions different from their own.

Giussani's educational theory, articulated in his work *The Risk of Education*, begins with the claim that education must be "an introduction to total reality" and is "conditioned and governed by reality both at its origin and destination."[22] He notes that every student who walks through the door of the classroom already holds some way of making sense of reality, what he calls

---

[20] Ibid., 42–43.
[21] Ibid., 42.
[22] Giussani, *Risk of Education*, 50.

"received traditions" full of various "hypotheses of meaning."[23] We are all given guiding values, beliefs, and narratives by our family, teachers, communities, and culture. Yet, as we have seen, an essential part of maturation is the critical analysis of these traditions, keeping those that prove helpful in making sense of the world and leaving behind those that do not.

The role of the educator, particularly the religious educator, is to consistently uphold a tradition, offering a hypothesis of meaning from this tradition (e.g., that all human lives have inherent dignity) for the student to "test" against reality. This process of "existential verification" is "the systemic work of helping the teenager draw the connection between what he [or she] has received ('tradition') and life."[24] Recognizing that our ideology stems from our experience, the educator creates experiential spaces where this wrestling with meaning can occur, and only then does the student come to recognize the validity (or inadequacy) of the proposed hypothesis. This method is ultimately oriented toward developing conviction in students: "Conviction is formed when we discover a vital link between the idea we embraced or received and our own predicaments, and find it relevant to our needs or projects . . . the result of a testing of the original idea or view that proves to be the keystone for all encounters."[25] By experiencing the validity of the proposed hypothesis of meaning time after time in their own lives, students become "devoted" to it. More importantly, they develop the "habit of comparing their positions not only with those of others but especially with the tradition they have received."[26] In other words, the students in Giussani's classroom have practiced being mindful carriers of a tradition, both convicted of its resonance with reality and capable of comparing their own tradition to others, trusting that this will only lead them closer to reality. While teaching the content of a tradition, the educator is also teaching students a practice with which they can navigate the challenges and "disruptive dilemmas" they encounter in the future.

To illustrate the potential of Giussani's method, consider a student who comes from a wealthy background and is a strong believer in the idea that anyone who isn't successful in life just hasn't put in the effort: God helps those who help themselves. In theology class this week, the teacher has been discussing the preferential option for the poor, one of the core elements of

---

23 Ibid., 8.
24 Ibid., 71–72.
25 Ibid., 67.
26 Ibid., 68.

Catholic social teaching, and applying it to the plight of migrants on the Mexico–United States border. This student has been resistant all week, because her hypothesis of meaning (most likely received from her parents and mainstream news outlets) is directly clashing against the hypothesis of meaning proposed by the teacher and Catholic tradition. The teacher can create a space where both hypotheses of meaning can be tested, perhaps by introducing students to the true stories of migrants as a way of investigating their motivations and experiences. By creating an opportunity to encounter and dig into the reality of the situation, the student may come to see that her guiding philosophy, while true in many respects, falls short in light of migrants' incredible efforts to secure a better life and the many systems of oppression that make this nearly impossible. She is able to keep what is good from what she has received—that there is dignity in striving for a good life— while nuancing it with the Christian notion that we share responsibility for ensuring that all persons have this opportunity to strive. Through engaging with and relating to narratives otherwise foreign to her own experience, the student has been given an opportunity to perceive reality more objectively and, potentially, to become convicted or converted in her posture toward this reality.

The example above is simple, and the reality is that one lesson, no matter how well prepared and profound, will not change a student's deeply ingrained beliefs. But this is precisely the point Giussani is trying to emphasize: religious educators do not teach a list of facts or beliefs within a tradition; they teach students the method for critically engaging with a tradition or, to use his terminology, the consistent *practice of verification* by which they become convicted (or suspicious) of the value and truth of a tradition through their embodied experience. It is the *process* of seeking truth together that is formative for the students, encouraging the habit of engaging with the complexity of the world instead of escaping from it.

However, it is important to remember that this process of verification, here through encountering difference, is "embedded" in a particular tradition. Giussani is skeptical of the efficacy of an uprooted, tradition-less, and therefore passive engagement with diverse opinions.[27] Rather, it is through wrestling with the traditions that are given to us, "embedded" in our own context, that we gradually grow into a sense of conviction that can engage with traditions other than our own. Catholic educators, or even Catholic school communities, should share clear and compelling visions of what belief in Jesus

---

[27]   Ibid., 58–62.

Christ offers to humanity, especially in a world where the Christian gospel is so often warped and co-opted by cultural and political forces. However, this also requires holding space for the traditions and contexts of non-Catholic or even non-Christian students, trusting that encounters among all of these perspectives, when encouraged, will only move us closer to reality.

In the end, this method of introducing students to a process of verification is oriented toward forming the student's freedom to engage the whole of reality. As Giussani writes, "If indeed history and life are vehicles for rediscovering values in new experiences, to whom does the task of discovery fall? The parent? The educator? Not at all, because this would simply be traditionalism. It is the student who must undertake the task, because only thus can his freedom truly develop."[28] In the end, the student must be the one who continues this process of verification in the world, and the teacher must increasingly take the risk of letting the student develop his or her freedom through this process. Ultimately, "The teacher must entrust to God, to the mystery of Being, . . . the ever wider spaces that the surprising paths of the pupil's freedom open up in his [or her] dialogue with the universe."[29] This is the horizon of mystery toward which all education, including moral formation, aspires. In many ways, this methodology reflects its own situated knowledge, a type of openness to the world rooted in the Catholic tradition's deep conviction that encountering others in all of who they are can only lead us deeper into Truth itself.

Practicing Encounter

I'd like to offer some practical applications of the insights shared here. Generally, any time we help students engage a perspective different from their own in a meaningful way, we are helping them develop the habit of engaging difference. One fundamental way to practice engaging difference in the classroom is through narrative. Stories can bring otherwise absent perspectives into the conversation, carrying the potential to be both disorienting dilemmas as well as moments of solidarity. While there are many stories that can come from outside of the classroom, they are especially meaningful when they come from the students themselves. In a classroom with a diverse student body, the students' own stories, which often go untold, carry a variety of perspectives that both challenge and support one another.

---

[28] Ibid., 81.
[29] Ibid., 82.

Somewhat paradoxically, the process of telling one's own story is especially key to engaging other perspectives. After all, unless something is brought into relation with our own reality, it will remain other to us, and telling our own story grounds us in our reality. The way in which Constance, Charlie, and Orange make sense of the content of the class *will* differ, simply because their lives are different. There are various ways that educators can invite students to tell their own stories. For example, in a unit on the dignity of human life, students might be asked to share a story from their own life, not an abstract principle, that has either affirmed or challenged their views on the issue. Telling their story engages the content of the course as well as the content of their own lives, assessing comprehension of the material while also providing opportunities for students to relate this material to their own diverse experiences.

The key is to bring these stories into relation to the perspectives that challenge them to think differently. While always being mindful of respecting students' privacy and comfort, there are a variety of ways to bring in students' stories and perspectives into conversation. For example, Socratic seminars and other democratic teaching methods could be adapted to help students share their experiences, while giving them the freedom to determine how much they are comfortable sharing. Small groups of students, perhaps even meeting consistently over the course of the semester to develop rapport, can provide low-stake arenas, rather than whole-class discussions, to practice difficult conversations and to begin learning other peers' perspectives. The reality is that the outcomes of experiences where students engage with difference can never be predicted, but at the very least, becoming aware of whether or not we are increasing the possibility of these encounters and developing students' free engagement with difference is a principle worth keeping in mind while we are lesson planning, building curriculum (especially outside of social justice and world religions electives), and planning school events.

Conclusion

What does it mean to be a Catholic school that proposes a certain narrative and yet engages in the process of moral formation of *all* of its students, regardless of the narratives they bring? What does the work of conscience formation actually look like for the classroom where Charlie, Amina, Francesco, Constance, Orange, and Steven are sitting next to each other, each testing reality against a different multifaceted narrative? Hopefully, the insights shared here provide inspiration that it is both necessary and possible to form students capable of encountering and engaging diversity as a part of this formation. As Catholic high schools grow more diverse, the classroom will continue to be a privileged space where students bump shoulders daily with peers whose lives are at once familiar and also significantly different from their own. Too often, these perspectives are never brought into conversation with one another, even though it is through the process of engaging the differences among us, not ignoring them or smoothing them over, that forms convicted and mature consciences. In the end, the telos of educating toward difference is reflective of the world's needs: young women and men who are free yet grounded agents, convicted pursuers of the common good with a fundamental openness to others. In spiritual terms, these would be young people open to being "invaded by the power of eternity and to be continuously enriched by it."[30] Catholic schools, whose very mission is rooted in intellectual *and* spiritual formation, offer a potent space where the work of this holistic moral formation can occur.

---

[30] Ibid., 85.

Transgender Students in Catholic Schools, Probabilism, and Reciprocity of Conscience

Lisa Fullam

Transgender students in Catholic schools have become the newest hostages in culture clashes in the church. On June 10, 2019, the Congregation for Catholic Education (CCE) released "'Male and Female He Created Them:' Towards a Path of Dialogue on the Question of Gender Theory in Education"[1] (M&F), the first developed consideration of gender identity from the magisterium. The document was welcomed by (among others) Bishop Michael Barber, SJ, chair of the U.S. Conference of Catholic Bishops' Committee on Education, who said that "In a difficult and complex issue, the clarity of Church teaching, rooted in the equal dignity of men and women as created by God, provides the light of truth and compassion that is most needed in our world today."[2] Others were less impressed: Deacon Ray Dever is concerned that "This document will be used as a reason for Catholic schools and parishes to unjustly discriminate against transgender students, and in the process do some real harm to them and their families."[3]

My task here is to provide resources for school administrators to navigate this complicated territory: first, I will explore M&F and its hostile assessment of transgender identity. Second, I will offer some insights from the contempo-

---

[1] Congregation for Catholic Education, "'Male and Female He Created Them:' Towards a Path of Dialogue on the Question of Gender Theory in Education," February 2, 2019, www.vatican.va. Hereinafter M&F.

[2] "U.S. Bishops Chairman for Catholic Education Welcomes the Release of Male and Female He Created Them," Public Affairs Office, USCCB, June 11, 2019, www.usccb.org.

[3] Deacon Ray Dever, "The Vatican's New Document on Gender: Is There Hope?" Bondings 2.0, New Ways Ministries Blog, June 13, 2019, www.newwaysministry.org.

rary science of sex and gender. I will then put that into the context of Catholic teaching on conscience and probabilism in dealing with controverted moral issues. Transgender people will be cited throughout.[4]

"Male and Female He Created Them":
The CCE on Gender Theory

In M&F, the CCE sounds the alarm against "gender theory," which, according to the document

> denies the difference and reciprocity in nature of a man and a woman and envisages a society without sexual differences, thereby eliminating the anthropological basis of the family. . . . Consequently, human identity becomes the choice of the individual, one which can also change over time.[5]

The CCE cites no advocates of this definition of gender theory. I will unpack their concern in three steps: basic definitions, gender constructivism vs. essentialism, and gender complementarity.

First, definitions. Sex is a biological category, like male, female, or intersex. A polyfactorial reality, biological sex itself is extraordinarily complicated, "involving not only anatomy but an intricate choreography of genetic and chemical factors that unfold over time. . . . The more we learn about sex and gender, the more these attributes appear to exist on a spectrum."[6]

Sex is constituted by or reflected in any number of biological structures and functions: genes, epigenetics, hormones, genitalia, secondary sex traits like breasts and Adam's apples, and brain function. M&F recognizes that sex is multifactorial, but rests on the genetic argument: "male cells (which contain XY chromosomes) differ, from the very moment of conception, from

---

[4] This may seem obvious but is often overlooked even by those who are at least provisionally sympathetic. "Nothing about us, without us" should apply (i.e., the voices of those being discussed should be included in the discussion), especially in cases in which the legitimacy of a human person's identity is challenged.

[5] Pope Francis, *Amoris Laetitia*—"On Love in the Family" (2016), no. 56, www. vatican.va (quoting the *Relatio Finalis* of the bishops). Hereinafter *AL*.

[6] Amanda Montanez, "Beyond XX and XY: A Host of Factors Figure into Whether Someone Is Female, Male, or Somewhere in Between," *Scientific American*, September, 2017, 50–51.

female cells (with their XX chromosomes)."[7] What is unclear is how this is to be determined in the day-to-day work of Catholic schools: must all children in Catholic schools be genotyped to affirm the sex recorded on their baptismal certificates? What happens to a child who is genetically XY but due to androgen insensitivity or a mutation of the SRY (sex-determining region Y protein) gene was labeled a girl at birth and baptism? Is she male? Or is he a girl?

Gender, by definition, is a matter of masculinity or femininity, the socially and culturally determined attributes associated with biological maleness or femaleness—or not associated with maleness or femaleness, in an individual. The Canadian Institutes for Health Research defines gender as the *"socially constructed roles, behaviors, expressions and identities of girls, women, boys, men, and gender-diverse people. It influences how people perceive themselves and each other, how they act and interact, and the distribution of power and resources in society."*[8]

The issue in Catholic circles isn't whether sex and gender are corporeal *or* socially/culturally determined. Fundamental Catholic anthropology affirms that we are incarnate beings, body/soul composites—for example, this is why we affirm the resurrection of the body, not only the soul. Further, we are social by nature: one facet of that natural sociality is that we are creatures of and creators of culture. The real question in Catholic circles is the relationship of sex as a biological/bodily reality to gender as a social/cultural reality.

The second step: gender essentialism and gender constructivism. Extreme gender essentialism holds that everything or almost everything about gender is determined by biological sex. The Venn diagram of sex and gender overlaps completely or almost completely. Conversely, extreme gender constructivism holds that gender can be thought of as independent of sex. The Venn diagram of sex and gender shows two nonoverlapping areas. It is helpful here not to think of a binary between gender essentialism and gender constructivism, but rather of a spectrum of degrees of overlap with these extremes at the poles.

Extreme gender constructivism, I believe, is incompatible with Catholic anthropology, especially given the importance it places not just on bodies but on sexuality. Here's the *Catechism* on sexuality: "Sexuality affects *all aspects of the human person* in the unity of . . . body and soul. It especially concerns affectivity, the capacity to love and to procreate, and in a more general way the

---

[7] M&F, no. 24.

[8] Canadian Institutes for Health Research, "What Is Gender? What Is Sex?", https://cihr-irsc.gc.ca/e/48642.html.

aptitude for forming bonds of communion with others."[9] Extreme constructivism ignores the way bodily realities, including the effects of hormones, body
size, and musculature, influence one's experience of self and social experiences
based on those traits. Extreme constructivism is also in tension with the experience of many (but not all) trans men and women, for whom the medical
alignment of aspects of their bodies with their gender identity is extremely
important. As Rev. Carol Stone puts it, while transitioning she was "looking
forward to that moment when I will consider myself to be a matching head
and body and heart."[10]

Extreme gender constructivism seems to be the target of M&F: "It is
vital to bear in mind the distinction between the ideology of gender on the
one hand and the whole field of research on gender that the human sciences
have undertaken, on the other."[11] Pope Francis's 2015 apostolic exhortation *Amoris Laetitia* states, "It needs to be emphasized that 'biological sex
and the socio-cultural role of sex (gender) can be distinguished but not
separated.'"[12]

Extreme gender essentialism is just silly. Sociocultural norms for men and
women are too varied across space and time to sustain extreme essentialism.
Are pants for men only,[13] or high heels for women only? Can women exercise previously male prerogatives like voting, practicing medicine or law, or
being astronauts? Can men nurture children as fathers, teachers, therapists,
or day care workers? The challenge, then, is how to construct a relationship

---

[9] Pope John Paul II, *Catechism of the Catholic Church* (1992), para. 2332, emphasis
added.

[10] Quoted in Justin Tanis, *Transgendered: Theology, Ministry, and Communities of
Faith* (Cleveland: Pilgrim Press, 2003), 46. Like cis-gender people (those whose gender
identity aligns with the gender assigned at birth), transgender people have differing
experiences of how they become aware of, embrace or reject, and express their gender
identity. No single stance can capture the experience of gender identity for all. Siân
Tayldor does express her decision to transition as a choice: "I say [I] 'wanted to be a
woman' because that's how it was, plain and simple." Quoted in Susannah Cornwall,
Controversies in Queer Theology (London: SCM Press, 2011), 60. NB: transgender
people are cited here as they are in the works from which they're taken—first and last
names, first names only, or pseudonyms.

[11] M&F, no. 6.

[12] *AL*, no. 56, citing *Relatio finalis*.

[13] It's worth noting that Joan of Arc was burned at the stake by the British not
for hearing voices, defeating British armies, or for holding theological heresies, but for
wearing men's clothing. See Régine Pernaud, *Joan of Arc: By Herself and Her Witnesses*
(New York: Scarborough House, 1994 [1962]), 228.

between sex and gender that is robust enough to satisfy Catholic anthropological holism but also to reflect and respect the range of gender expression that exists within and among the sexes.

This brings us to the third step, sex/gender complementarity. Pope John Paul II developed a very strongly essentialist notion of sex/gender in his "Theology of the Body," presented in a series of public audiences from 1979 to 1984. Basing his assessment of male and female human nature on the Genesis creation narrative, the late pope posited personal, social, and affective aspects of masculinity and femininity that are seen in males and females, respectively.

According to John Paul II our integrity as body/soul composites means that our character and social roles are largely determined by our biological sex, which is regarded in strictly binary terms. People's social roles (like, e.g., leadership in the church) must reflect their male-masculinity/female-femininity. In John Paul II's thought, women are essentially called to motherhood, giving themselves in nurturant service to others (which is in conflict with, e.g., leadership in the church). Women's sense of their vocations in the world either reveal this maternal truth about feminine nature, or are wrong.

Complementarity is hugely influential in the church, and its traces are evident throughout M&F. For example, the document asserts the interchangeability of sex and gender, opposing a false freedom to decide one's gender irrespective of sex:

> In this [contemporary] cultural context, it is clear that sex and gender are no longer synonyms or interchangeable concepts. . . . The problem here does not lie in the distinction between [sex and gender], . . . but in the separation of sex from gender. . . . the concept of gender is seen as dependent on the subjective mindset of each person, who can choose a gender not corresponding to his or her biological sex, and therefore with the way others see that person (transgenderism).[14]

The notion that transgender people "choose" their gender is starkly at odds with the experience of most trans people. To be trans is neither a whim nor an act of philosophical rebellion. Thomas puts it simply:

---

[14] M&F, no. 11. The word transgender appears only one other time in M&F, and is incorrectly conflated with the intersex condition: "Efforts to go beyond the constitutive male-female sexual difference, such as the ideas of 'intersex' or 'transgender,' lead to a masculinity or feminity [sic] that is ambiguous" (M&F, no. 25).

"'Gender identity' is not about choosing which gender you would rather be, but noticing which gender you already are, as a gift given to you by God."[15]

M&F worries that acknowledging transgender identity would lead to a relativism "in which everything that exists is of equal value and at the same time undifferentiated, without any real order or purpose."[16] It is hard not to read this sentence as a reaffirmation of patriarchy, couched as it is in a discussion of sex and gender difference. After all, if equal value is relativistic, then someone must be determined to be lesser. This risk of relativism—or is it "equal value"?—is described in terms of transgender identity, sexual orientation, gender fluidity, and family structure. "In fact, the generic concept of 'non-discrimination' often hides an ideology that denies the difference as well as natural reciprocity that exists between men and women."[17]

Intriguingly, M&F both reaffirms John Paul II's strong gender essentialism, *and* quotes Pope Francis's gentle pushback: "It is true that we cannot separate the masculine and the feminine from God's work of creation, which is prior to all our decisions and experiences, and where biological elements exist which are impossible to ignore. But it is also true that masculinity and femininity are not rigid categories."[18]

In sum, M&F reflects the strongly gender-essentialist viewpoint of John Paul II, which carries water for the strict sex/gender binary complementarity that upholds many of the current magisterial teachings relating to sex. But sex is not a simple binary, nor does gender identity track unerringly with sex: the question of how trans kids (and genderqueer and genderfluid kids,[19] and others who challenge traditional gender norms) should be treated in Catholic schools arises because of this. There's a further problem: the sex assigned at

---

[15] Eloise Blondiau, "5 Trans Catholics on the Vatican's Rejection of Their Gender Identity," *Vox*, June 12, 2019, www.vox.com.

[16] M&F, no. 20.

[17] M&F, no. 21.

[18] *AL*, no. 286.

[19] Genderqueer people are those who reject the roles assigned with either pole of a gender binary, while genderfluid people are those whose gender identity ranges within the spectrum of gender identity. A final category may be helpful here: gender expression is how a person publicly presents themselves as masculine or feminine, or in between. For example, tomboys, girls who prefer typically masculine styles of dress and activity, are not usually transgender, but rather expressing femininity in the way they feel represents them best.

birth is given a significance in M&F that the science of sexual development does not support: a physician's scrying of infant genitalia says nothing about most of the other components of sex, and cannot determine one's gender identity. Let's look at the science.

Transgender Identity and Science

The number of trans people is difficult to ascertain, but one estimate suggests that about 1.4 million adult Americans are transgender, and at least 150,000 youth (aged thirteen to seventeen).[20] The *Diagnostic and Statistical Manual of Mental Disorders* (*DSM-5*) term for transgender identity is gender dysphoria, and is defined as a marked incongruence between one's experienced/expressed gender and assigned gender of at least six months' duration, manifested by at least six of eight criteria, one of which must be "a strong desire to be of the other gender or an insistence that one is the other gender (or some alternative gender different from one's assigned gender)."[21] Sean writes,

> My mother kept insisting on doing awful things to me like curling my hair and making me wear dresses like my sister instead of letting me wear suits to church like my brother. . . . I couldn't understand why they kept trying to turn me into a girl. I had put up many valiant struggles against my mother to try and show her how wrong she was about me, but she just wasn't getting it![22]

Emerging research shows that children who had more intense symptoms and distress, who were more persistent, insistent, and consistent in their cross-gender statements and behaviors, and who used more declarative statements ("I am a boy [or girl]" rather than "I want to be a boy [or girl]") were more likely to become transgender adults.[23] Some kids begin to show cross-gender

---

[20] Williams Institute, UCLA School of Law, "LGBT FAQs," https://williamsinstitute.law.ucla.edu/quick-facts/lgbt-faqs/.

[21] See Garima Garg, Ghada Elshimy, and Raman Marwaha, *Gender Dysphoria (Sexual Identity Disorders)* (Treasure Island, FL: StatPearls, 2020), https://www.ncbi.nlm.nih.gov/books/NBK532313/.

[22] Fortunate Families, "Stories by LGBTQ+ Persons and Their Family Members," www.fortunatefamilies.com.

[23] Thomas D. Steensma, PhD, Jenifer K. McGuire, PhD, MPH, Baudewijntje P.C. Kreukels, PhD, Anneke J. Beekman, BSc, and Peggy T. Cohen-Kettenis, PhD, "Factors Associated with Desistence and Persistence of Childhood Gender Dysphoria:

behavior at age two to four, when kids usually begin to express gendered behaviors and interests. Others begin to express cross-gender identity (or their identity becomes a more urgent matter) at puberty. Thus, kids might arrive at school with a transgender identity already asserted, or this might emerge later. Melissa writes,

> The intensity of my transsexual feelings definitely got stronger and more difficult to overcome as I got older largely because of the changes brought about by adolescence and puberty. As my body began to change, it got further and further away from where I wanted it, and more importantly, where I felt it needed to be.[24]

There is legitimate concern about whether gender dysphoria is prematurely or casually diagnosed in people who will eventually change their minds, perhaps seeing themselves instead as lesbian or gay, or responding to therapy to reconcile themselves to their assigned gender, or seeing themselves as expressing gender nonconformity. The DSM-5 diagnostic criteria are significantly more stringent than previous iterations.[25] Kristina Olson points to problems in earlier research: some studies that showed a large proportion of children "desitioning" back to their assigned gender did not originally meet the criteria for gender dysphoria. In other words, kids who were not trans remained not trans.[26]

One study showed that trans kids who had socially transitioned showed gender-typed preferences and behaviors consistent with their (nonassigned) identity. Their gender development was not different from that of cis-gender siblings or control subjects.[27] Despite being raised according to the sex

A Quantitative Follow-Up Study," *Journal of the American Academy of Child & Adolescent Psychiatry* 52, no. 6 (June 2013): 582–90.

[24] Fortunate Families, "Stories by LGBTQ+ Persons and Their Family Members."

[25] And while this designation was made in order to allow access to appropriate treatment for transgender people, others find that it still represents/creates stigma. See Roy Richard Grinker, "Being Trans Is Not a Mental Disorder," *New York Times*, December 6, 2018, www.nytimes.com.

[26] Kristina R. Olson, "Prepubescent Transgender Children: What We Do and Do Not Know," *Journal of the American Academy of Child and Adolescent Psychiatry* 55, no. 3 (March 2016): 155–56.e3.

[27] Selin Gülgöz, Jessica J. Glazier, Elizabeth A. Enright, Daniel J. Alonso, Lily J. Durwood, Anne A. Fast, Riley Lowe, Chonghui Ji, Jeffrey Heer, Carol Lynn Martin, and Kristina R. Olson, "Similarity in Transgender and Cisgender Children's Gender Development," *PNAS* 116, no. 49 (December 3, 2019): 24480–24485; first published

assigned at birth, these kids "self-socialized" in parallel with their cis-gender peers. In other words, refusing social transitioning does not prevent or reverse transgender identity. The authors conclude:

> Children develop a sense of identity at an early age, that this identity is not necessarily determined by sex assigned at birth, and that children may hold on to this identity even when it conflicts with others' expectations. . . . Our findings also demonstrate that once a child is living in line with an identity different from the one they were assumed to have at birth and were initially socialized to have, they are likely to show the same patterns of gender development as a child who develops a gender aligning with their assigned sex and socialization.[28]

A 2016 report from the Human Rights Campaign, the American College of Osteopathic Physicians, and the American Academy of Pediatrics concludes that "competent clinicians generally can tell transgender kids apart from other gender expansive children."[29]

Some object to transgender identity by labeling it purely a psychological (that is, nonbiological) condition, and that respect for trans identity reflects a body/mind dualism that devalues the body. Those objections fail in light of current brain research. The European Network for the Investigation of Gender Incongruence (ENIGI) is the largest study of transgender people in the world. Among their findings are *functional* MRI similarities of the brains of transgender and cis-gender people. There are gendered differences between blood flow to parts of the brain in use.[30] For example, men and women tend

---

November 18, 2019. "Cis-gender" refers to people whose gender identity corresponds with the sex they were assigned at birth.

[28] Selin Gülgöz et al., "Similarity in Transgender and Cisgender Children's Gender Development."

[29] Human Rights Campaign, the American College of Osteopathic Physicians, and the American Academy of Pediatrics, *Supporting and Caring for Transgender Children*, Sept., 2016, citing Marco A. Hidalgo et al., "The Gender Affirmative Model: What We Know and What We Aim to Learn," *Human Development* 56, no. 5 (2013): 285–90.

[30] Earlier research had posited structural similarities of the brains of trans people with their gender identity (not the sex assigned at birth). Here, though, as with other sexually dimorphic traits like height, brain structures fall more along continua than strict binaries. There is correlational evidence that gender forges epigenetic changes on the brain, altering sex. See Laura R. Cortes, Carla D. Cisternas, and Nancy G. Forger,

to use different parts of their brains when rotating objects in their minds. A scan of the brains of a group of twenty-one transgender boys who had recently begun testosterone treatment, showed them to more closely resemble cisgender boys than girls.[31] Other studies are showing similar results: a 2017 Amsterdam study showed similar fMRI results with 160 trans kids.[32] This research is ongoing, but increasing bodies of data are pointing to a biological foundation for trans identity that is not reducible to psychology or the effects of socialization alone.[33]

It is becoming clearer that hormone treatments for those who choose to transition[34] are safe, with few side effects. What does change with hormonal treatment is a marked reduction of anxiety and depression.[35] Earlier intervention and use of puberty blockers are also associated with better mental health outcomes.[36] A National Institutes of Health longitudinal study of trans teens and puberty blockers[37] is under way.

"Does *Gender* Leave an Epigenetic Imprint on the Brain?" *Frontiers in Neuroscience* 13:173 (2019). There is a common-sense correlate of this as well: transmen on testosterone, e.g., may note psychological and social effects of the hormone that transcend its "merely" physical effects, which can in turn affect gender expression.

[31] Sara Reardon, "The Largest Study Involving Transgender People Is Providing Long-Sought Insights about Their Health," *Nature* News Feature, April 24, 2019, www.nature.com.

[32] Nienke M. Nota, Baudewijntje P. C. Kreukels, Martin Den Heijer, Dick J. Veltman, Julie Bakker et al., "Brain Functional Connectivity Patterns in Children and Adolescents with Gender Dysphoria: Sex-Atypical Or Not?," *Psychoneuroendocrinology* 86 (August 2017): 187–95.

[33] Francine Russo, "Is There Something Unique about the Transgender Brain?" *Scientific American Mind*, January 1, 2016, www.scientificamerican.com.

[34] Again, there is no univocal transgender experience. Some transgender people opt for living socially as the other sex with no medical intervention, others for hormonal intervention only, others for surgeries that don't affect genitalia (such as mastectomy or brow ridge/Adam's apple reduction), and others for surgical intervention involving removal of gonads and reconstruction of genitalia. What most transgender people DO agree on is that the medical state of their bodies is personal; questions from strangers regarding their medical care are intrusive and usually unwelcome.

[35] Reardon, "The Largest Study Involving Transgender People Is Providing Long-Sought Insights about Their Health."

[36] Julie Moreau, "Early Care Leads to Better Mental Health for Transgender Youths, Study Finds," NBCnews.com, September 29, 2020.

[37] Johanna Olson-Kennedy, MD, Yee-Ming Chan, MD, PhD, [. . .], and Stephen Rosenthal, MD, "Impact of Early Medical Treatment for Transgender Youth: Protocol

A statement signed by more than three hundred medical professionals opposing antitransgender legislation in the southern United States pointed to

> the growing consensus in the medical community that improving access to gender-affirming care is a central means of improving health outcomes for transgender people … Many credible studies of trans youth populations have demonstrated that gender-affirming care is linked to significantly reduced rates of depression, anxiety, substance abuse, and suicide attempts. Gender-affirming care reduces reliance on self-prescribed and self-administered hormone use, which can be dangerous without the oversight of a physician. To put it plainly, gender-affirming care saves lives and allows trans young people to thrive.[38]

Indeed, those who insist that a person must, through sheer force of will, embrace a gender identity in conflict with the deepest truths they discern about themselves is a far more dualistic (and body-denying) stance than the one that body-mind-spirit holism regarding transgender identity affirms. Personal identity is at stake. As Mary Ann S. Saunders writes,

> As my body changed and people's perceptions of me changed, so did my understanding of myself and my identity. Hormone replacement therapy seemed to loosen the constraints I had placed on the "feminine" part of my identity—now I was able to acknowledge and embrace it, growing into it emotionally, psychologically and physically. I was surprised to find I really liked the physical changes, the most obvious of which was breast growth. My breasts seemed completely consistent with who I was and who I was becoming. Soon I couldn't imagine my body without them. Most importantly, I realized that my body finally belonged to me.[39]

---

for the Longitudinal, Observational Trans Youth Care Study," *JMIR Res. Protocols* 8, no. 7 (July 2019):: e14434.

[38] Campaign for Southern Equality, "Southern Medical Professionals Oppose Legislation Prohibiting Medically Necessary Care for Transgender Youth," www.southernequality.org.

[39] Mary Ann S. Saunders, "Of Back Hair and Body Image: My Transgender Body," *Visions Journal* 12, no. 1 (2016): 18.

What can we conclude about this foray into the science of transgender identity? Just as we once thought that all humans were "naturally" right-handed, or that all people are "naturally" heterosexual, a growing body of scientific evidence points to the biological foundation of trans identity. The witness of transgender people and the science of gender identity militate against the notion that cis-gender identity encompasses human nature and that transgender identity is a whim or a psychopathology.

Catholic school administrators, then, find themselves confronted with irreconcilable claims regarding trans children. M&F insists on a binary of sex and gender, strong gender essentialism, and complementarity of the sexes/ genders. This stance strains credulity in light of many, if not most, people's experience of the relationship of sex and gender, and stands in conflict with the voices of trans people, their allies, and emerging science. How should schools proceed? How should administrators make decisions in good conscience regarding trans students? Next, a look at some resources from Catholic tradition for this condition of conflicting truth claims.

Conscience, Probabilism, and the Development of Knowledge

In this section, I will make two points: first, probabilism provides a foundation from within Catholic tradition for affirming transgender identity. Second, the nature of conscience and its connection to human dignity demands that trans kids be respected *as* trans. Catholic schools and the church itself fail in their mission otherwise.

First, conscience and probabilism. The obligation to follow one's conscience is one of the rare absolutes in Catholic moral theology. On one hand, conscience is "the most secret core and sanctuary of a man. There he is alone with God, whose voice echoes in his depths."[40] On the other hand, that voice of God is an echo, not a clear call: a decision of conscience is invariably the product of fallible human reason. How can we be obliged to follow what we know might be wrong?

Thomas Aquinas wrestled this question to a draw, declaring that one who follows an inculpably wrong conscience is "excused" from the penalty for that error unless the error was about "what one ought to know."[41] This

---

[40] Vatican Council II, Pastoral Constitution on the Church in the Modern World, *Gaudium et Spes* (1965), 16.

[41] Thomas Aquinas, *Summa Theologiae*, I IIae, Q. 19.6, Second and Revised ed.

distinction is framed in Catholic moral tradition as the distinction between vincible (morally culpable) ignorance and invincible (morally not culpable) ignorance. But what if there are multiple reasonable stances on a given topic? Commenting on Thomas's *Summa Theologiae*, Bartolomeo de Medina wrote, "It seems to me that, if an opinion is probable, it is licit to follow it, even though the opposite opinion is more probable."[42] De Medina nuanced Thomas's distinction between vincible and invincible ignorance into a recognition of plural reasonable (probable) stances.

Because conscience seeks truth, it is always wrong to reject what one knows (or believes after appropriate investigation) to be true. It is also wrong to assert as true what is not known to be true; dealing with the latter is the work of probabilism. It is an underused resource for dealing with doubt in matters of conscience, including the doubt that is intrinsic to science and especially in new or rapidly developing scientific questions.[43] Probabilism affirms that in areas of uncertain knowledge, one's conscience weighs the degree to which varying stances are supported by good arguments (intrinsic probability) and/or held by experts (extrinsic probability), and is free to choose among probable opinions. As knowledge develops, the balance of probabilism shifts in keeping with greater understanding of the matter at hand, and what

---

(Fathers of the English Dominican Province, 1920), www.newadvent.org/summa. Others, for example, Alphonsus Liguori, thought that a person obeying an inculpably wrong conscience was good, if wrong: "When a person did not perceive any sin, there was no sin, and if the person acted out of love or charity when committing the error, then not only is the person 'inculpable,' but also good." James F. Keenan, "Can a Wrong Action Be Good? The Development of Theological Opinion on Erroneous Conscience," *Église et Théologie*, 24 (1993): 205–19, at 214.

[42] Bartolomeo Medina, *Expositio in Summae Theologiae* Partem I II, q 19, a. 6, cited in Albert R. Jonsen and Stephen Toulmin, *The Abuse of Casuistry: A History of Moral Reasoning* (Berkeley: University of California Press, 1988), 164.

[43] See Lisa Fullam, "Dealing with Doubt: *Epikeia*, Probabilism, and the Formation of Medical Conscience," in *Conscience and Catholic Health Care*, ed. David DeCosse and Thomas Nairn (Maryknoll, NY: Orbis Books, 2017), 49–62. Two extreme positions regarding probable stances have been condemned by ecclesiastical authority: tutiorism or rigorism holds that one must always follow the relevant moral rule rigorously, even if there are more probable opinions against it; and laxism, which grants any flight of fancy standing as probable cause to dispense from the moral rule. Moderate stances, like probabilism, probabiliorism (follow the rule unless stronger arguments against it exist), and equiprobabilism (the conscience is free where the arguments are more or less equally convincing) remain as tools in the Catholic moralist's toolkit (ibid., 52–53). See also Carol A. Tauer, "The Tradition of Probabilism and the Moral Status of the Early Embryo," *Theological Studies* 45 (1984): 3–33, at 16.

may once have been a probable opinion (e.g., "humans don't cause climate change") may drift into moral disrepute as improbable.

For Catholic schools deciding how to handle conflicts between those who would welcome trans kids and those who would exclude them (or exclude them by forcing them to dress and behave in conflict with their gender identities), probabilism offers a starting point for conscience. Since there are good scientific arguments and experts (especially trans people themselves, who are experts in their own lives) affirming trans identity, the state of this moral question is at least open.

But there's more to say regarding conscience. Decisions of conscience are not merely cogitations concerning right action in context. Rather, those very discernments reveal the array of virtues that one strives to realize in one's life—our decisions of conscience reveal the values we hold as central to our character. If conscience is the "secret core and sanctuary" where we attend to the voice of God, our decisions of conscience build and reflect our sense of who God is calling us to be. The work of conscience, then, is the fulfillment of integral personhood, the living into the vision of flourishing, individual and social, that we are given to discern by God. This is true for all who engage moral questions seriously.

This does not mean that we must accept any stance held by another as true because it is a matter of conscience. Rather, forming conscience requires dialogue. We seek truth together, and we learn from others' decisions, including—perhaps especially—those with whom we disagree. And where those disagreements are matters on which people of good will hold varying positions on a stance—where there is more than one probable opinion— refusing to hear the other is refusing to form our own consciences rightly. It is an affront to the God whose voice echoes in every human heart.

Conscience formation is a reciprocal and ultimately social process. Bernard Häring writes,

> The uniqueness and creativity of conscience is not just for one's own sake; it is for co-humanity in and for the reciprocity of consciences. Hence, discernment concerns the common good in Church and society, and the good of each of our fellowmen. . . . We have to listen to the prophets even if they shake us and unmask our errors.[44]

---

[44] Bernard Häring, "Conscience: The Sanctuary of Creative Fidelity and Liberty," in *Introduction to Christian Ethics: A Reader*, ed. Ronald P. Hamel and Kenneth R. Himes, OFM (Mahwah, NJ: Paulist Press, 1989), 270.

James F. Keenan, SJ, points to this collective or social model of conscience as formed in Europe in the wake of Christian complicity in the Holocaust. In our time antiracist theologians and ethicists, he writes, are issuing "a call that needs to be heard in our consciences, the source of our collective moral agency."[45] Keenan notes the stirrings of a new theology of "redeeming conscience," which finds common ground with many of the theologies of liberation—Black, Latin American, feminist, womanist, LGBTQ, and others.

"Redeeming conscience" requires of Catholic schools a stance of active welcome of trans kids *as* trans kids. First, because trans kids are worthy of the same respect and welcome as any other child of God. Their identity as trans is well-supported by relevant science, and school officials can help them most by making sure they have access to adequate medical care and social support.

Second, as liberation theologies of all kinds have observed, justice requires a preferential option for those who are outcast or marginalized by broader society. We've heard the grim statistics. Trans people are murdered at a rate 50 percent higher[46] than lesbian and gay people, who themselves are victims of hate crimes disproportionately. Too often families try to force children into a gender identity that does not fit, a kind of abuse that can also be deadly.[47] Transgender respondents who experienced rejection by family and friends, discrimination, victimization, or violence have a higher risk of attempting suicide. A preferential option for trans kids may well save their lives.

Third, the integrity of the church as a community of discernment is undercut if we fail to welcome trans students. Hilary writes,

> There will be a few transgender Catholics who will take [the CCE] at their word and use the title to promote a dialogue. If they want to have one, I am ready. But there will be many more who will finally concede that the church is just too irrelevant to life in the 21st century and will find other spiritual homes. Then there are those who

---

[45] James F. Keenan, SJ, "Redeeming Conscience," *Theological Studies* 76, no. 1 (2015): 129–47, at 137.

[46] James Nichols, "Trans Murders 50 Percent Higher than Gays, Lesbian in July," *Huffington Post*, August 27, 2013, www.huffpost.com.

[47] Williams Institute, UCLA School of Law, "Suicidal Behavior and Coming Out Milestones in Three Cohorts of Sexual Minority Adults" (June 2021), http://williamsinstitute.law.ucla.edu/research/suicide-attempts-among-transgender-and-gender-non-conforming-adults/.

will be attacked and marginalized by people who will find justification for their prejudice in [M&F]. All of that is heartbreaking.[48]

Finally, the integrity of Catholic schools as communities that seek to model the love and mercy of God is threatened if we do not welcome trans kids. Kelsey Pacha, a consultant on transgender issues, writes, "I never questioned in terms of whether I thought God would love me and support me in transitioning." But that's not the God he met in the Catholic Church:

> Pacha, who grew up in a devout Catholic family in Iowa, no longer identifies as Catholic, which he noted is "for my own survival." In dealing with church congregations, Pacha asks: "What is the fruit that you are bearing when you reject people who are transitioning?" Nodding to statistics from the American Academy of Pediatrics that some forty percent of non-binary American youth have attempted suicide, Pacha said the answer to his question is: "That we die." And when it comes to transgender people being rejected by their family, "there's a huge overlap with religiosity," he said.[49]

Conclusion

I began this essay with a discussion of the argument in the 2019 document "Male and Female He Created Them," showing it to be based on a sex/gender essentialism that is no longer tenable in light of contemporary science and experience. Conversely, the extreme gender constructionism that seems to be the target of M&F is incompatible both with the experience of many trans and cis-gender people and with fundamental Catholic anthropological claims about incarnate human personhood. I turned to science: the probability of a given position shifts as science develops. Trans people bring their experience to bear on this question, of course. Both of these, I hope, have established that a more open welcome to transgender men and women in the church and to trans kids in Catholic schools is justified as a probable stance. The first conclusion of this essay is a modest one: transgender identity transcends psychopathology or whim.

---

[48] Blondiau, "5 Trans Catholics on the Vatican's Rejection of Their Gender Identity."

[49] Don Clemmer, "Transgender Catholics Criticize Retiring Archbishop's Letter on 'Gender Ideology,'" *National Catholic Reporter*, August 26, 2020, www.ncronline.org.

Transgender people, persistent, insistent, and consistent in declaring that they are not as they were labeled at birth, model a kind of courage that is extraordinary. Those who worry that calling kids by their preferred pronouns or letting them dress according to their gender identity will sway them into trans identity have failed to notice the too-often dangerous lengths trans people are forced to go as they pursue the body-mind-spirit holism that Catholic tradition affirms. The equal humanity of trans people demands that we respect their discernments of conscience and enter into true dialogue with them. In addition, the shift of probability, along with the marginalized, endangered status of transgender people in church and society, make denial of trans identity a morally culpable affront to their human dignity. And here is the second conclusion of my essay: we, the church, must do better.

Cultivating Conscience
in Catholic Higher Education

Patrick O'Kernick

New college students find themselves wielding altogether new powers of agency. There is an expansion in scope as they are now relatively free to spend their days as they choose. The reach of agency extends in time as they entertain the commitments that will establish their identities and the trajectories of their lives. And the quality of agency is enhanced as students have new experiences and develop greater cognitive, emotive, and social facility. Developmental psychologists refer to this stage of life as "emerging adulthood"; it is an in-between and instable period of self-focus, exploration, and optimism, "when hopes flourish and people have an unparalleled opportunity to transform their lives."[1] In this context of increasing agency and expanding opportunity, the immature, superego-ish conscience of adolescence is no longer serviceable. There is, of course, no simple fix—no way somehow to swap in sound moral sensibility, existential poise, prophetic concern. Yet, entering this period of "emerging adulthood," students are more in need of these than ever. To address this situation, I propose that educators at Catholic colleges and universities adopt a *cultivation approach* to conscience development. Cultivators attempt to bring about in persons conditions hospitable to mature experiences of conscience. For new college students this means, first of all, establishing greater self-awareness and self-command—so far as I see it.

In this essay I describe the cultivation approach and its suitability for Catholic college/university classrooms. Then I present the *State of the Self Series*, a program of assignments designed to address the considerable self-ignorance I believe to be typical of many students. This program of assignments exemplifies the cultivation approach. I offer it in the hope that it can be integrated into generally required introductory courses.

---

[1] Jeffrey Jensen Arnett, *Emerging Adulthood: The Winding Road from the Late Teens through the Twenties* (Oxford: Oxford University Press, 2015), 9.

A Cultivation Approach

Cultivation may be considered an aspect of conscience formation or altogether distinct, depending on how "formation" is defined.[2] At any rate, four things are characteristic of cultivation. First, an attempt is made to meet people where they are. This means that the starting point for development is the acknowledgment of what is already there. Rather than imposing the "right" ways and answers, people are encouraged to investigate, assess, and then choose. Second, a broad notion of conscience is assumed. Conscience may be experienced in an ongoing way, not only in discrete instances of decision and judgment. All people, maybe emerging adults most of all, are ever caught up in orienting and disposing of themselves, of committing their energy and attention, of implicitly if not explicitly choosing this rather than that. In addition, entangled with, implicated in, even partially constitutive of conscience, are a broad range of unconscious/irrational and semiconscious/semirational psychological factors, including emotions, attitudes, and personal constructs.[3] Third, it is assumed that conscience can develop in certain ways without the explicit adoption of Catholic beliefs and values. This notion is consistent with, for example, the belief that God is the source and fullness of truth, beauty, and goodness, as when Pope Francis writes,

> As believers, we also feel close to those who do not consider themselves part of any religious tradition, yet sincerely seek the truth, goodness and beauty which we believe have their highest expression and source in God. We consider them as precious allies in the commitment to defending human dignity, in building peaceful coexistence between peoples and in protecting creation.[4]

---

[2] As Bryan N. Massingale argues, there is no consensus vision of "conscience formation" and no account altogether adequate to the psychological and sociological complexities involved in experiences of conscience ("Conscience Formation and the Challenge of Unconscious Racial Bias," in *Conscience & Catholicism: Rights, Responsibilities, & Institutional Responses*, ed. David E. DeCosse and Kristin E. Heyer [Maryknoll, NY: Orbis Books, 2015], 61–64).

[3] On the role of automatic processes, see Stephen J. Pope, "Conscience, Catholicism, and the New Science of Morality," in DeCosse and Heyer, *Conscience & Catholicism*, 39–52. Massingale addresses unconscious bias ("Conscience Formation," 53–68). Richard M. Gula, SS, associates "character" and "vision" with conscience (*Reason Informed by Faith: Foundations of Catholic Morality* [New York: Paulist, 1989], 138–45).

[4] Pope Francis, *Evangelii Gaudium*—"The Joy of the Gospel" (2013), no. 257. Likewise, all persons are believed to be obliged in conscience to seek truth (Vatican II,

Finally, it is assumed that experiences of conscience may be prayerful in quality even when there is no explicit reference to God. When agency is treated with reverence; when the sheer vulnerability of others *to what I do* is registered; when realities like truth, goodness, beauty, justice, mercy, and love are in question; then conscience is touched by God's presence, however implicitly.

A cultivation approach is optimal for the Catholic college/university classroom; it addresses five typical realities. First, students are diverse in their religious and ethical beliefs. In cultivation, the development pursued is consistent with Catholic belief but credible regardless of belief. Second, as emerging adults, students have a (laudable) tendency to insist upon thinking and deciding for themselves (indeed, college is a place to foster critical attitudes).[5] In cultivation, students are asked to investigate, consider, and choose for themselves with the expectation that they can distinguish between better and worse. Third, self-identifying Catholics are likely reconsidering their commitment to Catholicism and are susceptible to concluding that belief is an impediment to growth.[6] In cultivation, there is no demanding that students give assent to teachings or conform to beliefs; rather, students are encouraged to mature, empowered to take command of their orientation to life.[7] Fourth, students are secular natives and often not at home in the internal logic of religious ideas. Even within self-identifying Catholics there is an "intertwining of religious and secular citizenship" such that they engage religious discourse with expectations derived from secular discourse—that is, most importantly, they are open to appeals to reason and prone to dismiss would-be authoritative impositions.[8] Cultivation is informed by psychological and sociological perspectives that appeal to reason and empirical research. Finally, some self-identifying Catholic/Christian students have routine recourse, in their thinking and speaking, to the trappings of Christianity but nevertheless

---

Declaration on Religious Liberty [*Dignitatis Humanae*], nos. 1 and 2). Additionally, for example, it is sometimes the case that students identifying as *spiritual but not religious* are complacent in a permissive, incoherent relativism. The consciences of such students may mature in certain ways, if they become "reflexive spiritualists"—see Kelly Besecke, *You Can't Put God in a Box: Thoughtful Spirituality in a Rational Age* (Oxford: Oxford University Press, 2014).

  [5] Arnett, *Emerging Adulthood*, 226–27.

  [6] This is the principal concern I address in Patrick O'Kernick, "The Catholic Church as a Cultivator of Conscience," *Jesuit Higher Education* 4, no. 2 (2015): 98–107.

  [7] It may be productive to introduce such students to the possibility of the doctrinally legitimate position of "sincere non-assent" (Michele Dillon, *Postsecular Catholicism: Relevance and Renewal* [Oxford: Oxford University Press, 2018], 28).

  [8] Ibid., 12–13.

approach life in a superficial manner.[9] In cultivation, emphasis is placed on harmonizing one's operative self with one's explicit views and beliefs.

To illustrate the cultivation approach, I describe the problem of student self-ignorance and then present the *State of the Self Series*.

The Mark Scenario

Mark is a (hypothetical) freshman at a Catholic university. Like most people, Mark has an enduring desire to be worthwhile—his every experience of conscience is intertwined with this.[10] However, Mark is ignorant in certain fundamental ways: he is unaware that he already has major assumptions about human existence; he is unaware what his assumptions are; he is unaware that his assumptions continually influence his thinking, feeling, perceiving, and action; and he has no idea how to access his assumptions, let alone how to rework them. Indeed, he has little competency in self-observation; he lives each day largely unaware of the feelings that color how he views himself, and the fears, wants, and concerns that occupy his attention. To top it all off, he is unaware of just how easy it is for him to let his own sense of responsibility be curtailed.

In this state of ignorance, Mark is unlikely to have a mature experience of conscience. He does not have the wherewithal to challenge his visceral reactions and routine sensibilities, neither proactively (to grow), nor contextually (to navigate the complexities typical of so many situations), nor collegially (to engage in substantive dialogue with others). In the worst of cases, Mark may even identify his reactions and sensibilities with the voice of God, placing them beyond scrutiny and deluding himself. Meanwhile, Mark is continuously deciding and acting: college offers manifold academic and social opportunities and Mark chooses whether and how to engage them. Little by little, he is setting the trajectory of his life. Day by day, he is meeting or missing opportunities to serve others. All the while, through his comportment of himself, he is affecting others for better or worse. Mark is at the mercy of his self-ignorance and his default dispositions; without intervention, he will happen along ill attuned to those depths of his person where conscience might sound.

---

[9] An explicitly Christian/Catholic terminology does not ensure the mature functioning of conscience; indeed, some students may disdain Christian language and yet choose and act in ethically enlightened ways.

[10] In Jason J. Howard's account of conscience, to which I am deeply indebted, a desire to be worthwhile is at the very root of conscience (*Conscience in Moral Life: Rethinking How Our Convictions Structure Self and Society* [New York: Rowman & Littlefield, 2014], 64–65).

Intervention: *State of the Self Series*

The *State of the Self Series* aims to acquaint students with themselves, specifically with aspects of their persons that routinely influence and orient the exercise of their agency. The aspects treated are *existential metrics, emotions of self-assessment, possible selves,* and *responsibility throttles.* The series includes eight assignments: a proposal, a discussion, three introspection trials, two reflections, and a final report. The "State of the Self Series Schedule" (Table 1)[11] shows how these assignments may be distributed across a standard sixteen-week semester. Below, I describe each of the topics and assignments in the order of the schedule.

Existential Metrics

Whether or not people explicitly recognize the legitimacy of distinguishing between "good" and "bad/evil," they are nevertheless oriented to life as though there really are some ways of failing/being worthless (to be avoided) and some ways of flourishing/being worthwhile (to be pursued). Any construct employed to distinguish forms of human failing/worthlessness from opposite forms of human flourishing/worthwhileness is what I am calling an *existential metric.* Any sort of distinction may serve as a metric (*callous vs. compassionate, indifferent vs. committed, suffering vs. comfortable, phony vs. authentic, inconsequential vs. consequential, judging vs. accepting,* etc.). Some metrics are relatively shallow (*being poor vs. being rich*). Some metrics are reprehensible (*dark-skinned vs. light-skinned*). The classic virtues and vices constitute a formal set of metrics (*foolhardy vs. courageous, cowardly vs. courageous*). A metric may be elaborated into a continuum, as in this example of an *ignorant vs. aware* metric:

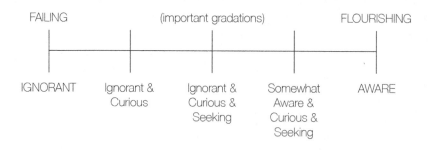

---

[11] All tables may be found at the end of this essay.

While some people may explicitly assert the legitimacy of a certain set of metrics, all people implicitly follow some set of metrics every time they act—especially when they fear, avoid, desire, or pursue. These operative metrics govern the orientation of one's agency, rendering certain avenues of action obvious and others literally unthinkable.[12] This governance is tyrannical for a person so long as the operative metrics are hidden, so long as the person remains unaware that the metrics themselves may be reimagined. Mark is just such a person. The goal of the first two assignments is to raise the question of existential metrics so that students are in a better position to one day discover and adjust their operative metrics.

Existential Metrics Proposal (750 words, weeks 1-2): Students are introduced to the idea of *existential metrics* and then asked to indicate the five metrics that they believe best describe the possibilities of human existence, the ways in which humans can ultimately fail and flourish. For each metric, students come up with the key terms (_____ *vs.* _____), plot them at opposite ends of a continuum, plot any important gradations, and (in about 150 words) describe the metric and explain why they considered it to be one of the five most important. This is submitted electronically in one week and receives a cursory review grade ("0" [incomplete]; "√−" [deficient]; "√" [satisfactory]; or "√+" [well done]).

Existential Metrics Discussion (online, weeks 3-5): Students' proposals are made available in an online forum (identifying features removed). Students are given three weeks to comment on at least four proposals, as follows:

- List anything that has been appealed to in order to support each proposed metric.
- Acknowledge anything that seems to be well-conceived or especially thoughtful.
- Offer an objection to anything that seems troublesome or problematic.
- Indicate anything you found surprising/interesting and explain why.

The educator adds to the discussion whatever is missing and gives each student a cursory review grade according to their level of engagement.

---

[12] In this way metrics function at the level of (what is popularly called) "worldview."

Emotions of Self-Assessment

The emotions of self-assessment are guilt, pride, shame, and hubris. Guilt reflects a negative assessment of a specific act done, under consideration, or neglected (*I did a bad thing*); pride reflects a positive assessment of a specific act (*I did a good thing*). Shame reflects a negative assessment of the entire self (*I am rubbish*); hubris, a positive assessment of the self (*I am the greatest*).[13]

Experiences of shame and hubris tend to be detrimental to well-being. Both typically involve obsessive self-preoccupation and distorted perception. In shame, the person feels hopelessly compromised; in hubris, assuredly superior.[14] Guilt and pride are more likely to promote positive social behavior.[15] Even with guilt and pride, however, people vary considerably in their propensities and each person's propensities are formed throughout life. From childhood (in response to caretakers and authority figures) through adolescence (in response to peer groups and media influences) propensities to guilt and pride are calibrated. Throughout these early years, calibration is largely a *passive* process. Moreover, it is predominately an *indiscriminate* process insomuch as that which is internalized may be rooted in anything (a parent's whim or bias or desire to keep one safe, a peer's genuine friendship or self-conscious projection, or a news organization's ratings-driven culture war); what is internalized is not necessarily rooted in sound principles or coherent notions of existence.[16] Experiences of guilt and pride constitute immediate, visceral evaluations of the depravity/worthwhileness of one's behavior and thus exercise considerable force in determining the orientation of one's agency. Whatever the merits of the influence, people merely suffer experiences of guilt and pride until they investigate the sources of these experiences and endeavor to manage them—to recalibrate them *deliberately*, in accordance with their developing (hopefully increasingly substantive) outlooks on life.[17]

---

[13] June Price Tangney, Jeff Stuewig, and Debra J. Mashek, "Moral Emotions and Moral Behavior," *Annual Review of Psychology* 58 (2007): 348–49 and 360.

[14] On shame, see ibid., 349–52. On hubris (hubristic pride), see Jessica L. Tracy, *Take Pride: Why the Deadliest Sin Holds the Secret to Human Success* (New York: Houghton Mifflin Harcourt, 2016), 51–52.

[15] On guilt, see Tangney et al., "Moral Emotions," 350–55. On pride, see Tracy, *Take Pride*, 51–52.

[16] I develop distinctions between conscience and superego in O'Kernick, "Catholic Church," 99–103.

[17] The formability of one's propensities to guilt, pride, and shame are central to Howard's account of conscience (*Conscience in Moral Life*, 49–85). Howard is more

Mark certainly experiences emotions of self-assessment and sometimes even modifies his behavior because of them. But he is hardly aware of any of this. He grants the emotions authority passively. He rarely subjects the experiences to scrutiny. The goal of the following two assignments is to familiarize students with their emotions of self-assessment so that they are ready to further investigate and ultimately manage these emotions on their own.

Introspection Trial I: Emotions of Self-Assessment (journal, weeks 2–5): Students are introduced to the emotions of self-assessment and asked to be vigilant for such experiences. Students are to document these experiences as follows:

- Note the date, time, and location of the experience.
- What emotion was experienced (guilt, pride, shame, or hubris)?
- How powerful was the experience (on a scale from 1 to 10)?
- What brought about the experience?
  - For guilt and pride, indicate the *behavior* at issue, including whether you *did something, failed to do something,* or *refrained from doing something.*
  - For shame and hubris, indicate the context (the occasions, the company of certain people) that prompts bouts of the emotion.
- Describe the experience. (Note any somatic characteristics [*My stomach was off*] as well as psychological characteristics [*I kept imagining my father looking on, disapproving*]).[18]

After one week, the educator checks in with each student (reviews sample entries or meets with each student one-on-one) to make sure that the documentation is being done correctly. The documentation is submitted with the final report.[19]

---

hopeful than I am concerning the potential for experiences of shame to be constructive (ibid., 74–76 and 79).

[18] For best results with the introspection trials, students should document the events as immediately as possible. Some may find it useful to make an audio recording right away and then put things in writing later. Moreover, students should refrain from judgment—the goal is to observe. Students are encouraged to document as many experiences as possible without being obsessive. The entries should be intelligible but do not need to be polished.

[19] Across the series, students are being asked to share with the educator rather personal information. In the best of cases, the educator will develop the rapport with students necessary for them to feel comfortable sharing. Assurances should be given that everything will be confidential (so long as students do not report anything criminal

Reflection I: Emotions of Self-Assessment (500 words, weeks 6–7): After the four weeks of documentation, students reflect upon their records of experiences in a two-part paper. For the first part, the educator provides students with an electronic copy of "The Disposition of My Emotions of Self-Assessment Template" (Table 2). Using their documentation, students fill in their information (expanding the template as necessary). Thus, they create personalized accounts of the current disposition of their emotions. For the second part, students choose the seven items in their accounts that they believe to be the most influential in their day-to-day lives (e.g., the top three guilt-inducing behaviors, the top two pride-inducing behaviors, the top one shame trigger, and the top one hubris trigger). For each of the seven (in about seventy words each), the student responds to the following prompt: *How did this propensity develop in you? Who/what influenced you, when, and in what way that now you are prone to experience bouts of guilt/pride because of this behavior or shame/ hubris in connection with this context?* The educator provides substantive feedback and a cursory review grade.

Possible Selves

A person's routine concerns often come to expression in the form of experiences of *possible selves*. Hazel Markus and Paula Nurius describe "possible selves" in this way:

> An individual's repertoire of possible selves can be viewed as the cognitive manifestation of enduring goals, aspirations, motives, fears, and threats. Possible selves provide the specific self-relevant form, meaning, organization and direction to these dynamics . . . The assistant professor who fears he or she will not become an associate professor carries with him or her much more than a shadowy, undifferentiated fear of not getting tenure. Instead the fear is personalized, and the professor is likely to have a well-elaborated possible self that represents this fear—the self as having failed, as looking for another

---

or indicative of an intention to harm themselves or others). Some students may want to "censor" their official documentation; these students should still be encouraged to document sensitive experiences, even if they do not submit that documentation or refer to it in their reflections. It is also important that educators know their limits and encourage students to make use of the appropriate campus resources (counselors, therapists, support groups) when appropriate.

job, as bitter . . . Similarly the person who hopes to lose 20 pounds does not harbor this hope in vague abstraction, but rather holds a vivid possible self—the self as thinner, more attractive, happier, with an altogether more pleasant life.[20]

Markus and Nurius delineate six categories of possible selves: personality (the possible confident self), lifestyle (the possible world-traveler self), physical state (the possible sexy self), general abilities (the possible good-public-speaker self), others' feelings (the possible hated self), and occupation (the possible desk-job self).[21]

Experiences of possible selves typically come about automatically, as attention becomes fixated for a time upon this what-if person, this daydream, or that nightmare self. Unlike people's conscious expressions of their concerns, goals, fears, and motives (what they tell themselves, what they tell their friends), experiences of possible selves are immediate, unvarnished expressions: they are thus highly reliable disclosures. Mark is largely unaware of the possible selves that preoccupy his attention, let alone what they might tell him about himself. The goal of the two assignments that follow is to prompt students to notice possible-self experiences and to capitalize on the revelatory potential of these experiences.

Introspection Trial II: Possible Selves (journal, weeks 6–9): Students are introduced to the idea of possible selves and asked to be vigilant for experiences. They are to document these experiences as follows:

- Note the date, time, and location of the experience.
- How powerful was the experience (on a scale from 1 to 10)?
- Was it a threatening self (something you fear to be) or an aspirational self (something you desire to be)?
- Was the self relevant to the short term (days to months) or long term (months to years)?
- Describe the possible self (what characteristics did it have?).
- Note any other prominent aspects of the experience (e.g., *My friend was seeing me as this person*).

---

[20] Hazel Markus and Paula Nurius, "Possible Selves," *American Psychologist* 41, no. 9 (1986): 954.

[21] Ibid., 958–59.

The educator checks in with each student after one week and the documentation is submitted with the final paper.

Reflection II: Possible Selves (500 words, weeks 10–11): Students are to reflect upon their records in a two-part paper. For the first part, the educator provides students with a copy of "My Repertoire of Possible Selves Template" (Table 3). Students review their documentation, devise short-hand names for each possible self, and then enter each name into the appropriate box in the template (expanding it as necessary). In this way students create personalized repertoires of possible selves. For the second part, students respond to the following prompt: *Imagine that your journal and repertoire of possible selves is not yours. Instead, it belongs to Alex K., a student whom you've never met. Using only the journal and repertoire, do your best to infer the five existential metrics most operative in Alex K.'s day-to-day life. Support your inferences with evidence and explain the metrics.* Along with substantive feedback, the educator gives the paper a cursory review grade.

Responsibility Throttles

People are very adept at behaviors that minimize their sense of responsibility; I refer to these behaviors as *responsibility throttles*. I summarize the range of minimizing behaviors in "Standard Ways to Throttle a Sense of Responsibility" (Table 4). The table includes twenty-one throttles organized into four major categories.[22] There are "implicit" throttles (categories "A" and "B"): behaviors that effectively diminish a sense of responsibility although this diminishment was never altogether intended (e.g., A2 *be preoccupied*). These are by and large mixtures of self-serving ignorance and apathetic tendencies. There are "explicit" throttles (categories "C" and "D"): behaviors whereby one purposely attempts to excuse oneself from being held responsible (e.g., C2a *reinterpret/deny injury*). There are throttles that pertain to the commission of a bad act (categories "A" and "C")—e.g., C1 *outright deny* as in *"I didn't do it."*). And there are throttles that pertain to the failure to do a good act (categories "B" and "D")—e.g., D1 *outright deny* as in *"Not my problem!"*).[23]

---

[22] Although the organization and much of the phrasing is original, "Standard Ways" relies heavily on Stanley Cohen, *States of Denial: Knowing about Atrocities and Suffering* (Cambridge: Polity, 2001), especially his description of three types of denial (7–9), bystander effects (15–16), and techniques of neutralization (60–61—which Cohen adopts from Gresham M. Sykes and David Matza, "Techniques of Neutralization: A Theory of Delinquency," *American Sociological Review* 22, no. 6 [1957]: 665–70).

[23] In "Standard Ways," each of the twenty-one throttles is labeled in terms of a verb

I would hazard to say that most people have engaged in most of the twenty-one behaviors at one time or another. In the worst of cases, these behaviors can altogether thwart a person. When the adoption of dubious self-justifications has become routine, and when the contenting of oneself in desensitized states has become practically undetectable, then self-governance completely miscarries. For most, I suspect, some degree of inclination to throttling behaviors poses a continuous challenge to good self-governance—indeed, to realizing experiences of conscience and to acting accordingly. Mark is likely very inclined to implicit throttling and moderately inclined to explicit throttling. Worse still, he is little aware of his throttling behaviors. The goal of the following assignment is to prompt students to recognize their throttling tendencies in the hopes that they will combat them and come to adopt a more self-suspicious attitude.[24]

Introspection Trial III: Responsibility Throttles (journal, weeks 9–12): Students are introduced to *responsibility throttles* and provided a copy of "Standard Ways." Students are asked to be vigilant for their own engagement in this behavior and to document throttling episodes:

- What kind of throttling took place?
    - If listed in "Standard Ways," give the letter-number designation and name (e.g., D2b *deny competence*).
    - If not listed in "Standard Ways," give the category where it would fall (A, B, C, or D) and create a name.
- When and where did it happen?
    - For explicit throttling, give the date, time, and location of the event.
    - For implicit throttling, describe the period of time over which it took place.
- What was at issue: what was the bad act done or the good act not done?
- Describe in detail the throttling event and how you came to recognize it.
- Is the sense of responsibility gone or do you still feel responsible in this case?

The documentation is submitted with the final report.

(e.g., A1 *be privileged*, D2c *reinterpret the issue*); each implicit throttle is described (e.g., A3 *be anesthetized* is described thus, *be so dulled by substances/comforts that wrongs done go unnoticed*); and each explicit throttle is exemplified by way of the sort of statements that typically manifest the behavior (e.g., C2c *blame the victim* is exemplified in the statements, *"He hit me first." "He had it coming." "She was asking for it."*).

[24] Students will also be better equipped to recognize the throttling rhetoric of others.

Final Report:
State of the Self (1000 words, weeks 13–14)

Throughout the series, students have been gathering information about four aspects of their persons. The goal of the final report is to get students to assess themselves according to this information and to identify avenues for improvement. Students respond to the following prompt:

- (250 words) Review your *Existential Metrics Proposal*. How accurate do you find the proposal now (on a scale from 1 to 10)? Do you still believe that the metrics you proposed are the five best at capturing the possibilities of human existence? Explain. Be sure to demonstrate that you've carefully considered alternative metrics.
- (250 words) Review your emotions of self-assessment documentation and reflection. How dependable are your propensities to experience emotions of self-assessment? Do they guide you toward ultimately worthwhile living? Do emotions arise when it is not appropriate [*I feel guilty about this but I shouldn't*] or fail to arise when it would be appropriate [*I should feel guilty about this but I don't*]? How would you adjust your propensities to make them more dependable?
- (250 words) Review your possible-selves documentation and reflection. How dependable are your propensities to experience possible selves (on a scale from 1 to 10)? Do they guide you toward ultimately worthwhile living? How would you adjust your repertoire of possible selves to make it more helpful—what selves would you remove/ change/add?
- (250 words) Review your responsibility throttling documentation. How susceptible are you to responsibility throttling (on a scale from 1 to 10)? What sorts of throttling are particularly common for you? Identify at least three concrete ways that you can combat your tendencies to throttle.

Students submit this paper along with a portfolio, including all the materials they have produced for the *State of the Self Series*. Taking into consideration such things as the review grades, the apparent level of engagement, and the trajectory toward/away from improvement, the educator gives the entire portfolio a grade, worth about 30 percent of the course grade.

Conclusion

I realize that adding something like the *State of the Self Series* to a THEO-1001-type course is a "big ask": the semester is short, educators already have running lists of content they wish they could include, and the assignments do not seem especially "theological."[25] I contend, nevertheless, that this series (or something comparable) should have priority. There are, I believe, many students like Mark, alienated from conscience to one degree or another by self-ignorance and self-incompetence. The duty to intervene in such cases falls squarely upon Catholic higher education. Insomuch as the church recognizes the dignity of personal conscience, it thereby assumes a responsibility to empower individual persons to engage in mature conscience experiences. The college/university classroom is perhaps the only forum in which this may be done *en masse*. The first year of college is the earliest good opportunity, as young students have only now assumed relatively adult powers of agency, only now entered "emerging adulthood." I hope that all educators will give this program serious consideration and that all will find additional ways to enact a cultivation approach. There is tremendous potential here for educators to have a profound impact on student lives, the church, and society.

---

[25] If well-integrated into the course, the series may augment students' engagement with more traditional "religious/theological" subject matter. For example, "existential metric," may serve as a common term to put students' views into dialogue with Christian outlooks. Sections of Pope Francis's *Gaudete et Exsultate* [*Apostolic Exhortation on the Call to Holiness in Today's World* (2018)] may be helpful here. Francis contrasts the possibility of living a "dull and dreary mediocrity" [no. 138] with holy ways of living; in numbers 67–94 he concludes each reflection on a beatitude with a definition of holiness, as in, "Knowing how to mourn with others: that is holiness" [no. 77]). These metrics derived from the beatitudes could be introduced into the online discussion or otherwise treated in class—challenging students to reimagine how existence might be measured.

Table 1: State of the Self Series Schedule			
Week	*Assigned*	*Due*	*Ongoing*
1	• Existential Metrics Proposal (750 words)		
2	• Introspection Trial I: Emotions of Self-Assessment (journal)	• Metrics Proposal	• Trial I
3	• Existential Metrics Discussion (online)		• Trial I • Metrics Discussion
4			• Trial I Metrics Discussion
5			• Trial I Metrics Discussion
6	• Reflection I: Emotions of Self-Assessment (750 words) • Introspection Trial II: Possible Selves (journal)		• Trial II
7		• Reflection I	• Trial II
8			• Trial II
9	• Introspection Trial III: Responsibility Throttles (journal)		• Trial II • Trial III
10	• Reflection II: Possible Selves (750 words)		• Trial III
11		• Reflection II	• Trial III
12			• Trial III
13	• Final Report: State of the Self (750 words)		
14		• Final Report	
15			
Exams			

Table 2: The Disposition of My Emotions of Self-Assessment Template (with Examples)				
	Guilt-Inducing Behavior	*Pride-Inducing Behavior*	*Shame Triggers*	*Hubris Triggers*
High Intensity/ Frequency	time-wasting	grade-making	mealtimes	Tom & Bernie
Low Intensity/ Frequency				

Table 3: My Repertoire of Possible Selves Template (with Examples)				
	Aspirational Selves		*Threatening Selves*	
	Short-term	*Long-term*	*Short-term*	*Long-term*
High Intensity/ Frequency	playmaker self	nurse self	lonely self	lives with parents self
Low Intensity/ Frequency				

Table 4: Standard Ways to Throttle a Sense of Responsibility		
	Responsibility for Doing a Bad Act	*Responsibility for Failing To Do a Good Act*

Implicit	**A**
	1. be privileged
	  enjoy benefits from social practices with (concealed) inherent injustices
	2. be preoccupied
	  be so absorbed in accomplishing some goal that wrongs done along the way go unnoticed
	3. be anesthetized
	  be so dulled by substances/ comforts that wrongs done go unnoticed
	4. be callous
	  be so compromised in ability/ desire to empathize that wrongs done are imperceptible
		B
		1. be privileged
		  lack inclination to challenge unjust social practices that harm others
		2. be preoccupied
		  be so absorbed in accomplishing some goal that opportunities to do good are overlooked
		3. be anesthetized
		  be so dulled by substances/ comforts that opportunities to do good pass by unnoticed
		4. be callous
		  be so compromised in ability/ desire to empathize that opportunities to do good are imperceptible

Explicit	**C**
	1. outright deny "I didn't do it."
	2. rationalize
	  a. reinterpret/deny injury
	    "I didn't steal it, I borrowed it."
	    "It was mischief not vandalism."
	    "What happened wasn't rape."
	  b. deny intention
	    "I didn't mean to."
	    "I didn't know what I was doing."
	    "I wasn't in control of myself."
	  c. blame the victim
	    "He hit me first."
	    "He had it coming."
	    "She was asking for it."
	  d. condemn the condemners
	    "They're all corrupt."
	    "She has it in for me!"
	  e. assert necessity
	    "It was unavoidable"
	    "It couldn't be helped."
	  f. appeal to higher loyalties
	    "I had to, he's family."
	    "It was a favor for a friend."
		D
		1. outright deny "Not my problem!"
		2. rationalize
		  a. appeal to others' competence
		    "They're just as capable as me, why don't they do something?"
		  b. deny competence/availability
		    "What was I supposed to do about it?"
		    "I don't have time for that."
		    "I can't take care of everybody."
		  c. reinterpret the issue
		    "Is it really that big of a deal?"
		    "What's happening isn't all bad."
		  d. condemn the condemners
		    "Don't be so naïve."
		    "You're such a weirdo."
		    "Welcome to the real world."
		    "Don't act so perfect."
		  e. assert inescapability
		    "That's just how it's done."
		    "It's always been that way."

"Liberating Conscience" and Latinx Students at Catholic Universities

Moral Consciousness, Power, and *Nos/otrx*

Pearl Maria Barros

For Latinx communities—as for many communities that are historically marginalized—the ability to name our own experience is a radical act.[1] Part of being in a marginalized community is the experience of being defined (and constrained) by others; it is the experience of not having authority—the authority to name and shape reality.[2] How then do we—college

---

[1] Although I use "Latinx" and "Chicanx" in my own scholarship to challenge binary constructions of gender, I refer to Latinx authors by the terms they use to refer to themselves in the texts I engage. For example, in the texts I quote from Ada María Isasi-Díaz she refers to herself as "Latina," so I therefore refer to her as "Latina." Relatedly, throughout this essay, I will use the term "Latinx women" and only use "Hispanic Women" or "Latinas" if the authors use these terms in their writings. Although the shifts between these terms might be initially confusing for readers unfamiliar with Latinx theologies and decolonial theories, the variation is itself indicative of important scholarly debates regarding the power of naming and identity formation. See, for example, Ada María Isasi-Díaz, Elena Olazagasti-Segovia, Sandra Mangual-Rodriguez, Maria Antonietta Berriozábal, Daisy L. Machado, Lourdes Arguelles, and Raven-Anne Rivero, "Roundtable Discussion: *Mujeristas* Who We Are and What We Are About," *Journal of Feminist Studies in Religion* 8, no. 1 (1992): 105–25. For important analyses of the term *Latinx*—including how the term is debated—see, for example, Edwin David Aponte and Miguel de La Torre, "Who Are Latinx Peoples?," in *Introducing Latinx Theologies*, rev. ed., ed. Edwin David Aponte and Miguel de La Torre (Maryknoll, NY: Orbis Books, 2020), 1–40; "About One-in-Four U.S. Hispanics Have Heard of Latinx, but Just 3% Use It," Pew Research Center, Washington DC (August 2020), https://www.pewresearch.org/hispanic/wp-content/uploads/sites/5/2020/08/PHGMD_2020.08.11_Latinx_FINAL.pdf; John Paul Brammer, "Digging into the Messy History of 'Latinx' Helped Me Embrace My Complex Identity," *Mother Jones* (May/June 2019 Issue), https://www.motherjones.com.

[2] As Nancy Pineda-Madrid writes, "Even though oppression may be described as racism, sexism, classism, heterosexism, and so forth, or be understood as the

professors at Catholic universities in the United States—educate marginalized students in conscience when so many of the conversations around conscience emphasize personal agency and authority? To tell a marginalized student that she can find "sanctuary"[3] within herself—when she has been consistently socialized to locate authority outside of herself—is not necessarily an immediately "liberating" educational moment for her and instead can feel a lot like being blamed for what she cannot control. The line between intended empowerment and unintended disempowerment is thinner than we imagine, and how we navigate that line is usually connected to our own positionality. How, then, do we form students in conscience in a way that attends to both the possibilities of interior authority and the constraints of systemic injustices?

In this essay, I examine how *mujerista* ethicist Ada María Isasi-Díaz's understanding of "moral consciousness and conscientization," feminist and decolonial critiques of knowledge production, and the notions of "self" operative in these writings collectively point to the need for an understanding of conscience as critical consciousness.[4] While I am not arguing that "conscience" and "consciousness" are synonymous, I find it significant that

cumulative and interconnected effect of several 'isms' (which is often the case for Latinas and others), ultimately oppression means being prevented from naming our world and ourselves," in "Notes Toward a ChicanaFeminist Epistemology (And Why It Is Important For Latina Feminist Theologies)," in *A Reader in Latina Feminist Theology: Religion and Justice*, ed. María Pilar Aquino, Daisy L. Machado, and Jeanette Rodríguez (Austin: University of Texas Press, 2002), 241–66, at 241. I engage Pineda-Madrid's article more fully later in this essay.

[3] Pope Paul VI, *Gaudium et Spes*—"Pastoral Constitution on the Church in the Modern World" (1965), no. 16. Hereinafter *GS*.

[4] While definitions of "consciousness"—like definitions of "conscience"—abound, Isasi-Díaz is, in part, drawing her understanding of consciousness from the work of Jesuit theologian Bernard Lonergan, particularly as she reads Lonergan through the work of Charles Curran and Walter Conn (see Ada María Isasi-Díaz, "Conscience, Conscientization, and Moral Agency in *Mujerista* Theology," in Ada María Isasi-Díaz, *En La Lucha/In the Struggle: Elaborating a Mujerista Theology* (Minneapolis: Fortress, 2004), 150–75, at 161, footnote 56). Indeed, Conn also defines conscience as consciousness, writing: "A little etymological study tells us, in fact, that conscience *is* consciousness—the distinctive moral consciousness of the responsible, existential subject concerned with value, with moral judgment, decision, and choice" (see Conn, *Christian Conversion: A Developmental Interpretation of Autonomy and Surrender* [Eugene, OR: Wipf & Stock, 1986], 33). I address Isasi-Díaz's engagement of Lonergan, Curran, and Conn—including her rethinking of them from a *mujerista* perspective—later in this essay.

many Latinx Catholic theologians do not discuss "conscience" as much as they discuss "conscientization" and "consciousness."[5] I think that this preference for "consciousness" is inherently tied to the notions of "self" acknowledged and unacknowledged by "conscience" and to the decolonial critique of this notion of "self" found in Latinx theologies.[6]

This essay is divided into three parts that follow Isasi-Díaz's description of the steps involved, for her, in the process of conscientization: "(1) recognizing the distinction between nature in its inevitability and culture in its change-ability; (2) unmasking the myths that allow oppressors to dominate society by blurring this distinction; and (3) exploring the alternatives available under the fundamental 'generative theme' of our epoch, namely, liberation."[7] In the first part of this essay, I trace Isasi-Díaz's theory of moral development, showing how it challenges understandings of conscience that appeal to moral knowledge as that which is best mediated by external authority (e.g., the Catholic Church's magisterium and Protestant "fundamentalist" biblical interpretations) and draws from Bernard Lonergan's understanding of consciousness as constitutive of the subject.[8] I argue that while she retains the distinction between nature and culture, her theory of moral development gestures toward the difficulty of making this distinction precisely because she highlights how

---

   [5] For an excellent survey of the field of Latino/a/x Christian ethics, see María Teresa Dávila, "Latino/a Ethics," in *The Wiley Blackwell Companion to Latino/a Theology*, ed. Orlando O. Espín (Oxford: John Wiley & Sons, 2015), 249–67. It is notable that the term "conscience" does not appear in the "key themes" of *mestizaje, la lucha, teología en conjunto, acompañamiento*, and *dignidad*" that Dávila identifies as characteristic of Latinx ethics and theologies (ibid., 250; on 264 in footnote 5 she also mentions other concepts such as *Religión popular, fiesta*, and *comunidad* but again does not mention conscience).
   [6] See, for example, Miguel A. De La Torre, "Doing Latina/o Ethics from the Margins of Empire: Liberating the Colonized Mind," *Journal of the Society of Christian Ethics* 33, no. 2 (2013): 3–20; Nichole M. Flores, "Latina/o Families: Solidarity and the Common Good," *Journal of the Society of Christian Ethics* 33, no. 2 (2013): 57–72; Roberto S. Goizueta, "*Nosotros*: Toward a U.S. Hispanic Anthropology," *Listening: Journal of Religion and Culture* 27, no. 1 (1992): 55–69; Mayra Rivera, *Poetics of the Flesh* (Durham, NC: Duke University Press, 2015).
   [7] Isasi-Díaz, "Conscience, Conscientization, and Moral Agency in *Mujerista* Theology," 161.
   [8] Although Isasi-Díaz critically engages the role of biblical interpretation in Protestant—and more specifically, "fundamentalist, Pentecostal, and storefront"—churches and its impact on Latinx women's moral development, I focus on her critique of the promotion of "authoritarian conscience" by Catholic bishops in this essay (see ibid., 159–60, 152–59).

external authorities that mediate moral truths are already shaped by—and function as mediators of—cultural norms.[9]

In the second part, I turn to the work of Chicana Catholic theologian Nancy Pineda-Madrid and philosopher Eduardo Mendieta to show how feminist and decolonial critiques of epistemology attempt to "unmask the myths that allow oppressors to dominate society by blurring" the distinction between nature and culture. Importantly, I highlight how thinkers such as Mendieta actually lead us to wonder whether nature and culture can ever be understood outside of each other. In other words, feminist and decolonial theories not only remind us that nature and culture are already "blurred," but also even posit that the supposed line between the two may not exist.

In the third and final part, I explore the implications of this feminist and decolonial insight about the relationship between nature and culture as an "alternative available" for helping us imagine how to foster a "liberating conscience and consciousness" in our students and in ourselves—in who I call "*nos/otrx*."[10] Drawing on the concept of "*nosotros*" in Latinx theological anthropologies and "*nos/otras*" in the work of Chicana theorist Gloria Anzaldúa, I offer three pedagogical guidelines that have helped my own students and me—*nos/otrx*—examine our own positionalities and enter into difficult conversations. Throughout the essay, I argue that reframing our conversations about "conscience" as a "critical consciousness" of an ever-evolving self can enable *nos/otrx* to find within the complexity of our identities the capaciousness necessary to create a more just and inclusive world.

Learning to Recognize:
Mujerista "Moral Consciousness and Conscientization"

Ada María Isasi-Díaz's "Conscience, Conscientization, and Moral Agency in *Mujerista* Theology" begins as much of her work often does, namely, with *lo cotidiano*, the everyday experiences of "Hispanic Women" as a site of (and for) theological and ethical reflection.[11] In particular, she attempts to understand

---

[9] Ibid., 161.

[10] I first started using the term "*nos/otrx*" publicly in December 2020 during my homily for the Feast of *La Virgen de Guadalupe* for Catholic Women Preach. Similar to my reasons for using the term "Latinx," I wanted to use a form of "*nos/otros*" or "*nos/otras*" that would be inclusive of those who identify as nonbinary. See Pearl Maria Barros, "Feast of Our Lady of Guadalupe," Catholic Women Preach (December 12, 2020), https://www.catholicwomenpreach.org.

[11] Isasi-Díaz, "Conscience, Conscientization, and Moral Agency in *Mujerista*

"the significance and the role that conscience plays" in their lives.[12] Reflecting
on "[phrases] often heard among Hispanic Women" like "*Mi conciencia me
dice*" ("my conscience tells me") and "*haz lo que tu conciencia to indique*"
("do what your conscience tells you"), she seeks to show how these and other
everyday phrases heard in "regular conversations" reveal a sense of moral
agency present in Latinx women.[13]

Central to her project of rethinking conscience from a *mujerista* theological perspective is a concern about the possible stifling of this moral agency,
specifically "in the context of Hispanic Women's religious experience in the
U.S.A.," by external authorities such as the Roman Catholic Church.[14] For
Isasi-Díaz, the Roman Catholic Church holds more power over "Hispanic
Women's" lives in the U.S. context than in their "countries of origin" for two
main reasons. "First, the Roman Catholic Church is operative at the neighborhood level through well-organized parishes that provide a strong presence
of the official church among the people."[15] She argues that this structural

---

Theology." For a thorough definition of *lo cotidiano* as it is understood in her work, see
Ada María Isasi-Díaz, "Mujerista Discourse: A Platform for Latinas' Subjugated Knowledge," in *Decolonizing Epistemologies: Latina/o Theology and Philosophy*, ed. Ada María
Isasi-Díaz and Eduardo Mendieta (New York: Fordham University Press, 2012), 44–67,
at 47–56. It is also important to note that Isasi-Díaz's work—particularly her coined
term *mujerista*—has not been without critique by other Latina/x theologians. See, for
example, María Pilar Aquino, Daisy L. Machado, and Jeanette Rodríguez, "Introduction," in Aquino et al., *A Reader in Latina Feminist Theology*, xiii–xx, at xiv–xv, and
footnotes 3 and 4. For a brief comparison and contrast of *mujerista* and Latina feminist
theologies, see Michelle A. Gonzalez, *Created in God's Image: An Introduction to Feminist Theological Anthropology*, (Maryknoll, NY: Orbis Books, 2007), 92–93. Another
critique of Isasi-Díaz's work is her reliance on "experience" (usually the experience of
"Hispanic Women"/"Latinas"); seeming to engage this critique, she writes, "In valuing
the experience of the oppressed, I want to highlight their epistemological contribution.
I make a difference between 'raw data,' what happens, which I am quick to admit we
never know except through the lens that we use to see it, and experience, which has two
elements: what happens and how we explain it. For a theoretical framework to understand the point I am making," Isasi-Díaz contines, "see Paula M. L. Moya, *Learning from
Experience: Minority Identities, Multicultural Struggles* (Berkeley: University of California Press, 2002), 38–39"; Isasi-Díaz, "Mujerista Discourse: A Platform for Latinas'
Subjugated Knowledge," footnote 9.

[12] Isasi-Díaz, "Conscience, Conscientization, and Moral Agency in *Mujerista*
Theology," 150.
[13] Ibid.
[14] Ibid., 151.
[15] Ibid.

presence is missing in Latinx women's "countries of origin, where, because of lack of priests and because the concept of belonging to a parish is not operative in most cases, the church lacks tight organization and is not able to exert significant control."[16] Second, the Catholic Church holds more influence over the lives of Latinx women in the United States "because of the availability of means of communication" that allow the church to "[reach] people much more frequently than in Latin America and the Caribbean."[17] For Isasi-Díaz, the particularities of the Catholic Church's authoritative presence in the lives of Latinx women in the United States shapes—and challenges—the way *mujerista* theologians engage the formation of conscience in Latinx women. She writes, "Therefore, our task as *mujerista* theologians is much more extensive in regard to encouraging the growth of moral agency. Not only do we have to support and enhance its development but we also have to argue for it and help Hispanic Women to defend their right and duty to develop their own moral agency."[18]

The *mujerista* imperative to help Latinx women in the United States "defend their right and duty to develop their own moral agency" is a response, according to Isasi-Díaz, to the growing "curtailment of freedom of conscience" by Catholic bishops.[19] Tracing how members of the church hierarchy have "[vested] their opinions with the same authority as the word of God" (as exemplified in John Paul II's 1988 address to moral theologians), she argues that Catholic bishops have promoted an "authoritarian conscience" that attempts to elicit total obedience from the faithful and quell dissent.[20] Importantly, in critiquing this authoritarian conscience, she is not arguing for moral relativity, but rather that "the hierarchy of the church [. . .] carry out vigorously its theological task of increasing religious education, of assisting in the formation of conscience, including imparting knowledge about what many call the best kept secret in the church: primacy of conscience."[21] For her, a goal of *mujerista* theology is a robust formation of conscience that aims to foster moral consciousness and agency in Latinx women. But how does she differentiate between conscience and moral consciousness? And what is the process she proposes for forming this moral consciousness?

---

[16] Ibid.

[17] Ibid.

[18] Ibid, 151–52.

[19] Ibid.,152–53.

[20] Ibid., 152–59.

[21] Ibid., 158–59.

"Conscience," Isasi-Díaz notes, "should not be understood as a faculty or power but instead should be identified with the 'moral consciousness' of the person."[22] Significantly, in identifying "conscience" with "the moral consciousness of the person" Isasi-Díaz is drawing on Jesuit philosopher Bernard Lonergan's cognitional theory.[23] While it is not possible to fully engage Lonergan's theory here, a brief summary can prove helpful in understanding possible resonances between *mujerista* conceptions of conscience and conscientization and Lonergan's understanding of the person and consciousness.[24] Importantly, Isasi-Díaz notes that she reads Lonergan through the work of theologians Charles Curran and Walter Conn, particularly as they connect his theory to conscience. In Conn's *Christian Conversion: A Developmental Interpretation of Autonomy and Surrender*, he argues that in order to understand

---

[22] Ibid., 161.

[23] Ibid. See especially her footnote 56 where she writes, "This concept of moral consciousness was developed by Bernard Lonergan. I have used the work of both Curran and of Conn to guide me through Lonergan's exposition" (ibid., 228). See Bernard J. F. Lonergan, *Insight: A Study of Human Understanding* (New York: Philosophical Library, 1970); Lonergan, *Method in Theology* (New York: Herder and Herder, 1972); Lonergan, *The Subject* (Milwaukee, WI: Marquette University Press, 1968). See also Walter Conn, *Conscience: Development and Self-Transcendence* (Birmingham, AL: Religious Education Press, 1981), especially 121–24, 133, and 138; and Charles E. Curran, *Directions in Fundamental Moral Theology* (Notre Dame, IN: University of Notre Dame Press, 1985). Importantly, Isasi-Díaz also notes in footnote 63, "Following Curran's lead in *Directions in Fundamental Moral Theology*, 240–43, my starting place for this analysis of moral consciousness was Bernard Lonergan, *Method in Theology* (New York: Herder and Herder, 1972), 103–5. I have changed his schema significantly to reflect what I have learned from the Hispanic Women whose voices are presented in this work. See also Carol Gilligan, *In a Different Voice* (Cambridge: Harvard University Press, 1982), 160" (228). For an excellent concise summary of Lonergan's theory, see Francis Schüssler Fiorenza, "Systematic Theology: Task and Methods," in *Systematic Theology: Roman Catholic Perspectives*, 2nd ed., ed. Francis Schüssler Fiorenza and John P. Galvin (Minneapolis: Fortress Press, 2011), 36–41.

[24] Interestingly, Catholic theologian M. Shawn Copeland also notes the possible resonances between Lonergan's work and decolonial theories as she writes: "Jesuit philosopher and theologian Bernard Lonergan would not be considered a decolonial thinker, but his cognitional theory worked out during the 1950s anticipates and addresses similar concerns about the relation between knowing and doing, ethics and action, subjectivity and objectivity, and love as incarnate human authenticity" (see M. Shawn Copeland, "Enfleshing Love: A Decolonial Theological Reading of *Beloved*," in *Beyond the Doctrine of Man: Decolonial Visions of the Human*, ed. Joseph Drexler-Dreis and Kristien Justaert [New York: Fordham University Press, 2020], 91–112; 106, footnote 12).

conscience, "The personal subject must be explicitly understood in the very concreteness of its consciousness and becoming."[25] Tracing Lonergan's distinction "between the subject-as-subject (consciousness) and the subject-as-object (reflexive intentionality)," Conn writes, "Consciousness, according to Lonergan's theorem, not only reveals the subject-as-subject, but constitutes it."[26] Elaborating on the constitutive nature of consciousness, Conn states, "The 'I,' the subject who feels, understands, and decides, is not only revealed to itself as such in consciousness, but is made capable of feeling, understanding, and deciding only through consciousness."[27] Echoing Conn's reading of Lonergan, Isasi-Díaz writes, "In *mujerista* moral theology conscience is understood as the agent herself as morally conscious, and since consciousness is constitutive of the human person as agent, the formation of moral consciousness has to do with enabling the process of conscientization of the person."[28] This understanding of consciousness as constitutive of the human person is one of the strongest resonances between Lonergan's theory and *mujerista* moral theology because it reminds us that how and what we know is who we are and might become—an insight that has profound ramifications in the struggle for liberation that is at the heart of *mujerista* theology.

If how and what we know—our epistemologies—constitute our consciousness and our consciousness constitutes us, then changing our ways of knowing can change our consciousness and thus change us. For Isasi-Díaz, changing our ways of knowing can be achieved through the process of conscientization, and this conscientization must be in the service of liberation.[29] In

---

[25] Walter E. Conn, *Christian Conversion: A Developmental Interpretation of Autonomy and Surrender* (Eugene, OR: Wipf & Stock, 1986), 33. Although the primary focus of Conn's book is conversion, he begins his analysis by examining the relationship between conscience, consciousness, and personal development (see, especially, chapters 1 and 2 of *Christian Conversion*). These discussions echo insights from his earlier work, *Conscience: Development and Self-Transcendence* (Birmingham, AL: Religious Education Press, 1981), which Isasi-Díaz cites.

[26] Conn, *Christian Conversion*, 34.

[27] Ibid.

[28] Isasi-Díaz, "Conscience, Conscientization, and Moral Agency in *Mujerista* Theology," 161.

[29] She writes, "Conscientization is an integral part of the understanding of an [*sic*] the struggle for liberation," Isasi-Díaz, "Conscience, Conscientization, and Moral Agency in *Mujerista* Theology," 161. *Mujerista* theology is, firstly, a liberation theology, drawing on the insights of Latin American Liberation theologian Gustavo Gutiérrez's *A Theology of Liberation: History, Politics, and Salvation*, (Maryknoll, NY: Orbis Books, 1973) and philosopher and educator Paulo Freire's *Pedagogy of the Oppressed* (New

other words, conscientization is a conscientization toward liberation—our own and that of others. As previously mentioned, this process entails "(1) recognizing the distinction between nature in its inevitability and culture in its changeability; (2) unmasking the myths that allow oppressors to dominate society by blurring this distinction; and (3) exploring the alternatives available under the fundamental 'generative theme' of our epoch, namely, liberation."[30] In Isasi-Díaz's theory of moral development, we see her carrying out the first step of this process, attempting to help Latinx women "recognize the distinction" between nature and culture by urging them to listen to their own authority (*"Mi conciencia me dice"* / "My conscience tells me") rather than an external authority mediated by the Catholic Church (or Protestant fundamentalist biblical interpretation). In encouraging Latinx women to listen to their own consciences—to themselves, Isasi-Díaz invites them to reflect on the discrepancies between what they know to be true and what they are told to be true. Again, this does not mean that she is advocating for moral relativism but that for her the first step in developing moral consciousness is the ability to question whether something is "natural" or whether it is a cultural norm masquerading as God-given. The ability to recognize between the two becomes particularly imperative when the cultural norm perpetuates injustice. For Isasi-Díaz, our becoming aware of injustice—our conscientization—should shift our moral consciousness so that we push against injustice, thus *becoming* agents of liberation.

Although Isasi-Díaz's insight that we can only become agents of liberation if we are aware of injustice is helpful for understanding the imperative to shift moral consciousness toward liberation, her concept of the process of conscientization maintains the problematic distinction between "nature" and "culture." As feminist and decolonial theorists (among others) have

---

York: Bloomsbury, 1970). It calls for people to be in solidarity with the oppressed and to actively counter injustice. In Isasi-Díaz's later writings, she acknowledges the critical engagement of the term "liberation" by decolonial and other theorists and theologians. She writes, "Though mujerista theology and ethics have used the language of liberation discourse, they certainly understand liberation not as a project possible within Western civilization but rather one that has as its goal radical structural changes. Our attempt has always been to enable and further Latinas' thinking, that is, to shed light on the epistemological richness that emerges from our lived experiences and to value what we know and how we know it as our contribution to building a different world" (Isasi-Díaz, "Mujerista Discourse," 45).

[30] Isasi-Díaz, "Conscience, Conscientization, and Moral Agency in *Mujerista* Theology," 161.

noted, nature and culture are not easily untangled—if they are even separate threads to begin with—because what we know to constitute "nature"
is always already discursively embedded.[31] To state it plainly, knowledge is
never neutral. Indeed, Isasi-Díaz's example of the "authoritarian conscience"
promoted by Catholic bishops is an excellent example of how knowledge—
in this case moral knowledge—is always already situated within a particular
world of meaning that is conditioned by its sociocultural context and
dynamics of power. Furthermore, the knowledge of Latinx women to which
she appeals is also similarly situated. Knowers, like knowledge, are never
neutral. Thus, while Isasi-Díaz argues for an understanding of conscience
as the moral consciousness of the person that is formed through a process
of conscientization toward liberation, she retains the distinction between
nature and culture that feminist and decolonial theories highlight as one of
the fundamental "oppressor's myths" used to enable injustice.

"Unmasking the Oppressor's Myths": Power of Knowledge/Unknowledge

Feminist and decolonial critiques of knowledge production provide powerful
reminders of how knowledge is inextricably connected to power.[32] In Pineda-
Madrid's "Notes Toward a Chicana Feminist Epistemology (And Why It Is
Important For Latina Feminist Theologies)," she writes, "At its root, oppression—as both a social and an internalized phenomenon—has to do with who
controls the creation and validation of knowledge, with *epistemology*; and

---

[31] See, for example, Michel Foucault, *The History of Sexuality: An Introduction*,
vol. 1, trans. Robert Hurley (New York: Vintage Books, 1978); Judith Butler, *Gender
Trouble: Feminism and the Subversion of Identity* (New York: Routledge, 1990); Mayra
Rivera, "Carnal Relations," in *Poetics of the Flesh* (Durham, NC: Duke University Press,
2015), 133–52.

[32] See, for example, María Lugones, *Pilgrimages/Peregrinajes: Theorizing Coali-
tion against Multiple Oppressions* (New York: Rowman & Littlefield, 2003); Walter
Mignolo, "Decolonizing Western Epistemology/Building Decolonial Epistemologies," in Isasi-Díaz and Eduardo Mendieta, *Decolonizing Epistemologies*, 19–43; Chela
Sandoval, *Methodology of the Oppressed* (Minneapolis: University of Minnesota Press,
2000). For an insightful critique of Mignolo's work and the implications of that critique
for Catholic theology, see Susan Abraham, "Postcolonial Hermeneutics and a Catholic
(Post)Modernity," in *Beyond Dogmatism and Innocence: Hermeneutics, Critique, and
Catholic Theology*, ed. Anthony J. Godzieba and Bradford E. Hinze (Collegeville, MN:
Liturgical Press, 2017), 203–27.

with the ability to act on that knowledge, with *humanization*."[33] Drawing on the work of feminist (and other) theorists, Pineda-Madrid notes that their work "calls attention to the inherent relationship between epistemology and politics."[34] Elaborating on this relationship she argues, "on the one hand, epistemology must never be reduced to politics; but on the other, any credible epistemology cannot ignore the sociopolitical dimensions of knowledge."[35] Although she does not use the categories of "nature" and "culture" (as Isasi-Díaz does), Pineda-Madrid signals a distinction between epistemology and politics that, at least initially, suggests some knowledge might exist beyond (yet ever-in-relation to) politics. Yet, she immediately follows that idea with this statement: "Nonetheless, epistemological commitments, whether implicit or explicit, serve as the rational foundation for all intellectual work and have implications for the pursuit of truth. In striving toward the truth of God, theologians invariably assume an epistemology."[36] Here, the initial distinction Pineda-Madrid makes between epistemology and politics begins to break down, since she asserts that "epistemological commitments" function as the "rational foundation for all intellectual pursuits." Even if we assert theologically that "the truth of God" ultimately transcends politics (hence our "*striving toward*" it), it is nevertheless mediated to us through language that is always tied to structures of power. Thus, for humans, epistemology and politics—nature and culture—are inextricably connected to each other.

In "The Ethics of (Not) Knowing: Take Care of Ethics and Knowledge Will Come of Its Own Accord," Mendieta explores this nonneutrality of knowledge. He writes, "There is no knowledge that is not situated, historical, and thus woven into a whole culture of what can be known, how it can be known, and by whom it can be known."[37] Knowledge production is never neutral because it occurs within existing social systems that maintain themselves by policing the boundaries of what can (and cannot) be known and by whom. Importantly, he explicitly connects this key insight of feminist and decolonial theories to ethics. Central to his argument is not only that "the production of knowledge is also the production of unknowledge" but

---

[33] Pineda-Madrid, "Notes Toward a Chicana Feminist Epistemology," 241.

[34] Ibid., 242.

[35] Ibid.

[36] Ibid.

[37] Eduardo Mendieta, "The Ethics of (Not) Knowing: Take Care of Ethics and Knowledge Will Come of Its Own Accord," in *Decolonizing Epistemologies: Latina/o Theology and Philosophy*, ed. Ada María Isasi-Díaz and Eduardo Mendieta (New York: Fordham University Press, 2012), 247–64, at 249.

also that we are *responsible* for the "unknowledges" our knowledges produce. Or put differently: we are culpable for what we make unknown—what we erase or obscure—through what we know. He writes, "To the crime of innocence there corresponds the responsibility for ignorance. Knowing ignorance and ignorant knowing are always morally suspect."[38] Drawing on Charles Mills's concept of "moral ignorance"—"which is not just not knowing what the ethical thing to do is but also that what we do not know itself has moral effects"—and Toni Morrison's idea of "the crime of innocence," Mendieta highlights how "such 'innocence' is a luxury of a power position."[39] For Mendieta, "not to know is a luxury afforded by a social situation in which epistemic assets, powers, and standpoints are unequally and prejudicially distributed."[40] Such an insight is particularly useful in our consideration of conscience formation and Catholic education since producing and validating knowledge—as college professors and universities do—is a participation in a multi-intersectional system of power that is used to empower and/or oppress. Thus, we need to ask the following: What are the "knowing ignorances" that we produce? How do the knowledges we share with our students possibly obscure and perpetuate oppression?

Taking Pineda-Madrid and Mendieta's arguments together, both not only remind us that knowledge is always constructed in relation to power but also that this power demands accountability since, as Mendieta writes, "knowing is always itself an ethical act."[41] Furthermore if, as Pineda-Madrid argues, "at its root, oppression" is tied to "who controls the creation and validation of knowledge" and who is able "to act on that knowledge," then I think it can also be argued that the possibility of countering oppression—uprooting it—can also paradoxically be found in the production of knowledge and the action(s) informed by this knowledge. Finally, if producing "knowledge" is also always an act of producing "unknowledge," then it is imperative that the knowledges we produce within Catholic universities contain a critical reflexivity that continually pushes against injustices they may unknowingly perpetuate. It also means that we must form students—knowers—who can engage in critical self-reflection that inspires action against injustice. But how might we do this?

---

[38] Ibid., 255.
[39] Ibid., 260.
[40] Ibid., 260–61.
[41] Ibid., 249.

Liberating Alternatives: Imagining "*Nos/otrx*"

The construction of the person in Latinx theological anthropologies and in Anzaldúan[42] thought can illuminate how we might form students who can engage in critical self-reflection and who ultimately know that the unknowledge produced by their knowing demands accountability. Although the extent of Latinx theological anthropologies and Anzaldúan constructions of the "self" cannot be fully analyzed here, I think that both taken together offer us a profound insight as to how we might approach the formation of conscience in our students, both those who identify as Latinx and those who do not.[43] In fact, I believe that forming Latinx students in conscience should not be seen as entirely different from forming non-Latinx students. To think so only perpetuates the violence of othering and tokenization that people from historically marginalized communities already suffer. Indeed, the main insight from Latinx theological anthropologies and Anzaldúan thought that I want to highlight—the concept of "*nosotros*" and "*nos/otras*" (respectively)—pushes against this violence precisely because it reminds "us" that "we" are always in relation to each "other."

In Catholic theologian Roberto Goizueta's "*Nosotros*: Toward a U.S. Hispanic Anthropology," he argues that a fundamental aspect of Latinx theological anthropology is that the subject is understood as "constituted by community."[44] He writes, "In an authentic community, the identity of the 'we'

---

[42] Chicana theorist Gloria Anzaldúa is best known for her concept of borderlands consciousness as developed in *Borderlands/La Frontera: The New Mestiza*. See Gloria Anzaldúa, *Borderlands/La Frontera: The New Mestiza* (San Francisco: Spinster/Aunt Lute Books, 1987).

[43] In a forthcoming article, I analyze the idea of the "self" in Anzaldúan thought and its ramifications for Catholic theological anthropologies.

[44] Roberto S. Goizueta, "*Nosotros*: Toward a U.S. Hispanic Anthropology," in *Listening: Journal of Religion and Culture* 27, no. 1 (1992), 55–69, at 57. As Barros notes, "Importantly, Goizueta also acknowledges how a *nosotros* understanding of identity is also connected to sin and suffering (as well as grace) since it is tied to *mestizaje*, which is 'characterized by suffering.' He continues, 'The experience of *mestizaje*, as a dual marginalization, is first an experience of suffering, alienation, homelessness, non-identity, oppression, and exile; it is an experience of the cross' (Goizueta, "Nosotros," 58). This resonates with Anzaldúa's discussions of the borderlands as '*una herida abierta*' (an 'open wound') and the problematics of *mestizaje* in *Borderlands/La Frontera*, especially in Chapters 1 and 7," (Pearl Maria Barros, "Rethinking Women's Suffering and Holiness: Gloria Anzaldúa's 'Holy Relics,'" *Journal of Feminist Studies in Religion* 36, no. 2 (2020): 7–24, at 23, footnote 54).

does not extinguish the 'I'; the Spanish word for 'we' is *'nosotros*,' which literally means 'we others,' a community of *otros*, or others."[45] Similarly, Chicana theorist Gloria Anzaldúa "often uses *'nos/otras'* instead of 'we'" in her later writings.[46] As Barros elaborates, "Pushing against dichotomous thinking that posits 'us' against 'them,' [Anzaldúa] plays with the Spanish word for 'we'— *nosotros(as)*—by splitting it into *'nos/otras'* to show how any reference to ourselves always includes a reference to others."[47] Both Goizueta and Anzaldúa show how understanding ourselves as part of the other and the other as part of us can radically shape our way of being in the world. Being *nos/otrx* reminds us that we are not only in constant relationship with the other, but we are also responsible for each other. There is no place between "us" and "them" to hide from the demands of this accountability. Such an insight has profound implications for how we might go about forming our students in conscience—or, to return to Isasi-Díaz's words, how we shape the moral consciousness of our students through a process of conscientization that is oriented toward liberation. We now turn to a few pedagogical guidelines that, I think, can help in teaching and learning how to be *nos/otrx*.

In my own teaching practice, I have found the following guidelines—and the practices they inspire—to be helpful in fostering a critical consciousness that is oriented toward creating a more just and inclusive world. They are by *no* means meant to be proscriptive, but are more akin to sharing notes from the field in the hope of contributing to what is, and likely will always be, an ongoing conversation. Furthermore, they are not original to me, and thus you will likely hear in them echoes from the writings of other theologians, philosophers, theorists, and Christian mystics.

---

[45] Goizueta, "*Nosotros*," 57.

[46] Barros, "Rethinking Women's Suffering and Holiness," 23. In briefly summarizing borderlands consciousness (which is synonymous with "mestiza consciousness") in Anzaldúan thought, Barros writes, "The term 'borderlands' refers to the national border between the United States and Mexico as well as to the tension of living between seemingly contradictory markers of 'self.' Calling this 'borderlands' *'una herida abierta'* ('an open wound'), Anzaldúa recognizes the pain inherent to living with conflicting markers of 'self' but also points to the possibilities for transformation that can stem from '[living] *sin fronteras*' ('without borders') and thus '[being] a crossroads' between seemingly disparate worlds" (Barros, "Rethinking Women's Suffering and Holiness," 10).

[47] Barros, "Rethinking Women's Suffering and Holiness," 23. She also notes, "Furthermore, [Anzaldúa] uses the female form of the Spanish 'we' as a way of destabilizing the androcentric tendencies of language since Spanish grammar dictates that any general use of the term 'we' should always take the masculine form" (Barros, 23, footnote 52).

1. **Critical self-reflection begins with the self.** In order to teach students how to engage in critical self-reflection, we must also do so. In examining our own positionalities, we ask the following: What are the sites of privilege and oppression within my own life? How do they inform each other? How do they inform my teaching and scholarship? How will I use them to push against injustice? Importantly, this is not a one-time practice, but like the Ignatian Examen and other forms of prayer meant to help growth in self-awareness and grace, it must be done continually.[48]

2. **Be suspicious of perfectionism.** In attempting to dismantle multi-layered, intersectional structures of injustice through our teaching and scholarship—and through our very being—we need to remember that we will make mistakes. We will say the wrong thing, fail to be as inclusive as we hope to be, and find ourselves facing our own strong emotions in the midst of trying to guide students through heated moments in the classroom. Sometimes we will be able to correct ourselves in the moment, but often, we will fail to do so. Paradoxically, the danger of these failures is not the failures themselves, but their ability to convince us that we should "stick to what we know" rather than challenge ourselves to grow. Perfectionism does not allow for the real growth and transformation that comes through the process of learning—a process that usually involves mistakes.[49]

3. **Don't forget to cultivate hope.** Engaging in critical self-reflection with an orientation toward justice, and teaching students to do the same, is exhausting work. We can become overwhelmed by the task at hand, especially when we know the magnitude of the issues we face. Sexism, racism, classism, homophobia, ableism, and all other systems of injustice are difficult to eradicate precisely because they are insidious and often mutate to continue perpetuating themselves. To keep going in the struggle for justice, we need to find ways of cultivating hope. By "hope" I do not mean naïve "optimism," but rather the fundamental Christian belief that death and destruction never have the last word. It is the hope of resurrection. As Latin American and U.S. Latinx liberation theologians remind us, cultivating this resurrection hope

---

[48] For an example of the Ignatian Examen written to challenge racial injustice, see the Association of Jesuit Colleges and Universities (AJCU), *Eyes to See: An Anti-Racism Examen*, https://www.ajcunet.edu/eyes-to-see.

[49] For an engaging reflection (intended for a popular audience) on the relationship between perfectionism, vulnerability, and growth, see Brené Brown, *Daring Greatly: How the Courage to Be Vulnerable Transforms the Way We Live, Love, Parent, and Lead* (New York: Avery, 2012).

does not detract us from our efforts to bring about the "kin-dom of God" in the here and now.[50] Instead, it gives us strength for the hard work of justice.

Conclusions

To conclude this essay, I want to return to the question I posed at the beginning, namely, how do we (college professors) form students in conscience in a way that attends to both the possibilities of interior authority and the constraints of systemic injustices? I have argued that the way we answer this question is often tied to our own positionalities, to the sites of privilege and oppression that we occupy (or that occupy us?) in our own lives. Examining Isasi-Díaz's understanding of conscience as a moral consciousness that must be conscientized toward liberation as well as feminist and decolonial critiques of the relationship between knowledge and power, I have tried to show how appeals to inner authority that do not take account of systemic injustice ring false to most people who belong to marginalized communities. To tell a young Latinx student to take comfort in the inner "sanctuary"[51] within herself even as she finds no sanctuary in the world around her can be, as Mendieta cautions us, a moment in which our knowledge produces "unknowledge." In thinking that we are offering empowerment, we might actually be disempowering her by obscuring the realities of oppression that constrain her life. What, then, can we do? Paradoxically, I think that an answer to this question lies in the fact that it resists easy answers; the tension between desiring to affirm the possibilities of interior authority while also challenging the systemic injustices that threaten it can lead *nos/otrx* to imagine ways of educating students in conscience that allow space for constant critical reflexivity.

---

[50] Ada María Isasi-Díaz, "Popular Religiosity, Spanish, and *Proyecto Histórico*: Elements of Latinas' Ethnicity," in Isasi-Díaz, *En La Lucha/In the Struggle*, 52–79, at 53.

[51] *GS* no. 16.

On Grieving for the Garden of the World

Catholic Education and the Cultivation of an Ecologically Sensitive Conscience

Daniel P. Castillo

A Planetary Emergency

Today, the world exists in a state of planetary emergency. Human activity has become a primary driver of biophysical change on a global scale.[1] The effects of this change are manifold and daunting. Already, the sixth great extinction is unfolding, with the survival of myriad species threatened as the cumulative effects of the human enterprise decimate ecosystems and habitats.[2] Concentrations of carbon in the atmosphere continue to escalate at an alarming rate, inducing a rise in Earth's temperature. As the planet continues to warm, both the fluctuation and the extremes in weather patterns will intensify.[3] Moreover, the poor of this world, those who have contributed to and benefited from the acceleration of exploitative human activity the least, are also the most vulnerable to the negative effects of the increasingly unstable biosphere.[4] Today, Earth—its ecosystems, its flora and fauna, its human life—demands our attention and responsiveness in urgent and unprecedented ways.

This essay considers how Catholic education, as it is animated by the Christian imagination, might contribute to the vital task of forming the

---

[1] See Will Steffen, P. J. Crutzen, and J. R. McNeill, "The Anthropocene: Are Humans Now Overwhelming the Great Forces of Nature?" *Ambio* 36 (2007): 614–21.

[2] See Elizabeth Kolbert, *The Sixth Extinction: An Unnatural History* (New York: Henry Holt, 2014).

[3] See "Fourth National Climate Assessment, Volume II: Impacts, Risks, and Adaptation in the United States," https://nca2018.globalchange.gov/.

[4] See Robin M. Leichenko and Karen L. O'Brien, *Environmental Change and Globalization: Double Exposures* (New York: Oxford University Press, 2008).

consciences of communities of faith and learning so that these communities might respond appropriately to the planetary emergency. I begin by first exploring the ambiguous heritage of Catholic Christian thought regarding the value of the earth and nonhuman creation. In so doing, I demonstrate that the Christian imagination has resources within its traditions, narratives, and systems of symbolism that can help to attune the consciences of persons and communities to the "travail of creation" (Rom 8:22). At the same time, I acknowledge that this imagination frequently has been developed in ways that dampen and marginalize concern for the earth. Second, in light of this ambiguity, I consider how Pope Francis's concept of "integral ecology" can help to organize the Christian imagination (and by extension the Catholic conscience) in a manner that is fruitful for hearing and responding to the cries of the earth and poor. Third, in continuing to draw on the insight of Pope Francis, I suggest that his interpretation of key passages of the book of Genesis can further illuminate the concept of integral ecology and ground this concept more deeply in traditional sources of Christian revelation. I consider specifically how Francis's interpretations of Genesis 2:15 and of the narrative of Cain and Abel help to clarify the human vocation to the "love of earth" as an essential dimension of the mission of Catholic education. Finally, I conclude by positing that it is vital for institutions of Catholic education to conceive of themselves as institutions of integral ecology so as to form properly the consciences of the persons and communities they serve.

Throughout this essay, I appeal to Judith Butler's notions of "grievable-ness" and "framing" in order to think about the virtues, failures, and promise of the Christian imagination as a resource for cultivating a conscience that is attentive to the cries of the earth and the poor. I begin, therefore, by briefly considering how Butler develops her terms.

(Un)grievable Life and Catholic Education

The question of what makes life grievable, what renders a life worthy of mourning, lies at the heart of Butler's exploration of how public discourse and media imagery act to shape how we, as humans, perceive others.[5] Butler is particularly concerned with how our ways of speaking of and portraying others (or failing to speak of and simply ignoring others) can function to diminish the value that we ascribe to their lives, even subjecting their lives to total erasure from our epistemological horizon. When we "frame" lives in

---

[5] Judith Butler, *Frames of War: When is Life Grievable?* (New York: Verso, 2016).

derogatory ways or leave them out of the frame altogether, we fail to perceive these lives as grievable. In other words, we judge these lives to be unworthy of care and of love.[6]

The question of when life is grievable is not only a question of love but also fundamentally one of conscience. Our perceptions of lives as being worthy or unworthy of mourning engages our affective drives. These drives, in turn, orient and energize our ethical considerations and actions.[7] To perceive a life as valuable, and thus the loss of that life as grievable, catalyzes an emotive responsiveness on the part of the perceiver. This initial responsiveness, Butler argues, brings with it the offer (even the demand) of responsibility. Our appraisals of the grievableness of life shape our understanding of to whom and to what we are responsible.

It bears emphasizing that no person exercises complete control in determining the ways in which they frame the lives of others. Our perception of whose life is worth mourning is always significantly shaped by the cultural and ideological formations that discipline our own internal value systems. As Butler writes, "Our affect is never merely our own: affect is, from the start, communicated from elsewhere."[8] This observation is particularly pertinent for the present study. It points to the influence that the communities, institutions, and ethos that comprise and orient Catholic education can have on learners formed by this system of education. Institutions and communities of Catholic education play a vital role in cultivating the effect of their constituents. They help these constituents (students, teachers, administrators, parents, etc.) discern who and what is worth loving, who and what is worth grieving. Indeed, the cultivation of these evaluative frameworks might be understood as the most important task of a system of moral education.

In her own work in reflecting on the grievableness of life, Butler does not focus on questions pertaining to environmental ethics. Instead, her reflections are prompted by, and center on, the initiation of the United States's purported "war on terror." Thus, Butler examines how the administration of George W. Bush, in its attempt to justify the violence it sanctioned, deployed various

---

6 Ibid., 6–12 and 23–29.

7 For a helpful discussion of the recent insights of moral psychology into the relationship between the affective and rational dimensions of human conscience, see Stephen J. Pope, "Conscience, Catholicism, and the New Science of Morality" in *Conscience and Catholicism: Rights, Responsibilities, and Institutional Responses*, ed. David E. DeCosse and Kristin E. Heyer (Maryknoll, NY: Orbis Books, 2015), esp. 39–43.

8 Butler, *Frames of War*, 50.

sociopolitical and cultural mechanisms and strategies in order to depict millions of lives (of predominantly brown bodies) as essentially ungrievable. Nonetheless, Butler's observations with regard to how the framing of life gives rise to both affective and ethical responses are particularly germane to my concerns here. In order to understand why this is the case, I turn to consider the influential critique of the Judeo-Christian worldview proffered by the twentieth-century historian of science Lynn White Jr.

Ecological Consciousness and the Problem of the Christian Imagination

In his 1967 essay, "The Historical Roots of Our Ecologic Crisis," White argues that the Judeo-Christian worldview is the fundamental cause of the widespread human-induced ecological degradation that arises in the modern era. "Christianity," he argues, "is the most anthropocentric religion the world has seen." For White, the Christian way of seeing, especially in its Western forms, endows only humans with any sort of inherent value amongst creation. Thus, Christianity's ethos has "insisted that it is God's will that man exploit nature for his proper ends."[9] This ethos, continues White, came to exert significant cultural and sociopolitical influence over the West, sanctioning and sanctifying the West's historical projects of environmental abuse and exploitation so that, by the middle of the twentieth century, these historical projects had pushed the world into a state of emergency.

Set in Butler's terms, White maintains that the Christian worldview frames reality so as to render only human life grievable. Per White, Christianity engenders a way of perceiving nonhuman life (as well as the nonhuman elements that comprise the myriad ecosystems of the biosphere) that renders it innately unworthy of human love, care, and affection. Thus, the Christian worldview dampens, or even deadens, the affective and ethical connections and concerns that persons and communities might develop for nonhuman creation. Within this milieu of vitiated concern for that which is not human, societies have unleashed veritable wars of domination against the earth without evoking moral outrage from its (Westernized) peoples.

---

    [9] Lynn White Jr., "The Historical Roots of Our Ecologic Crisis," *Science* 155 (1967): 1205. I have left the gendered language here without augment since the Christian worldview throughout much of its traditions has been and remains problematically androcentric.

White's argument raises clear difficulties when considering how Catholic education might contribute to the development of an ecologically responsive conscience. If the communities of faith and learning that are formed by Catholic education are meant to be rooted in and oriented by the Christian imagination and the truth claims that form this imagination, one must ask whether it is possible for these communities to develop consciences capable of feeling aggrieved by the "cry of the earth" that rises up amidst the planetary emergency. Thus, the question emerges, "Can the Christian imagination be of moral and ethical aid in our contemporary planetary context?" In responding to this query, it is helpful to begin by noting that, while White's depiction of the Christian worldview is in some ways instructive (a point to which I return below), his analysis fails to account for many nuances within the Christian worldview and its diverse traditions.

White's claim regarding the radical anthropocentrism of the Christian worldview simply cannot be sustained when one considers the deeply rooted theological traditions that affirm the inherent value of the created order. From the earliest development of its tradition, Catholic Christian theology has confessed that creation is a good and beautiful gift given freely by God. Indeed, this confession echoes God's own judgment of the created order as it is articulated in the first chapter of Genesis—God saw that "it was good" (Gen 1:1–2:3). Moreover, the Catholic Christian tradition affirms that creation, in its goodness and beauty, offers praise to God. Thus, creation exists fundamentally because of and for God.

The Catholic Christian tradition, moreover, avers that the goodness and beauty of creation reflect, in manifold ways, something of God's own goodness and beauty. The medieval theologian Hugh of Saint Victor captures this view well, writing, "This whole sensible world is like a book written by the finger of God, that is, created by the divine power, and individual creatures are like certain characters invented *not by human judgment*, but by divine choice to manifest and to signify in some way the invisible wisdom of God."[10] As such, the created order should be understood in broadly sacramental terms. Creation is revelatory of the Divine.[11] This way of seeing, then, stands in stark contrast to White's presentation of the Christian worldview. From the perspective of these traditions, the whole of creation participates

---

[10] Hugh of St. Victor, "The Three Days of Invisible Light," cited in Jame Schaefer, *Theological Foundations for Environmental Ethics: Reconstructing Patristic and Medieval Concepts* (Washington, DC: Georgetown University, 2009), 74–75.

[11] See Schaefer, *Theological Foundations for Environmental Ethics*, 65–102.

in the goodness of God. Accordingly, it is not only the human person that is worthy of care and concern, but all of creation. On this account, nonhuman life is inherently grievable and demands a loving responsiveness on the part of human persons (particularly, one might add, when that life and the systems that support that life are rendered precarious by destructive societal norms and practices).

Nonetheless, White's critical account of the Christian worldview cannot be entirely dismissed. There are characteristics of the Catholic Christian tradition that, when taken in isolation, can orient persons and communities of faith toward a problematically anthropocentric view of the world and, by extension, contribute to the development of a destructively anthropocentric conscience. Particularly germane, here, is the Christian understanding of the vocation to love, which stands at the center of Christian life.

When a scribe asks Jesus to identify the greatest of the commandments, Jesus responds by citing Deuteronomy and Leviticus, saying,

> "The first is this: 'Hear, O Israel! The Lord our God is Lord alone! You shall love the Lord your God with all your heart, with all your soul, with all your mind, and with all your strength.' Jesus, then, continues, proclaiming, "The second is this: 'You shall love your neighbor as yourself.' There is no other commandment greater than these" (Mk 12:29–31).

From Jesus's response arises an important line of moral thought that numerous Christian thinkers have developed over the centuries. This tradition emphasizes both the close relationship between love of God and love of neighbor and the centrality of these two loves to the Christian life. The connection between the love of God and the love of neighbor is stressed, for example, in Augustine's reflections on moral and political theology.[12] This connection is likewise of central concern to the Thomistic tradition of moral thought.[13] In recent decades, various strands of liberation theology have underscored the closeness of the relationship between love of God and love of neighbor. Along these lines, Gustavo Gutiérrez writes that it is not enough to say that love of

---

[12] See Tarsicius J. Van Bavel, "Love," in *Augustine through the Ages: An Encyclopedia*, ed. Allan D. Fitzgerald (Grand Rapids: Eerdmans, 1999).

[13] The literature on Thomas Aquinas's conception of charity is vast. For a helpful overview of Thomas's thought on the subject, see Meghan J. Clark, "Love of God and Neighbor: Living Charity in Aquinas' Ethics," *New Blackfriars* 92 (2011): 415–30.

God is closely related to love of neighbor. Rather, Gutiérrez avers that love of God is expressed *through* love of neighbor, so that the two loves, though distinct, are fundamentally inseparable.[14] Even more recently, in reflecting upon a personalist conception of conscience, James Keenan writes that the Christian conscience is to be formed "in the pursuit of the good, animated by its call to love God, self, and neighbor." Here, one can note that Keenan modifies the standard terms of the Great Commandment to include the love of self within the moral framework he develops. He does so not to endorse selfish individualism, but rather to caution against the distortions and dangers of destructive self-hatred. Nonetheless, in his formulation, Keenan retains an emphasis on the love of God and neighbor. He goes on to affirm that conscience organizes "the way that the disciple hears and responds to the triple command to love through virtue."[15]

With regard to the vocation to love, then, one finds that White's critique of the Christian worldview acquires purchase. Throughout the Christian tradition, persons and communities of faith have consistently articulated the vocation to love in terms that, perhaps unintentionally, render the dignity of nonhuman creation invisible or, at least, of little concern. If one were to judge the tradition solely by its discourses on the call to love, they could conclude that nonhuman life is ungrievable and that the Christian worldview is unambiguously anthropocentric in its orientation. "Blessed are those who mourn for their human neighbors," the Christian tradition seems to affirm with regard to the vocation to love, but as to the cries of the earth, one can remain apathetic.

Modernity, Catholic Social Thought, and the Concept of Integral Ecology

In light of the foregoing analysis, it is apparent that the Catholic Christian tradition contains a tension with regard to its understanding of the value of creation. On the one hand, the tradition has consistently affirmed the beauty and goodness of the created order, understood the created order as a gift from God, and affirmed that this order, through its very being, both praises God's

---

[14] Gustavo Gutiérrez, *A Theology of Liberation: History, Politics, and Salvation*, 15th Anniversary Edition, trans. Caridad Inda and John Eagleson (Maryknoll, NY: Orbis Books, 1988), 114–15.

[15] James F. Keenan, "To Follow and to Form over Time: A Phenomenology of Conscience," in DeCosse and Heyer, *Conscience and Catholicism*, 12–13.

goodness and communicates something of that goodness to humanity. In these ways, the Christian imagination appears strikingly dissimilar to White's description of the Christian worldview. On the other hand, the Catholic Christian tradition has consistently marginalized, or left underdeveloped, concern with regard to the human person's responsibility to care lovingly for creation. Within traditional discourse on the Christian vocation to love, the love of earth does not appear to be of similar significance, or even related concern, to the love of God and neighbor. It bears emphasizing that, for much of the history of Christian thought, the sacramental strand of the tradition (which affirms the goodness of the created order) could be relied upon to correct traditional ways of conceptualizing the vocation to love. The vision of creation as sacramental implicitly required humans to approach creation with a posture of loving care.

At this juncture, it is important to observe that the emergence of Modernity in the West significantly marginalized the sacramental vision of the Catholic Christian tradition and, in so doing, greatly impaired the Christian imagination's ability to render nonhuman creation grievable. With the onset of Modernity—typified with the rise of the Enlightenment, the development of modern scientific epistemologies, the inception of classical economic theory, and the implementation of extractive colonial political economies—the dominant social imaginary of the West consistently construed nonhuman creation in instrumental terms. In other words, within the Modern Western imagination, the earth and the creatures of the earth appear as inherently valueless entities that humans are free to exploit and manipulate for their own ends (often for the maximization of profit). This view radically desacralizes nature.

The entanglement of the Christian imagination with that of Modernity—an entanglement that is deep and complex[16]—has tended to suppress the creation-embracing strands of the former. The traditional Catholic Christian way of seeing creation in sacramental terms largely became absorbed by a technocratic worldview that envisioned the world merely as brute matter. When this absorption occurred, it significantly weakened the ability of the Christian imagination to problematize or expand the narrow scope of the Christian vocation to love. As a result, the modern Western Christian imagi-

---

[16] For an important critical examination of these entanglements both with regard to race and place, see Willie James Jennings, *The Christian Imagination: Theology and the Origins of Race* (New Haven, CT: Yale University, 2011). See also Ileana M. Porras, "Appropriating Nature: Commerce, Property and the Commodification of Nature in the Law of Nations," *Leiden Journal of International Law* 27 (2014): 641–60.

nation became increasingly constrained in its capacity to form consciences sensitive to ecological concern.

Indeed, one finds the diminishment of concern for nonhuman creation reflected in the development of Catholic social teaching in the middle of the twentieth century, where the love of God and the love of neighbor are often construed over and against concern for nonhuman creation. For example, when, in *Populorum Progressio*, Pope Paul VI calls for the cultivation of "true development" (which has subsequently been interpreted as "integral development") amongst the peoples of the world, he articulates a vision of development that responds not only to the economic needs of the human communities but the cultural and spiritual needs of these communities as well.[17] Moreover, Paul VI's vision of integral development finds both its source and fullest realization in communion with God. Evident in Paul VI's vision, then, is a strong sense of the link between love of God and neighbor. Equally notable, however, is the instrumentalized and dominative language that the pope employs when discussing the earth. He writes, "In the very first pages of Scripture we read these words: 'Fill the earth and subdue it.' This teaches us that the whole of creation is for man, that he has been charged to give it meaning by his intelligent activity, to complete and perfect it by his own efforts and to his own advantage."[18] Similarly, Paul VI lauds the ways in which church missionary work has taught indigenous communities "how to take full advantage of natural resources."[19] In short, while working to unite the love of God and the love of neighbor, Paul VI embraces a technocratic vision of nonhuman creation, framing nonhuman creation in a manner that renders creation a mere "it."[20]

To be sure, not all strands of modern Catholic social thought have embraced Modernity's dominative way of perceiving the earth in instrumentalist terms. To their credit, the teachings of Pope John Paul II and Pope Benedict XVI increasingly sought to recover and foreground the sacramental imagination of the Catholic Christian tradition as a way of denouncing humanity's unrelenting exploitation of the earth.[21] Numerous bishops and

[17] Pope Paul VI, *Populorum Progressio*—"On the Development of Peoples" (1967), esp. 1–42, www.vatican.va.

[18] Ibid., no. 22.

[19] Ibid., no. 12.

[20] On this point see Michael J. Himes and Kenneth R. Himes, "The Sacrament of Creation: Toward an Environmental Theology," *Commonweal* (January 26, 1990), www.commonwealmagazine.org/sacrament-creation-toward-environmental-theology.

[21] See, for example, Jame Schaefer and Tobias Winwright, eds., *Environmental*

theologians have developed similar arguments.[22] These works of recovery and resistance have found a recent highwater mark in Pope Francis's encyclical *Laudato Si': On Care for Our Common Home*. In *Laudato Si'*, Francis responds explicitly to the unfolding planetary emergency.[23] In so doing, he elaborates a vision of the Christian faith that places human responsiveness to the travail of creation at the heart of Christian discipleship while also rejecting wholly instrumentalizing modes of relating to nonhuman creation.

At the center of *Laudato Si'* is Pope Francis's call for the construction of "integral ecology." The concept of integral ecology is a politico-ecological concept. It refers specifically to Francis's vision of a world in which human persons, in accordance with God's desire, organize their cultures and societies so as to hear and respond to the interrelated cries of the earth and poor. For Francis, integral ecology is made manifest when both the preferential options for the earth and the poor—options that the pope understands as fundamentally interrelated—are enacted and incarnated in the world. Thus, with the concept of integral ecology, Francis expands upon Paul VI's vision of integral development which, as I just observed, marginalized concern for creation. The concept of integral ecology exists in continuity with that of integral development in that both resist reductive economic conceptions of development. However, in discontinuity with the thought of Paul VI, Francis's concept places concern for nonhuman creation at the center of its framework.

In a manner that resonates with the arguments of his most recent papal predecessors, Francis locates the impetus for the cultivation of an integral ecology (or at least the "environmental" dimension of integral ecology) in the recovery of a sacramental vision of the world. The pope calls communities of

---

Justice and Climate Change: Assessing Pope Benedict XVI's Ecological Vision for the Catholic Church in the United States (Lanham, MD: Lexington Books, 2013). I should hasten to add that many of the teachings of these popes are enmeshed in, or at least not sufficiently critical of, the Eurocentric, sexist, and racist logics of what decolonial theorists describe as "the colonial matrix of power." As such, the virtues of these teachings ought to be critically affirmed. For a discussion of the ways in which racism, sexism, and anthropocentrism are entangled within the colonial matrix of power, see Walter Mignolo, "The Invention of the *Human* and the Three Pillars of the Colonial Matrix of Power: Racism, Sexism, and Nature," in Walter D. Mignolo and Catherine E. Walsh, *On Decoloniality: Concepts, Analytics, Praxis* (Durham, NC: Duke University, 2018), 153–76.

[22] The scholarship in this area in recent decades is immense. See, for example, the work of Denis Edwards.

[23] Pope Francis, *Laudato Si': On Care for Our Common Home* (2015), www.vatican.va. Hereinafter *LS*.

faith to cultivate a way of seeing creation that patterns itself after the loving "gazes" of St. Francis and Jesus, who both perceived the gratuitous goodness of God endowed in the earth and its creatures.[24] In relearning to perceive the beauty and goodness of creation, the pope charges persons and communities of faith to become "painfully aware"[25]—*aggrieved*, to use Butler's terminology—of the damage that human societies have wrought upon the earth when acting in accordance with the logic of "the technocratic paradigm." Thus, in *Laudato Si'*, Francis recovers and foregrounds a robust understanding of the Catholic sacramental imagination, framing nonhuman creation as intrinsically grievable and worthy of human responsiveness. Perhaps even more importantly, however, is the manner in which Pope Francis develops an argument in his encyclical that connects the love of earth to the Great Commandment.

The Symbol Gives Rise to Affect: Grounding Christian Ecological Conscience

The most theologically significant passages in *Laudato Si'* are found in Francis's engagement with "the wisdom of the biblical accounts" in the encyclical's second chapter. The pope's interpretation of the early chapters of Genesis are of particular importance for understanding how the Christian imagination can inform the cultivation of an ecologically sensitive conscience. There, Francis affirms that the symbolism of the narratives of Genesis portrays human life as "grounded in three fundamental and closely intertwined relationships: with God, with our neighbor, and with the earth itself."[26] Francis repudiates any interpretation of Scripture that would suggest God calls the human person to dominate creation, as White maintains.[27] Instead, the Pope highlights the significance of God's call to the human person in the second creation narrative of Genesis. There, God gives the human person the vocation "to 'till and keep' the garden of the world."[28] As the pope explains, "'keeping' means caring, protecting, overseeing, and preserving." In short, for Francis, the act of "keeping" connotes extending the actions of love to nonhuman

---

[24] Ibid., no. 11 and nos. 96–100.

[25] Ibid., no. 19.

[26] Ibid., no. 66.

[27] In "The Historical Roots of Our Ecologic Crisis," White never directly references the language of dominion and subjugation found in Genesis 1. However, that language is commonly connected to the critique he advances.

[28] *LS*, no. 67.

creation within the garden of the world. To draw further upon the imagery of
Genesis, God calls the human person to the symbolic vocation of "gardener,"
inviting the human person to care lovingly for the soil and all that comes from
the soil.[29] In the fulfillment of the vocation of gardener, the three intertwined
relationships fundamental to human existence are brought to perfection
through this threefold work of loving care. Indeed, one finds in the second
creation account that the human person's love of God is expressed through the
loves of neighbor and earth with the latter two loves as closely related as the
human person is to the soil itself.

If Pope Francis's interpretation of the second creation narrative of Genesis
intimates that God creates the human person to live in loving communion
with God, neighbor, and earth, then the pope's subsequent reading of Cain's
murder of Abel underscores, albeit in negative terms, this threefold call to
love. Moreover, here, Francis echoes Keenan's previously cited formulation by
also including a rightly ordered love of self as vital to the vocation to love. As
the pope writes, "In the story of Cain and Abel, we see how envy led Cain to
commit the ultimate injustice against his brother, which in turn ruptured the
relationship between Cain and God, and between Cain and the earth from
which he was banished." Pope Francis continues, observing, "Disregard for
the duty to cultivate and maintain a proper relationship with my neighbor,
for whose care and custody I am responsible, ruins my relationship with my
own self, with others, with God and with the earth. When all these relationships are neglected, when justice no longer dwells in the land, the Bible tells
us that life itself is endangered."[30] Here, Francis's interpretation of the Cain

---

[29] In the second creation account, God plants a garden in the fertile soil and forms
the human and the other living creatures out of those same soils. Although it is true that
the primordial woman is formed out of the rib of the primordial human and not out
of the earth itself, this should not be interpreted as creating a separation between the
woman and the soil. After all, the rib itself is composed of soil. The call to care for the
soil and all that comes from the soil, should be interpreted as including the woman as
both an object and agent of care. Rejecting any interpretation of this passage that would
suggest a subordinate or derivative status of the woman to the man, I affirm Phyllis
Trible's view that the rib signifies "solidarity and equality" between human sexes. See
Phyllis Trible, "Eve and Adam: Genesis 2–3 Re-read," *Andover Newton Quarterly* 13, no.
4 (1973): 253. Along these same lines, the vocation of gardener should be ascribed to
all human persons regardless of their sex. Moreover, especially in view of the patriarchal
and misogynist character of so much of the Christian imagination, the earth should not
be coded "female" in contemporary interpretations of this text.

[30] *LS*, no. 70.

and Abel narrative elucidates a vital point that, too often, has been overlooked in exegesis and moral reflection: the human person's sinful failure to love not only warps and violates the person's relationships with God and neighbor but with the earth as well.[31] Moreover, these distinct relationships are once again depicted not in separate and isolated terms, but rather as intimately interwoven with one another.

In the late twentieth century, the philosopher of language Paul Ricoeur made famous the dictum, "the symbol gives rise to thought."[32] For Ricoeur, thought and critical reflection emerge from the symbolic systems that are always at work within human cognition, mediating the human person's encounter with reality. In light of Butler's foregoing observations, we might expand upon Ricoeur's insight and affirm that the symbol also gives rise to affect. In other words, symbols play vital roles in framing for human persons and communities what aspects of reality are grievable or ungrievable, what things are worthy of love or suitable for neglect. In *Laudato Si'*, Pope Francis's retrieval of key symbols from the narratives of Genesis frame not only human persons as worthy of care but also the earth itself. The symbol of gardener intimates the human person's fundamental responsibility to the soil and all that comes from it. Likewise, the encyclical's interpretation of the symbol of sin underscores the grave losses that occur when this responsibility is neglected or perverted.

It bears noting that this symbolic construal of the vocation to love coheres well with the broader sacramental vision of creation discussed above. The goodness and sacramental character of nonhuman creation make plain that creation is worthy of human care and concern. Thus, in broadening the traditional understanding of the vocation to love and in affirming creation's sacramentality, *Laudato Si'* constructs a way of perceiving the world that demands human responsiveness not only to the cry of the poor but to the cry of the earth as well. Indeed, one finds that this way of seeing provides a manner of structuring both Christian affectivity and conscience so as to orient these faculties toward the desire to work toward the realization of integral ecology in history.

---

[31] Here, Francis also emphasizes a healthful relationship to oneself in a manner that echoes Keenan's previous affirmation of the positive role that a healthful love of self plays in the Christian life.

[32] Paul Ricoeur, *The Symbolism of Evil*, trans. Emerson Buchanan (Boston: Beacon Press, 1967), 347–57.

Conclusion: Catholic Education and
the Cultivation of a Christian Eco-Social Conscience

In this essay, I have argued that despite its ambiguous historical legacy, Christianity has within its traditions, narratives, and symbol systems, the resources from which to cultivate an ecologically responsive conscience. Indeed, I have maintained that *Laudato Si'* presents a vision of the Christian faith that locates at the very heart of the faith the need to cultivate this conscience. A vital task for Catholic education, then, is to work to form this conscience within its various constituent members.

In light of the unfolding planetary emergency and in view of the vision outlined in *Laudato Si'*, it may appear tempting to suggest that institutions of Catholic education each work to develop a "center of integral ecology" or run programs that explore this concept. This, in my view, falls short of what is required. Rather than constructing centers and programs that reflect upon the significance and demands of integral ecology, it is imperative that institutions of Catholic education *become* centers that both promote and embody integral ecology—centers where every facet of education is oriented toward responding to God through hearing and responding to the interrelated cries of the earth and poor.[33] Accordingly, the subject matter in math, the natural sciences, the social sciences, and the humanities should be intentionally and explicitly organized to help make manifest the preferential options for the earth and poor. Likewise, Catholic institutions of education must work to organize the buildings they inhabit, the lands upon which they dwell, their modes of consumption, and their financial investments, in ways that honor the integrity of creation. In order to ground and energize these tasks, these institutions of faith and learning must simultaneously work to develop the consciences of their constituents in ways that cohere with the symbol of "the gardener." That is to say, these institutions must work to cultivate structures of affect and thought that perceive the underlying unity between the love of God, neighbor, earth, and self, and likewise become aggrieved at the manifold

---

[33] Along these lines, the establishment of centers or institutions of integral ecology that are housed within schools or universities, *might* be taken as hopeful signs that these schools are moving toward realizing Francis's vision of an integral ecology. However, this phenomenon might also be a well-intended symptom of greenwashing—making a public facing show of virtue while the broader institution continues to form persons in accordance with the regnant neoliberal, technocratic, and neocolonial ideologies.

sufferings caused from the failure to love. Within the context of the planetary emergency and in response to God's call, these institutions and their constituents, by virtue of their very identity, would respond with acute sensitivity and urgency to the cries of the of earth and poor.

THE CONSCIENCE OF A
CATHOLIC FEMINIST WORKING
IN CATHOLIC EDUCATION

Julie Hanlon Rubio

Standing before my students, I meet them as a theologian, a professor, a formator of future ministers, and that increasingly rare commodity—a feminist who stays in the Catholic Church. I teach in Berkeley, California, a place where most religious progressives of any kind left long ago for yoga, meditation, brunch, or politics. Most of my students share my feminist worries about the church. In teaching them the theology I love, I am also teaching them how to remain within an imperfect system, a system that I, in some way, represent. I aim to give them hope, to encourage their vocations. Yet I am teaching them by example what it means to live with compromise. They are looking at me. They want to know, "How can I work it out in my head and heart?" They interrupt my lectures on this or that theologian. "But what do you think? What do you believe?"

In over twenty-five years working in Catholic education, I have known many Catholics who struggle with questions of conscience, but today the question of Catholic identity seems the most pressing conscience issue of all. The question is not, "Can I do this?" but "Can I be this?" A large majority of Catholics affirm their right to disagree with church teaching while remaining "good Catholics."[1] Only a minority attend Mass weekly; the rest have different ideas about what good Catholics do.[2] The tougher question for progressives is whether to continue to claim identification with a flawed institution. Many ask, "Is it possible for me to identify with a church that, while doing much

---

[1] Hart Research Associates, "The Shriver Report Snapshot: Catholics in America," http://www.shrivermedia.com/wp-content/uploads/2015/09/Key-Findings-from-Poll-of-Catholics.pdf, p. 7.

[2] CARA, "Frequently Asked Questions: U.S. Data Over Time," https://cara.georgetown.edu.

good in the world, also teaches harmful falsehoods and neglects serious evil?"[3] These questions become particularly salient for those whose very identity places them in tension with Catholic teaching and practice—LGBTQ Catholics, Black Catholics, and, the subject of this essay, feminist Catholics.[4]

Given widespread acknowledgment of the Catholic-feminist identity dilemma, especially among educators and other "professional Catholics," its neglect in the literature on conscience is puzzling. In the last several decades, with some notable exceptions, academic discourse on conscience has been dominated by men, so this may partially explain the gap.[5] Catholic feminist theologians have considered the question extensively, but conscience is not the primary language they use to describe the dilemma of their existence. Feminist identity thus presents an interesting case study for Catholic thought on conscience, an opportunity to expand a long and substantial conversation in the tradition. In this essay, I attempt to fill in the gap by examining themes in the recent literature on conscience (as inner sanctuary, well-formed, a process of coming to judgment, integrity, and a source of creative praxis) in order to narrate the struggle of a feminist seeking an authentic way to stand within institutional Catholicism.

Why Answering the Catholic Feminist Question Is Harder Now

Feminist theologians have offered many answers since the question first arose: Staying is the only way to change the institution. The church is mine and I won't leave. It's a part of me, my family, and my community. I love the liturgy and the sacraments, the incense, the gospel choir, Guadalupe. I believe in the Catholic social justice tradition and find inspiration in its saints and movements. The center—Jesus, the Eucharist, the church, the call to love—is true and, with feminist revisioning, rings true for me. Books of the 1980s and 1990s offered Catholic women paths "beyond anger" for living with a patriarchal tradition "beyond patching."[6] Though some women moved "beyond

---

[3] See, e.g., Rebecca Bratten Weiss, "Who Speaks for the Church?," *Patheos*, Jan. 31, 2021, www.patheos.com, on owning the complicity of being a practicing Catholic.

[4] See, e.g., Jim McDermott, "A Place for Us: On Being Gay in the Priesthood," *National Catholic Reporter*, January 26, 2021, www.ncronline.org; and Diana L. Hayes and Cyprian Davis, eds., *Taking Down Our Harps: Black Catholics in the United States* (Maryknoll, NY: Orbis Books, 1998).

[5] For an overview, see James F. Keenan, "Redeeming Conscience," *Theological Studies* 76, no. 1 (2015): 129–47.

[6] See, e.g., Maria Riley, *Transforming Feminism* (New York: Sheed & Ward, 1989);

God the father," right out of the church, most of those Catholic feminists stayed, and even today when more are leaving, a large majority remain.[7]

Though they have wrestled with the Catholic-feminist identity question for decades, few feminist theologians identify their dilemma as a matter of conscience, and even fewer focus their energy on this question. In a collection of essays titled, *Women's Consciousness, Women's Conscience: A Reader in Feminist Ethics*, three early Christian feminist ethicists bring feminist consciousness to bear on ethics (or matters of conscience). While rightly recognizing the need for women's voices in ethics and calling for feminist critique of "education, politics, laws, and religion," they include no essay addressing the central quandary of feminists like themselves who stay in a sexist church.[8] As in much feminist writing, consciousness is a more important category than conscience, and the use of conscience is evocative rather than technical. Combining women's experience, feminist theory, social analysis, and the best of their religious traditions, they turn their ethical lens outward. Like other progressives, they resolve the tension of conflicting identities by combining elements of both, bracketing neuralgic issues, and focusing on broader social concerns.

But as Notre Dame professor Mary Catherine Hilkert argued in a 1993 essay, "Experience and Tradition: Can the Center Hold?," it is not clear that the resolution upon which Catholic feminists like these relied can be sustained.[9] Feminist scholars have made the arguments for better interpretation of Scripture and tradition, more embodied sacramental theology, more varied God language, less hierarchical ecclesiology, more nuanced moral

---

Carolyn Osiek, *Beyond Anger: On Being a Feminist in the Church* (Mahwah, NJ: Paulist, 1986); and Sandra M. Schneiders, *Beyond Patching: Faith and Feminism in the Catholic Church* (Mahwah, NJ: Paulist, 1991, rev. ed. 2004).

[7] See Mary Daly, *Beyond God the Father: Toward a Philosophy of Women's Liberation* (Boston: Beacon Press, 1973); and Mary J. Henold, *Catholic and Feminist: The Surprising History of the American Catholic Feminist Movement* (Chapel Hill: University of North Carolina Press, 2008). Recent surveys show lower levels of religious practice among Millenial Catholic women, but only a small number consider leaving. See Mark M. Gray and Mary L. Gautier, "Proud to Be Catholic? A Groundbreaking Survey Asks Women about Their Lives in the Church," *America* (January 28, 2018), 12, www.americamagazine.org.

[8] Barbara Hilkert Andolsen, Christine E. Gudorf, and Mary D. Pellaur, eds., *Women's Consciousness, Women's Conscience: A Reader in Feminist Ethics* (San Francisco: Harper & Row, 1985).

[9] Mary Catherine Hilkert, "Experience and Tradition: Can the Center Hold?," in *Freeing Theology: The Essentials of Theology in Feminist Perspective*, ed. Catherine Mowry LaCugna (San Francisco: Harper, 1993), 59–82.

theology, and more inclusive liturgical practice, but daily life in Catholic institutions shows little evidence that decades of Catholic feminist thought has been received. Catholic feminists continue to identify with a tradition they hope will change, but change is not forthcoming.

In recent decades, the dilemma has deepened along with our sense of what it means to be a responsible, authentic self. Theologian Andrew Prevot argues that philosopher Charles Taylor captures something essential in naming the modern "ethics of authenticity," which shapes the individual search for a meaningful life. Prevot suggests that Black people, as well as women and other marginalized groups are similarly—if not equally—blocked from becoming their true, free selves even now, when authentic selfhood has never been more important.[10] Today, more than ever, we feel responsible for what we identify as and with, for the persons we become and the relationships we maintain. We feel obligated to disentangle ourselves from complicity with unjust institutions. Being a Catholic feminist is harder now, but Catholic literature on conscience, despite its inattention to this particular dilemma, can illuminate the feminist quest for authentic selfhood.

Conscience as Inner Sanctuary

"I close my eyes," my student said one day in Feminist Theology class. In our chapel, the walls are bare; there are no icons or statues of Mary or other holy women. The human faces in our school of theology and ministry are mostly male. She closes her eyes so that she can participate in the Eucharist she loves without drowning in ambient maleness. Other women use the inclusive language they long to hear—silently. Some continue to identify as Catholic, though the thought of entering a church right now, given their disagreement with teachings on sex and gender, is unbearable. All of these women might be seen as summoning conscience as sanctuary.

At Vatican II, the centrality of conscience was recovered from long roots in the Catholic tradition while its interiority was stressed. James Keenan describes how European theologians concerned about the cooperation of Catholics with Nazi Germany and fascist Italy insisted on individual claims to know the truth apart from external authority, and on the moral agency

---

[10] Andrew Prevot, "Sources of a Black Self: Ethics of Authenticity," in *Anti-Blackness and Christian Ethics*, ed. Vincent W. Lloyd and Andrew Prevot (Maryknoll, NY: Orbis Books, 2017), 85.

that flows from internal conviction toward responsibility.[11] In the famous paragraph number 16 of *Gaudium et Spes*, conscience is described as a secret core or sanctuary where we are alone with God whose voice echoes in our depths.[12] In this place, we are called to good, away from evil. We experience a pull to do this, not that; to stand here, not there; to speak truth rather than to lie. Recently, Pope Francis acknowledged that this long-standing Catholic teaching has not always been clearly affirmed or communicated. "We have been called to form consciences, not replace them," he said, suggesting a movement beyond the ecclesial propensity to identify the dignity of conscience with its conformity to church teaching.[13] In expanding the space for conscience, Francis has also underlined the need to approach the holy ground of the other with reverence and respect.[14]

In secular feminist thought, women have long claimed the need for space to nurture a sense of self and listen to the voice within. In 1929, Virginia Woolf tried to answer the question of why so few women have been writers. For a woman "to have a room of her own, let alone a quiet or sound proof room, was out of the question," she wrote.[15] Occupied by serving the needs of others, and told repeatedly of their lack of suitability for the creative arts, few women have had the experience of "freeing whole and entire the work that is in [them]" so that "the poetry flows from them," as it does for the best artists.[16] Nearly forty years later Tillie Olsen would write of the silences that remain in history because women were so busy being "the angel in the house" that they had no time for creative work of their own.[17] Around the same time, Betty Friedan looked closely at "the feminine mystique," the pervasive belief that women should be fulfilled by their role in the home, and at its devastating effects on the many women who wanted more in life than housework and parenting.[18] In these representative voices of liberal feminism, lies an implicit

---

[11]   Keenan, "Redeeming Conscience," 133–35.

[12]   Pope John XXIII, *Gaudium et Spes*— "The Pastoral Constitution on the Church in the Modern World," no. 16 (1965), www.vatican.va. Hereinafter *GS*.

[13]   Pope Francis, *Amoris Laetitia*— "The Joy of Love," no. 37 (2015), www.vatican. va. Hereinafter *AL*.

[14]   Pope Francis, *Evangelii Gaudium*— "The Joy of the Gospel," no. 169 (2013), www.vatican.va.

[15]   Virginia Wolfe, *A Room of One's Own* (New York: Harcourt Brace, Jovanovich, 1929), 54.

[16]   Ibid., 58.

[17]   Tillie Olsen, *Silences* (New York: Dell, 1965).

[18]   Betty Friedan, *The Feminine Mystique* (New York: Dell, 1963).

recognition of a stirring deep within that needs to be recognized, respected, and given space to grow.

Catholic feminists, too, have identified a space within from which strong convictions arise, though they differ from their secular sisters in connecting interiority with the Divine. Anne Patrick identifies the law written on the human heart as "the presence in us of the Holy Spirit."[19] Linda Hogan calls for a "personalist theology of conscience," rooted in recognition of "an individual's personal discernment of the Spirit in moral matters," an imperfect church, and a living tradition.[20] Both hoped that a better theology of conscience would ground mature faith and make space for authentic belonging.

Catholic feminists stand within the tradition of Catholic thought on conscience, claiming an interior space of their own and engaging in responsible critique of the tradition. While appreciating the depth of interiority recovered by contemporary Catholicism, they insist on recalling that the authors of *Gaudium et Spes* in 1965, in the heart of the second wave of the women's movement, did not see anything problematic about framing their discussion with androcentric language ("In the depths of his conscience, man detects a law which he does not impose upon himself, but which holds him to obedience."). Conscience as interiority gives Catholic feminists space to be, to speak out, and to grow.

Conscience as Formed and Malformed

Neither the Catholic tradition nor Catholic feminists hold a view of conscience as the voice within that reveals to the individual her truth full stop, and this commonality can ground authentic Catholic feminist identity. In the Catholic tradition a good conscience is not formed in isolation. Rather, it is relational, nurtured through encounters with other human beings (as "Christians are joined with the rest of men in the search for truth") and via encounter with Christ (for "only in the mystery of the incarnate Word does the mystery of man take on light").[21] Though Pope Francis urges respect for the conscience-based decisions of adult Catholics, he also affirms the church's part in forming the consciences of the faithful.[22] For

---

[19] Anne E. Patrick, *Liberating Conscience* (New York: Continuum, 1996), 178.

[20] Linda Hogan, *Confronting the Truth: Conscience in the Catholic Tradition* (Mahwah, NJ: Paulist, 2000), 189–90.

[21] *GS* nos.16, 22.

[22] *AL* no. 37.

Catholics, just because something feels right to me does not make it right. Ignorance (vincible or invincible) can lead to an erroneous conscience.[23] A believer is both obligated to form her conscience and duty-bound to follow conscience once duly formed. Because moral discernment is about striving to love, the obligation to better form conscience, so that the "intellect and will . . . enrich and deepen this permanent power to love within the recesses of the soul" is serious.[24]

Recent writing on conscience in theological ethics suggests that the work of formation is harder than we once thought. Bryan Massingale argues that Catholics have been slow to realize the pernicious influence of cultural forces shaping our perceptions and emotions.[25] Responsible conscience formation means working to overcome the unconscious bias that allows white people to remain unmoved by the social evil of racism. Similarly, Kristin Heyer calls for attention to "the complexities of pursuing the good amid structures that harm and internalized ideologies that conceal," and Elizabeth Block calls for an "engaged conscience" that "draws us out of ourselves and away from our own concerns" to responsibility for social sin.[26]

Feminists, too, value individual freedom while insisting that openness to critique and conversion is central to living a good life. Friedan's call for consciousness-raising in the 1960s assumed that women were so impacted by the feminine mystique that they could not hear "the voice within."[27] Internalized sexism led to the psychological problems reported by women in Friedan's study (and to male comfort with undue power and privilege). Women's distress, Friedan found, was due to their belief that they should be fulfilled

---

[23] On the authority of an erroneous conscience, see Bernard Häring, *The Law of Christ: Moral Theology for Priests and Laity* (Westminster, MD: Newman, 1961), 154–57.

[24] Ibid., 152.

[25] Bryan N. Massingale, "Conscience Formation and the Challenge of Unconscious Racial Bias," in *Conscience and Catholicism: Rights, Responsibilities, & Institutional Responses*, ed. David E. DeCosse and Kristin E. Heyer (Maryknoll, NY: Orbis Books, 2015), 53–68.

[26] Kristin E. Heyer, "Catholic Public Witness on Health Care Reform: Toward a More Capacious Model of Conscience," in *Conscience & Catholic Health Care: From Clinical Contexts to Government Mandates*, ed. David E. DeCosse and Thomas A. Nairn (Maryknoll, NY: Orbis Books, 2017), 79–90; and Elizabeth Sweeny Block, "A Call to Action: Global Moral Crises and the Inadequacy of Inherited Approaches to Conscience," *Journal of the Society of Christian Ethics* 37, no. 2 (2017): 79–96, at 90.

[27] Friedan, *Feminine Mystique*, 26–27.

in their purely domestic lives but were not. Women needed to come to terms with the trap of internalized sexism causing their distress and loss of self.[28]

In the language of the Catholic tradition, one might say that women were following their erroneous conscience in believing that domesticity would ensure bliss but were also heeding a more authentic call of conscience in recognizing and articulating their unhappiness. In listening to the voices of psychological and religious authorities, and taking in the cultural ethos that was everywhere around them, they came to a false consciousness. The remedy was better conscience formation, which would enable them to see things more clearly, claim their own identity, and better love themselves and others.[29]

However, women of color challenged white second-wave feminists, including Catholic feminist theologians, to come to a deeper awareness of the narrowness of their concerns.[30] Black women, many of whom were already working outside the home, were more concerned with racial discrimination than the feminine mystique. White women had to confront their own dependency on the domestic labor of women of color. In the language of the Catholic tradition, conscience formation needed to go deeper. Women needed to ask, "What seems to have happened to the victims of systemic injustice as the result of the way we are going about our work? Or, more positively: How might we do more toward promoting the values of God's reign?"[31]

Catholics and feminists both have nuanced ways of valuing the need for ongoing formation of conscience. Both honor deeply held convictions, challenge themselves to critically assess personal judgments in light of possible "false consciousness" or "erroneous conscience," and insist on the need for good formation. For a Catholic feminist today, awareness of the critical edges of both traditions can allow for authentic ecclesial belonging. Catholic feminists are formed by feminism not only to critique sexism in the Catholic tradition but to criticize their own biases. They are formed by Catholic tradition not only to love God and others, but to embrace feminism. Mary Henold's history of Catholicism and feminism in the mid-twentieth century

---

[28] Ibid., 356. "Drastic steps must now be taken to re-educate the women who were deluded or cheated by the feminine mystique."

[29] Ibid., 68–69.

[30] M. Shawn Copeland, "Toward a Critical Feminist Theology of Solidarity," in *Women & Theology*, ed. Mary Ann Hinsdale and Phyllis H. Kaminski, College Theology Society Annual Volume 40 (Maryknoll, NY: Orbis Books, 1995), 3–38.

[31] Patrick, *Liberating Conscience*, 212, discussing the need for Catholic ethicists to answer for neglect of racism.

shows that Catholic women came to feminist consciousness not only
through secular liberation movements but also through their own tradition,
in particular via the ecclesial renewal brought about by Vatican II.[32] "We are
feminists BECAUSE we are Catholic," they insisted, even as they called for
ecclesial reform.[33] This dual formation means that conscience formation is
an ongoing process. A Catholic feminist who stays embraces not certainty
but a radical openness to ongoing, multifaceted work of conscience formation and growth.

Conscience as Coming to Judgment

Conscience is not only a sanctuary or a faculty that can be formed well or
badly; it is also a process of decision-making. Anne Patrick, the Catholic
feminist who has done the most substantial work on conscience, offers a four-
pronged model for the process of what she calls "coming to judgement": (1)
focusing on the question to be decided, (2) understanding what is going on
inside yourself, (3) critically examining the situation in consultation with
others, and (4) acting once a decision is made.[34]

Applying Patrick's process to the dilemma of Catholic feminist identity, we could say that the question is, "Is it possible to remain Catholic and
Feminist?" For a Catholic educator, the question is further sharpened—"Is it
ethical to remain an official representative of the church, contributing to its
witness, and to the formation of the Catholic faithful? Is it moral to represent an institution that continues to deny women vote, leadership, and voice?"
Once the question is clear, it is important to assess what is going on inside
oneself, asking, "What is God calling me to in this moment?" Social analysis
would take a Catholic feminist deeper, allowing her to weigh the good she
could accomplish by remaining as well as the damage to self and others, both
real and potential.

As biblical theologian Sandra Schneiders wrote in *Beyond Patching: Faith
and Feminism in the Catholic Church*, the problem only deepens the longer a
Catholic feminist stays, for

> once she has begun to see, begun the critical process of analysis, she
> will necessarily gradually be overwhelmed by the extent, depth, and

---

[32] Henold, *Catholic and Feminist*, 83–115.
[33] Ibid., 113.
[34] Patrick, *Liberating Conscience*, 210–11.

the violence of the institutional church's rejection and oppression of women. This precipitates the inward crisis which the feminist Catholic inevitably faces: a deep, abiding, emotionally draining anger.[35]

And yet the ability to stand as a "professional Catholic" and speak feminist truths within the community of faith, to claim ground that has to this point not been claimed, to challenge authority on behalf of women and girls of the future, is a powerful thing. The significance of the work of feminist theologian is a strong example of what Catholic educators can do. Theologians like Schneiders, Ada María Isasi Díaz, and Elizabeth Johnson have been broadly influential in the U.S. Catholic Church. In the words of one woman who encountered Elizabeth Johnson's interpretation of Mary as "a spirited, scandalous, prophetic, poor, liberated, joyful refugee," instead of an obedient handmaid, "This is a Mary I can live with."[36] With feminist theology, ethics, biblical interpretation, spirituality, and liturgy, people who linger on the edges of the church can find space to let go of anger and breathe. They can find a faith they can live with. This mission to women and men within the church, a mission often understood as a calling, can counterbalance one's sense of complicity. Recalling Patrick's analysis along with Block's caution that conscience should take us beyond ourselves, it is also important to note that the suffering of racism, poverty, and violence also deserves consideration. In the face of the world's suffering, especially of the most vulnerable, and with deep appreciation for the work of the church to combat this suffering, a conscientious decision to stay can make sense.

Conscience as Integrity

Though much of the literature on conscience is about doing, the question of being is not completely neglected, and conscience as a space of finding integrity has particularly important resonances for feminists. As Terrence Merrigan notes, both St. Thomas More and John Henry Newman agree that "in the experience of conscience, the subject apprehends not only itself but also itself

---

[35] Schneiders, *Beyond Patching,* 98. See also Osiek, *Beyond Anger,* for an argument that staying entails taking up the cross and suffering for the sake of a better future church.

[36] Kathleen Cummings Sparrow, quoted in Julie Hanlon Rubio, "Honoring Our Mothers in Theology," *CatholicMoralTheology.com,* May 11, 2014, https://catholicmoraltheology.com/honoring-our-mothers-in-theology/.

as a subject in relation to God."[37] In wrestling with conscience, we not only come to judgment, we find ourselves, which for Christians can only be finding ourselves in God. Both More and Newman knew that this search for integrity in history was inevitably ambiguous. Newman's apologia or defense of Christian faith embraced the ambiguity of belonging to a church that could only "approximate . . . what it was called to be."[38] The remarkable lives of saints like More and Newman suggest that the self "is actualized in every authentic response to the voice of conscience."[39] In our consciously chosen actions, we find our integrity and become our true selves.

One might argue that feminists struggling with Catholic identity today face a choice of conscience as integrity. A generation of women who grew up Catholic and could not imagine leaving has been replaced by younger cohorts with weaker ties to organized religion.[40] Multiple waves of the clergy sexual abuse crisis have worn away the tenacious commitments of even the most devoted. Hope that the church will catch up with decades of work in feminist theology is giving way to resignation in the face of retrenchment. The depth of personal compromise and complicity felt by some Catholic feminists makes staying very hard to justify in conscience.

In her most recent book, Joan Chittister speaks movingly about the call to embrace prophetic speech and action in response to social suffering from a foundation in the gospel.[41] One might see her as a modern day More or Newman. But without an account of why feminists should continue prophetic work from inside the Catholic Church, which is not provided in Chittister's book, it is not clear why prophecy would be a choice of integrity. As noted earlier, many women today find existing answers insufficient. Most contemporary moral theologians argue that a Catholic can and should exercise moral responsibility including actively dissenting from problematic teachings and even speaking prophetically to call the church to be better, but this still begs the question of why one remains in such a difficult position.

Some feminists assert their belief in distinctively Catholic elements of the Christian tradition, in particular its sacramental imagination and social justice

---

[37] Terrence Merrigan, "Conscience and Selfhood: Thomas More, John Henry Newman, and the Crisis of the Postmodern Subject," *Theological Studies* 73 (2012): 851.

[38] Ibid., 858.

[39] Ibid., 868.

[40] Gray and Gautier, "Proud to Be Catholic?"

[41] Joan Chittister, *The Time Is Now: A Call to Uncommon Courage* (New York: Convergent, 2019).

teachings. As Lisa Sowle Cahill wrote in an address at Santa Clara University on being a Catholic feminist,

> In a Catholic sacramental vision, Christ's last supper and sacrificial death are reenacted in memory of his table fellowship with those who were social "outsiders," in honor of the mission of the early church to all peoples and nations, and in continuity with our historic Catholic social justice tradition that is committed to transforming the world.[42]

The connection between sacrament and social ethics, and the saints like Óscar Romero and Dorothy Day who so beautifully connected the two, is unique. The same tradition that enrages, also compels and convicts.

It also seems that some measure of appreciation for Christian teaching on the virtue of humility is necessary for the Catholic feminist to embrace her tradition with integrity. If she is not to divide herself in two, going to Mass on Sunday while bracketing the feminist consciousness that she carries with her the rest of the week, she may need to make space for what Margaret Farley calls "the grace of self-doubt."[43] Knowing that she once held views she later came to renounce, and continues to struggle with sin, she can bear with an imperfect church, knowing she, too, stands in need of conversion.

M. Shawn Copeland's vision of Eucharistic solidarity, which brings together humility, sacrament, and justice, best captures the integrity needed for Catholic feminist flourishing. Copeland centers her theology not on gender but on the raced body. Eucharistic solidarity is her response to the depths of Black suffering she narrates. She calls readers to acknowledge their own blindness, see their own complicity with sinful social structures, and trust in a tradition much larger than themselves, and embrace Eucharist as "counter-sign to the devaluation and violence directed toward the exploited, despised black body . . . [It] forms our social imagination, transvalues our values, and transforms the meaning of our being human, of embodying Christ."[44] Keeping the focus squarely on the victims of history, while embracing a prophetic

---

[42] Lisa Sowle Cahill, "On Being a Catholic Feminist," *Santa Clara Lecture* 9, no. 3 (2003), https://www.scu.edu/media/ignatian-center/pdf-files/Cahill-Lecture.pdf.

[43] Margaret A. Farley, "Ethics, Ecclesiology, and the Grace of Self-Doubt," in *A Call to Fidelity: On the Moral Theology of Charles E. Curran*, ed. James J. Walter et al. (Washington, DC: Georgetown University, 2002), 55–76.

[44] M. Shawn Copeland, *Enfleshing Freedom: Body, Race, and Being* (Minneapolis: Fortress Press, 2010), 127.

Catholic social anthropology, liturgy, and praxis makes it possible to hold Catholic and feminist identities in balance, to claim not innocence but integrity in the ambiguity of history.[45]

Conscience as Source of Creative Praxis

Moral theologian Bernard Häring's concept of "creative fidelity" suggests that conscience sometimes compels not submission to what is or wholesale rejection of it, but new modes of faithful belonging. In his influential *Free and Faithful in Christ,* Häring lays out his understanding of conscience as the place where we encounter God and learn how to live fully and freely into our true selves, for in "the depth of our being . . . the Spirit's creativity touches us and perfects us. It is where God's Word speaks to us and it is where we respond in the wholeness, the totality, of our personhood."[46] Conscience as source of creative praxis was criticized by Pope John Paul II but recovered by Pope Francis, who calls us in conscience to be open to the "God of surprises."[47]

Creative praxis is especially important for today's Catholic feminist. Feminist theologians writing in the 1990s often spoke of two paths: stay or go, reformer or radical, in or out.[48] Even then, they knew those categories were complicated. Today, Catholics generally claim many variations of Catholicism that allow them to retain Catholic identity in a manner different from the polarities of two decades ago: Catholic heritage, Catholic-ish, recovering Catholic, raised Catholic, cultural Catholic, etc.[49] They do not have to choose only between two opposing options. Likewise, for Catholic feminists, there are a multiplicity of "graceful exits" and ways of remaining.[50] This is even true for the professional Catholic who teaches or represents the Catholic

---

[45] James Alison makes a similar case for staying in the church in "Letter to a Young Gay Catholic," http://jamesalison.com/letter-to-a-young-gay-catholic/.

[46] Häring quoted in Matthew Levering, "Pinckaers & Häring on Conscience," *Journal of Moral Theology* 8, no. 2 (2019): 158. Levering considers the emphasis on creativity to be a weakness of Häring's and of revisionist moral theology in general.

[47] Compare Pope John Paul II, *Veritatis Splendor*—"The Splendor of Truth," nos. 54–56 (1993), www.vatican.va; and Pope Francis, "The God of Surprises," morning meditation, January, 20, 2014, www.vatican.va.

[48] Schneiders. *Beyond Patching*, 90–112.

[49] Tom Beaudoin and Patrick Hornbeck, "Deconversion and Disaffiliation in Contemporary U.S. Roman Catholicism," *Horizons* 40, no. 2 (2014): 255–62.

[50] Debra Campbell, *Graceful Exits: Catholic Women and the Art of Departure* (Bloomington: Indiana University Press, 2003).

faith. Her faith and her feminism shape her conscience and may lead her to creative praxis. We know from the survey data reviewed above that only about 27 percent of Catholics attend Mass regularly. We know less about what they might do in addition or instead. Anecdotal evidence suggests that some choose nongeographical parishes or small intentional faith communities. Others focus on devotions to the saints or Mary, participate less in Mass and more in family rituals and community festivals, or combine folk traditions with elements of Christian faith.[51] With "creative fidelity" to a church both loved and questioned, they construct hybrid spaces where they can practice Catholicism and feminism, together and apart.

Conclusion

I have argued in this essay that Catholic feminist identity represents a particularly difficult dilemma that has not yet been fully addressed in the literature on conscience. Using available categories, we might describe Catholic feminists who struggle to honor the authentic voice within, form their consciences, make judgments, achieve integrity, and use their creativity to find a coherent, faithful praxis. All of these ways of talking about conscience provide some assistance in unpacking the undeniable stresses and strains as well as the progressive living into responsibility that are inescapable for a Catholic feminist. Catholic feminist educators are in a particularly difficult spot, because of their representative, public role. Their institutional commitment is more visible, their cooperation, more direct. Yet, their integrity is also more visible, and their creative praxis has the potential to shape, inspire, and make possible new ways of faithful belonging.

Purity is not possible in this space. Teachings, rituals, community, and a deep sense of being called compel one to stay precisely where one feels most compromised, albeit with creative adaptation. The strife of double belonging, the pain of feeling torn, and the longing for a church that recognizes the gifts of all of its members, remain. Yet, with the many now and in times past who have felt similarly, Catholic feminists rejoice in life with brothers and sisters in Christ, and commit to bringing about the church as "it could be."

---

[51] See, along with other essays in this volume, for example, Anna Perkins, "Of (Befriending) Dragons and Escaping the Underworld: Two Voices in Caribbean Catholic Feminist Ethics," in Linda Hogan and A. E. Orobator, eds., *Feminist Catholic Theological Ethics in the World Church* (Maryknoll, NY: Orbis Books, 2014), 167–76.

CONTRIBUTORS

Pearl Maria Barros is assistant professor of religious studies at Santa Clara University. She holds a ThD in religion, gender, and culture from Harvard Divinity School. Her specializations are Christian theology with an emphasis on theological anthropology, feminist and other liberation theologies, Latinx cultural studies, and decolonial thought. She is the first-place winner of the *Journal of Feminist Studies in Religion's* 2020 Elisabeth Schüssler Fiorenza New Scholar Award.

Dr. Kevin Baxter is director of the Mary Ann Remick Leadership Program at the Alliance for Catholic Education at the University of Notre Dame. Prior to his current role, Dr. Baxter served as the Chief Innovation Officer for the National Catholic Educational Association; the Senior Director and Super-intendent of Catholic Schools for the Archdiocese of Los Angeles from 2015 to 2019; and the Superintendent for Elementary Schools in the Archdiocese of Los Angeles from 2009 to 2015. Dr. Baxter is the author of *Greatness in Smallness: A Vision for Catholic Microschools*.

Elizabeth Sweeny Block is assistant professor of Christian ethics at Saint Louis University. Her work in moral theology focuses on moral agency, sin, freedom, and conscience; sex and gender; and technology. She has recently published essays in the *Journal of the Society of Christian Ethics* and is at work on a forthcoming book called *Engaged Conscience: Moral Agency in a Broken World*.

Daniel P. Castillo is associate professor of theology at Loyola University Maryland and currently serves as director of the university's Master of Theo-logical Studies program. His first book, *An Ecological Theology of Liberation: Salvation and Political Ecology*, received the College Theology Society's 2020 Book Award. Presently, he is working on a monograph entitled *Confronting the Age of Cain: Christian Faith in the 'Anthropocene.'*

David E. DeCosse is director of Religious and Catholic Ethics at the Mark-kula Center for Applied Ethics at Santa Clara University, where he is also adjunct associate professor of religious studies. He coedited *Conscience and Catholicism: Rights, Responsibilities, and Institutional Responses* (with Kristin E. Heyer) and *Conscience and Catholic Health Care: From Clinical Contexts to Government Mandates* (with Thomas A. Nairn). His book, *Created Freedom Under the Sign of the Cross: A Catholic Public Theology for the United States,* is forthcoming from Cascade Books.

Lisa Fullam DVM, ThD, is professor of moral theology at the Jesuit School of Theology of Santa Clara University and associate veterinarian at New Baltimore Animal Hospital in West Coxsackie, NY. Her many works include "CRISPR and Catholic Ethics," forthcoming in a volume of essays on CRISPR from Praeger Press; "Dealing with Doubt: Epikeia, Probabilism, and the Formation of Medical Conscience," in *Conscience and Catholic Health Care*, and "Civil Same-Sex Marriage: A Catholic Affirmation."

Cathleen Kaveny is the Darald and Juliet Libby Professor of Law and Theology at Boston College. She is the author of many articles and books, including *Ethics at the Edge of Law: Christian Moralists and American Legal Thought.* She is currently working on a book exploring Flannery O'Connor's role in the American culture wars.

James F. Keenan, SJ, is Canisius Professor, director of the Jesuit Institute, and the Vice Provost of Global Engagement at Boston College. He is the author of many articles and books, including influential recent essays on the theology of conscience in *Theological Studies.* His next book, *A Brief History of Catholic Theological Ethics,* is forthcoming from Paulist Press.

Paul John Kuczynski, MA, MTS, is a graduate of both the Echo program through the McGrath Institute for Church Life at the University of Notre Dame and the School of Theology and Ministry at Boston College. After working as a high school theology teacher and in college campus ministry, he currently lives and works with people with intellectual and developmental disabilities as a member of the L'Arche Chicago community.

Michael G. Lawler is the Amelia and Emil Graff Chair Professor Emeritus of Catholic Theology, and **Todd A. Salzman** is the Amelia and Emil Graff Chair Professor of Catholic Theology, both at Creighton University. Together they have published many articles and books (including extensive work on the theology of conscience). Their most recent books include *Introduction to Theological Ethics: Foundations and Applications* and *Pope Francis and the Transformation of Catholic Health Care Ethics.*

Dr. Brandi Odom Lucas is the principal of Verbum Dei High School in Los Angeles, CA. She received her bachelor's degree in psychobiology from the University of California, Los Angeles, and obtained her master's degree in Catholic school administration and a doctorate in educational leadership for social justice at Loyola Marymount University. She is a leader in efforts to advance diversity, equity, and inclusion in academic institutions, Catholic and beyond.

Patrick J. O'Kernick is a doctoral candidate in theology at Marquette University. His dissertation is tentatively entitled "Moved with Compassion: Parables in Luke and the Envisioning Reader." His work on conscience has appeared in *Jesuit Higher Education: A Journal.*

Julie Hanlon Rubio is professor of Christian social ethics at the Jesuit School of Theology of Santa Clara University. She writes about family, feminism, sex, and politics and is the author of numerous articles and books including *Hope for Common Ground: Mediating the Personal and the Political in a Divided Church.* Her next book, *Catholic and Feminist: Is It Still Possible?* is forthcoming from Oxford University Press.

Sister Mary Angela Shaughnessy, SCN, JD, PhD, is a Sister of Charity of Nazareth who has served as teacher and administrator in Catholic schools. Currently, she is Senior Distinguished Fellow of Catholic Education in the Center for Catholic Education at Loyola Marymount University in Los Angeles. A practicing attorney, she has advised administrators and pastors on legal matters for over thirty years. She is the author of hundreds of articles and over thirty texts, and has written National Catholic Education Association's legal series articles since 1990.

Darlene Fozard Weaver is associate provost for academic affairs and professor of theology at Duquesne University in Pittsburgh, PA. Her publications include *The Acting Person and Christian Moral Life* and *Self-Love and Christian Ethics.* Weaver has a forthcoming essay on ethics and advocacy in Catholic higher education and is working on a book manuscript with the working title *Wrong: Ethics for Offenders.*

Index

Made in the USA
Las Vegas, NV
29 April 2022